'Increasingly, a company's market value reflects the value attributed by investors to people, knowledge, trust and relationships, none of which are visible in traditional financial and management information. *Accounting for Sustainability* is a thoughtful assessment of how we can develop accounting and reporting to better reflect what is material to assessing corporate performance today.'
Lise Kingo, Executive Vice President, Novo Nordisk Ltd

'The Connected Reporting Framework is the most practical way of reporting an organisation's strategic approach to sustainability available today. This publication will provide helpful guidance to anyone keen to learn from early adopters of the methodology.'
Sir Michael Rake, Chairman, BT Group plc

'The importance of sustainability to the long-term economic performance and survival of organisations can no longer be ignored. This book sets out a powerful case for embedding sustainability considerations across all organisational activities, with examples of how to translate them into practical actions.'
Justin King, Chief Executive, J Sainsbury plc

'We believe that it is important that organisations measure and disclose their environmental performance in their statutory annual reports and accounts. The case studies in this report show that it is possible to account for the environment in terms of physical and financial data and present environmental and sustainability information in a clear and meaningful way.'
Mark McLaughlin, Director of Finance, Environment Agency

'*Accounting for Sustainability* provides a rich and diverse collection of case studies to help all those organisations looking for a practical way of addressing the major challenges and risks posed by sustainability-related issues.'
Charles Tilley, Chief Executive, CIMA (Chartered Institute of Management Accountants)

'All too often when discussing sustainability issues the focus is on performance reporting and assurance – whilst the real focus of our attention really ought to be the embedding of sustainability principles, resulting in real change. This text provides excellent examples of real change in action and will be of interest to a broad spectrum of managers and accounting professionals.'
Helen Brand, Chief Executive, ACCA (Association of Chartered Certified Accountants)

'This book is a significant contribution to the practice of sustainability, demonstrating why and how it can be embedded in an organisation's thinking and action. This is done through a series of very perceptive case studies that move us beyond the theoretical to the practical.'
Michael Izza, Chief Executive, ICAEW (Institute of Chartered Accountants in England and Wales)

'This book provides major learning points on how environmental sustainability can be embedded in organisations and reported on, and the issues likely to arise. This should significantly reduce any "reinventing the wheel" in embedding sustainability in corporate culture.'
Alan Thomson, President, ICAS (The Institute of Chartered Accountants of Scotland)

'This is a significant contribution and a rich source of learning. It illuminates the practice of pioneers in sustainability reporting who are already reaping considerable benefit. Here is reporting that favours clarity and comparability, links financial and non-financial information, focuses performance and accountability, and has relevance for all sectors.'
Steve Freer, Chief Executive, CIPFA (Chartered Institute of Public Finance and Accountancy)

Accounting for Sustainability

Accounting for Sustainability

Practical Insights

Edited by Anthony Hopwood, Jeffrey Unerman
and Jessica Fries

publishing for a sustainable future

London • Washington, DC

Earthscan Ltd, Dunstan House, 14a St Cross Street, London EC1N 8XA, UK

Earthscan LLC, 1616 P Street, NW, Washington, DC 20036, USA

Earthscan publishes in association with the International Institute for Environment and Development

For more information on Earthscan publications, see www.earthscan.co.uk or write to earthinfo@earthscan.co.uk

ISBN: 978-1-84971-066-4 hardback
ISBN: 978-1-84971-067-1 paperback

Typeset by MapSet Ltd, Gateshead, UK
Cover design by Rob Watts

A catalogue record for this book is available from the British Library

Library of Congress Cataloging-in-Publication Data

Accounting for sustainability : practical insights / edited by Anthony Hopwood, Jeffrey Unerman, and Jessica Fries.
p. cm.
Includes bibliographical references and index.
ISBN 978-1-84971-066-4 (hardback) -- ISBN 978-1-84971-067-1 (pbk.) 1. Sustainable development reporting. 2. Environmental auditing. 3. Social accounting. 4. Sustainable development reporting--Case studies. 5. Environmental auditing--Case studies. 6. Social accounting--Case studies. I. Hopwood, Anthony G. II. Unerman, Jeffrey. III. Fries, Jessica.
HD60.3.A25 2010
658.4'083--dc22

2010005565

At Earthscan we strive to minimize our environmental impacts and carbon footprint through reducing waste, recycling and offsetting our CO_2 emissions, including those created through publication of this book. For more details of our environmental policy, see www.earthscan.co.uk.

Printed and bound in the UK by TJ International, an ISO 14001 accredited company. The paper used is FSC certified and the inks are vegetable based.

Mixed Sources
Product group from well-managed forests and other controlled sources
www.fsc.org Cert no. SGS-COC-2482
© 1996 Forest Stewardship Council
FSC

Dedication

This book is dedicated to the memory of Professor Anthony Hopwood. A few weeks before Accounting for Sustainability: Practical Insights was published we learned with great sadness that, after a long illness, Anthony had passed away. Characteristic of the vision that Anthony brought to bear throughout his illustrious career, the initial proposal for this book came from Anthony. His drive, energy and enthusiasm ensured not only that the project was undertaken by a team of distinguished academics researching leading organizations, but also that it was completed to a high standard within very tight timelines. His insight and guidance throughout the researching and writing of this book has been invaluable to us, his co-editors, and to the researchers who have written the individual case study chapters.

Anthony has left a large and impressive legacy, in particular through his contribution to accountancy. He was an inspirational member of The Prince's Accounting for Sustainability Project from its inception in 2004 and was heavily involved in the creation of many of the tools and methodologies developed. As one of his final projects, we believe that this book will appropriately add to his legacy, helping to foster a more sustainable future by encouraging the adoption of the principles of Accounting for Sustainability. On behalf of all those who have been involved in researching, writing and publishing this book, we hope that Anthony's contribution towards achieving brighter prospects for future generations will bring some additional comfort to his widow, Caryl, his sons Mark and Justin, and all his family.

Jeffrey Unerman and Jessica Fries, May 2010.

Contents

Foreword

CLARENCE HOUSE

I established my Accounting for Sustainability Project - over five years ago now - to help ensure that sustainability (considering what we do not only in terms of ourselves and today, but also of others and tomorrow) is not just talked and worried about, but becomes embedded in organizations' "DNA".

Climate change and the rapidly increasing destruction of the Earth's eco-systems are, to my mind, the greatest challenges facing the world. If unchecked, they will dwarf our current economic difficulties, resulting in millions of environmental refugees, lack of water and uncertain production of food, increasing spread of disease and, of course, growing social instability. They will affect the well-being of every man, woman and child on our planet.

Since the Industrial Revolution we have achieved extraordinary prosperity: many people live longer, have access to universal education, better healthcare and the promise of pensions. However, on the debit side, we in the industrialized world have increased our consumption of the Earth's finite natural resources to such an extent that our collective demands now exceed the planet's capacity to renew itself by some twenty-five per cent annually. In other words, we are consuming the Earth's capital as if it were income – and confusing capital for income is simply not sustainable in the long term.

It seems to me self-evident that we cannot have capitalism without capital and, very importantly, that the ultimate source of all economic capital is Nature's capital. We need to remember that the health and stability of our economy are dependent, at the end of the day, on the health and stability of both the natural environment and the people living within it and not the other way round. If we are to survive and prosper in the long term, we must learn to live within Nature's limits and to re-orientate our economic model from unconstrained growth to sustainable growth.

We are, however, having to face this challenge without the full and complete information needed to reach balanced conclusions and make the right decisions. At present, business decisions are generally taken on the basis of narrow financial information that does not encompass wider economic, social and environmental impacts – on the basis of information that fails to count all that counts and measure all that matters.

My Accounting for Sustainability Project has been working to develop practical tools and guidance to help ensure that we are not battling to meet 21st Century challenges with, at best, 20th Century decision-making and reporting systems – firstly, by suggesting how sustainability can be taken into account more effectively in day-to-day operations and, secondly, by developing a framework for reporting sustainability performance in a more connected, consistent, clear and concise way. I hope that the new approaches which the Project is developing will help organizations find the right balance between the short-term expectations of customers and investors and the actions needed to ensure long-term continuity and success.

This book is another important step in raising awareness and developing the techniques needed to incorporate broader and longer-term sustainability considerations into decision-making and reporting. It sets out a series of case studies that provide practical insights into how eight leading private and public sector organizations have sought to apply the guidance developed by my Accounting for Sustainability Project. I very much hope and believe that readers will find the case studies useful in helping them take practical steps towards addressing the daunting challenges which confront us.

A huge amount of work has been devoted to the Project and I could not be more grateful to the many busy people who have given up their time to research and write this book, and to the accounting bodies who have generously provided the funding.

List of Figures, Tables and Boxes

Figures

Tables

Boxes

List of Contributors

Alnoor Bhimani: Alnoor is Professor of Management Accounting and Head of the Department of Accounting at the London School of Economics. He possesses an MBA from Cornell University where he was a Fulbright Fellow and holds a PhD from LSE. He is also a Certified Management Accountant (Canada). He is author of 15 books and over 100 articles. His most recent books are *Management Accounting: Retrospect and Prospect* (CIMA/Elsevier, 2009) and *Management and Cost Accounting* (Prentice Hall, 2008). Alnoor has also edited several books with Oxford University Press that are widely cited. He has undertaken strategy, marketing, and management control related research in a variety of global enterprises and has presented his findings to corporate executives and academic audiences in Europe, Asia and North America. His current academic research focuses on strategic finance and management controls in digitized enterprises and on the global institutionalization of corporate governance.

Martin Brigham: Martin is a Lecturer in the Department of Organization, Work and Technology, Lancaster University Management School, Lancaster University. He was previously at the University of Warwick. Research interests include sustainability and organizational change, partnerships and non-governmental organizations (NGOs), and public sector modernization. His research has been published in a variety of journals including the *Journal of Management Studies*, *New Technology, Work and Employment*, and *Society and Business Review*. He convenes the Global Society and Responsible Management module on the Lancaster MBA. He is currently part of a consortium of universities organizing a seminar series over 18 months entitled 'When worlds collide: contested paradigms of corporate responsibility' funded by the Economic and Social Research Council (ESRC) and the Institute of Chartered Accountants in England and Wales (ICAEW).

John Burns: John joined Exeter Business School, University of Exeter in 2010, having held previous positions at Dundee, Colorado (USA) and Manchester. His research and professional interests primarily rest in management accounting, organizational change and institutional theory. He has published numerous refereed articles and book chapters in these areas, as well as numerous articles for professional accountancy bodies. John is currently an Associate Editor for *Management Accounting Research*, and a member of the Research Board for the Chartered Institute of Management Accountants (CIMA). He is also co-founder of the European Network for Research of Organizational and Accounting Change (ENROAC); and currently holds Visiting Professorships at WHU Otto Beisheim School of Management (Germany) and the Swedish Business School, Orebro (Sweden).

Colin Dey: Colin is a Senior Lecturer in the Division of Accounting and Finance at the University of Stirling specializing in business environment, social accounting and financial accounting theory. His research projects have explored accountability issues with a particular focus on corporate social reporting. He has worked with the fair-trade organization Traidcraft plc to develop new forms of social accounting and bookkeeping. Recent publications include 'Social accounting at Traidcraft plc: a struggle for the meaning of fair trade' (*Accounting, Auditing and Accountability Journal*, vol 20, no 3, 2007) and 'Developing silent and shadow accounts' (in Unerman, J, O'Dwyer, B and Bebbington, J (eds) *Sustainability Accounting and Accountability*, Routledge, 2007). He is also the chair of the communications sub-committee of the Centre for Social & Environmental Accounting Research.

David Ferguson: David is a research associate at Cranfield University School of Management and has broad experience working on developing and delivering projects and initiatives with the private, public and voluntary sector. More recently, he has completed a research fellow contract relating to 'Measuring Sustainability Value' as an in-company, action-research programme collaboration with EDF Group's Corporate University. David has just submitted his PhD thesis as an industry-sponsored, company case study investigating the operationalization of corporate sustainability performance. Recent publications include contributions to the International Association for Business and Society (IABS) conference in 2007 and 2009 and *Measuring Business Value and Sustainability Performance* (European Academy of Business in Society (EABIS) and the Doughty Centre for Corporate Responsibility, 2009).

Jessica Fries: Jessica is Director of The Prince's Accounting for Sustainability Project, on secondment from PricewaterhouseCoopers (PwC). She has worked with a wide range of companies, governments, investors and not-for-profit organizations to help them integrate sustainability into policy, decision-making and mainstream business practices. Jessica is a chartered accountant, has an MSc in Economics from the London School of Economics and a BA in Economics from the University of Cambridge.

Georgios Georgakopoulos: Georgios joined Amsterdam Business School in August 2008 as an Assistant Professor in Accounting with his teaching focused on capital market research, financial and managerial accounting. He has also worked as a Lecturer in Accounting in the Kemmy Business School of the University of Limerick in Ireland, as a teaching assistant in accounting in Strathclyde University, as an assistant economist in the Scottish Executive Environment and Rural Affairs Department in Scotland, and in Federated Agricultural Associations in Greece. Georgios holds an undergraduate degree and MSc in Agricultural Economics, a MSc in Business Economics, and a PhD in Accounting (2005). Georgios' research interests are wide ranging, primarily focused in the areas of risk theory, accounting and accountability. He also has research interests in agriculture and food safety, policy and regulation, environmental economics and sustainability issues, and capital markets.

Suzana Grubnic: Suzana is a Lecturer in Accounting and Finance at Nottingham University Business School and holds a PhD from the University of Derby. Her current research focuses upon performance management in local government and, more widely, sustainability in the public sector. Together with a team from the International Centre for Corporate Social Responsibility, she is also involved in a CIMA sponsored project on the relationships and specific issues of sustainability accounting systems along with traditional management accounting systems in order to assess their contribution to organizational strategic decision-making. Her research has been published in *Financial Accountability and Management*, and *Public Administration*, among other journals. She is also a committee member of the British Accounting Association Public Services Accounting Special Interest Group.

Anthony Hopwood: Educated at the London School of Economics and the University of Chicago, prior to moving to the University of Oxford in 1995 Anthony held professorships at the London Business School and the London School of Economics. He served as the Dean of the Saïd Business School during its formative years, from 1999 until his retirement in 2006. He was also the President of the European Institute for Advanced Studies in Management, Brussels from 1995 to 2003. In 2006 he was appointed Chairman of The Prince's Foundation for the Built Environment. A prolific author, Anthony was founder and Editor-in-Chief of the major international research journal, Accounting, Organizations and Society for 35 years. He served as a consultant to commercial, governmental and international organizations, and held honorary doctorates from universities in Denmark, Finland, Italy, Sweden and the United Kingdom and awards from the British, European and American Accounting Associations. In 2008 Anthony was elected to the Accounting Hall of Fame. Anthony sadly passed away in May 2010 after a long illness.

Paraskevi Vicky Kiosse: Vicky is Lecturer in the Department of Accounting and Finance at Lancaster University Management School. She received her PhD in Accounting and Finance from Lancaster University. Her research focuses on the areas of pension accounting, pension fund asset allocation, corporate disclosure policies, and the value relevance of pension accounting numbers. Vicky's work has been presented at the European Accounting Association and British Accounting Association conferences. Her research has been published in *Accounting and Business Research* and the *Journal of Business Finance and Accounting*.

Linda Lewis: Linda is a Senior Lecturer in Accounting and an Associate Dean within the Management School at the University of Sheffield. Her current teaching and research interests lie in corporate social responsibility, social and environmental reporting, accounting for sustainability, regulatory and institutional frameworks for sustainability and the relationship between management accounting for sustainability and externally reported information. Additionally, with financial support from ACCA and ICAEW, she has conducted research on local government environmental auditing, socially responsible investment and social and environmental accounting education. A number of research projects in recent years have been funded by the Engineering and Physical Sciences Research Council (EPSRC) and current grants are funding further research into applications of whole-life costing and the significance of stakeholders in the successful implementation of new developments (for sustainability) in water cycle management.

Karen McCulloch: Karen is a chartered accountant on secondment to The Prince's Accounting for Sustainability Project from KPMG LLP, where she provides audit and assurance services to a wide range of UK and international organizations operating in diverse fields such as pharmaceuticals, consumer products and automotive manufacturing. She has a strong interest in the environment and particularly in how businesses are impacted by social and environmental factors, and the degree to which sustainability reporting reflects the underlying reality of how sustainability is regarded and embedded within organizations.

Brendan O'Dwyer: Brendan is Professor of Accounting and Head of the Accounting Division at the Amsterdam Business School, University of Amsterdam. He holds a PhD in Accounting from the University of Dundee and is a Fellow of the Institute of Chartered Accountants in Ireland having trained as a chartered accountant with Ernst and Young. Brendan's academic research interests, on which he has published widely, embrace the areas of: corporate sustainability accounting, auditing and accountability; non-governmental organization (NGO) accounting and accountability; and accounting profession regulation. He is an Associate Editor of *Accounting, Auditing and Accountability Journal* and serves on the editorial boards of numerous international academic accounting journals.

David Otley: David is Distinguished Professor of Management and Accounting and Associate Dean (Finance and Resources) in the Lancaster University Management School. He is also current President of the American Accounting Association Management Accounting Section and Chairman of the Management Control Association. He is a Fellow of the British Academy of Management. His research interests are centred on the study of performance management and control systems in both the public and private sectors, examining the mechanisms used to help ensure that strategy is effectively implemented. He is particularly interested in the design of performance measures that avoid excessive dysfunctional behaviour, and has made extensive studies of the behavioural impact of accounting and budgetary control systems in practice. He has published extensively in leading accounting and management journals and acted as a main panel chair in the recent UK Research Assessment Exercise 2008.

David Owen: David is Professor of Social and Environmental Accounting based within the International Centre for Corporate Social Responsibility at Nottingham University Business School. He has held previous appointments at the universities of Huddersfield, Salford, Manchester, Leeds and Sheffield. David's main research interests lie in the fields of social and environmental accounting, auditing and reporting. He has published extensively in a wide range of professional and academic journals on topics such as social investment, corporate social audit, and corporate social and environmental reporting and assurance practice. David currently serves on the editorial boards of *Accounting, Organizations and Society*; *Accounting, Auditing and Accountability Journal*; *Accounting Forum*; *Accounting and Business Research*; *British Accounting Review*; *European Accounting Review*; and *Business Strategy and the Environment*. He is also an Associate Director of the Centre for Social and Environmental Accounting Research at the University of St Andrews.

Leonardo Rinaldi: Leonardo is Lecturer in Accounting at Royal Holloway University of London. Educated at the University of Florence, Leonardo earned a PhD in Managerial Accounting. His research examines the role of accounting in discharging corporate duties of accountability to a broad range of stakeholders. Recent projects in this area comprise: the theoretical centrality of stakeholder dialogue to widespread corporate accountability initiatives, to throw light upon the extent to which corporations are using the communicative capabilities of the internet to develop innovative stakeholder engagement; and issues related to the role of the visual in dissemination of corporate social responsibility practices. Leonardo's research is predominantly of a qualitative nature and he has published in international peer reviewed journals in this area such as *Business Strategy and the Environment*, and *Journal of Accounting and Organizational Change*.

Kazbi Soonawalla: Kazbi has a PhD from Stanford University and is a lecturer at the LSE. Her teaching and research interests include international financial reporting and reporting on environmental accounting, and social responsibility and governance. Kazbi has published a chapter in a book, 'Environmental management accounting' (in Bhimani, A [ed] *Contemporary Issues in Management Accounting*, Oxford University Press, 2006); and a paper in the area: 'From conformance to performance: the corporate responsibilities continuum' (*Journal of Accounting and Public Policy*, vol 24, no 3, 2005). Her other interests include accounting for business combinations, joint ventures, and share-based payments.

Laura J. Spence: Laura is a Reader in Business Ethics at Royal Holloway, University of London where she is Director of the interdisciplinary Centre for Research into Sustainability (www.rhul.ac.uk/management/CRIS). Laura is Vice-President of the International Society for Business, Economics and Ethics and Section Editor of the *Journal of Business Ethics*. She is best known for her agenda-setting research on ethics and social responsibility in small- and medium-sized enterprises. Her other research interests are many and varied including social responsibility in the supply chain, business and the environment, stakeholder relationship, ethics and family business, social capital, competitive intelligence gathering and social entrepreneurship. At Royal Holloway she leads two taught courses, 'Business, Sustainability and Society' and 'Responsible Entrepreneurship'. Her most recent book is the successful reader '*Corporate Social Responsibility: Readings and Cases in a Global Context*', which she coedited with Andrew Crane and Dirk Matten (Routledge, 2007).

Ian Thomson: Ian is a Reader at the Department of Accounting and Finance, Strathclyde Business School. His research is concerned with how accounting and other forms of evidence impacts in organizational decision-making; and operations that have a social and/or environmental impact. This has included interdisciplinary studies on implementation of cleaner technology, establishing industrial ecologies, effective stakeholder engagement, risk governance in water and salmon farming, and the role of indicators in government policy-making processes. He has acted as expert witness to the Scottish Parliament Finance Committee on the sustainability of the latest Budget round, Special Policy Advisor to the Scottish Parliament's Transport, Infrastructure and Climate Change Committee, consultant to World Wide Fund for Nature (WWF) Scotland, and is a member of the expert stakeholder panel for the Sustainable Development Commission (Scotland). His current interests include the potential role of Life Cycle Costing and Carbon Accountability in Government Sustainability Strategy Development and Implementation. He is also a board member of the Centre for Social and Environmental Accounting Research, St Andrews University.

Jeffrey Unerman: Jeffrey is Professor of Accounting and Accountability at Manchester Business School, University of Manchester, having previously served as a professor and other faculty positions at colleges of the University of London. His research, which has been widely published in leading academic journals, investigates the role of accounting (in both annual reports and less formal media such as corporate websites and face-to-face interactions) in discharging corporate and NGO duties of accountability to a broad range of stakeholders. A particular focus of this research is the potential and actual use of accounting in making the social and ecological impacts of organizational activities more transparent and in encouraging sustainability within organizational decision-making. Professor Unerman is co-editor of *Sustainability Accounting and Accountability* (Routledge, 2007) and co-author *of Financial Accounting Theory – European Edition* (McGraw-Hill Education, 2007). He is currently Joint Editor of *Social and Environmental Accountability Journal*, an Associate Editor of *Accounting, Auditing and Accountability Journal*, and General Secretary of the British Accounting Association. He is also a member of the ACCA Research Committee. He holds a PhD in social and environmental accounting from the University of Sheffield, is a member of the Institute of Chartered Accountants in England and Wales and the Association of Chartered Certified Accountants, and is an honorary member of CPA Australia.

Will Webster: Will is a chartered accountant with an MA in Economics from Edinburgh University who was seconded from Grant Thornton UK LLP to The Prince's Accounting for Sustainability Project for 18 months during 2008–2009. At Grant Thornton he provides business risk services to large and listed organizations, including a number of FTSE 250 companies for which he has been Internal Audit Manager. For six years he project managed the annual *Grant Thornton Corporate Governance Review*, which looks at disclosure within the FTSE 350, including corporate social responsibility.

Acknowledgements

We gratefully acknowledge the support of the members of the Consultative Committee of Accountancy Bodies who have provided the funding for this book: Chartered Accountants Ireland (ICAI), Chartered Institute of Management Accountants (CIMA), The Association of Chartered Certified Accountants (ACCA), The Chartered Institute of Public Finance and Accountancy (CIPFA), ICAEW Charitable Trusts, and The Scottish Accountancy Trust for Education & Research (SATER) and The Institute of Chartered Accountants of Scotland (ICAS).

We would also like to extend our sincere thanks to the numerous individuals and eight case study organizations who have contributed to the writing and publication of this book: the academics who have undertaken the research and their respective universities; the eight case study organizations who have given their time and financial support, as well as sharing their experiences and insights; Professor Jan Bebbington, Professor of Accounting and Sustainable Development at the University of St Andrews for her help and advice; Jonathan Sinclair Wilson and his team at Earthscan for their support and guidance; the team at The Prince's Accounting for Sustainability Project, particularly Karen McCulloch and Gordon Wilson who have overseen this project; and the A4S Executive Board, Supervisory Board and Advisory Group members who have been instrumental in developing A4S's recommendations

All royalties from the sale of this book will go to The Prince's Charities Foundation.

List of Acronyms and Abbreviations

A4S	The Prince's Accounting for Sustainability Project
AA1000	AccountAbility 1000
ACCA	Association of Chartered Certified Accountants
AGM	annual general meeting
AONB	Area of Outstanding Natural Beauty
BITC	Business in the Community
BREEAM	Building Research Establishment Environmental Assessment Model
CAA	Comprehensive Area Assessment
CCAB	Consultative Committee of Accountancy Bodies
CDP	Carbon Disclosure Project
CEO	chief executive officer
CIPFA	Chartered Institute of Public Finance and Accountancy
CO_2e	carbon dioxide equivalent
CPA	Comprehensive Performance Assessment (*now* CAA)
CR	corporate responsibility
CRC	Carbon Reduction Commitment (CRC) Energy Efficiency Scheme
CRE Panel	Corporate Responsibility and Environment Panel
CRF	Connected Reporting Framework
CSP	Corporate Sustainability Programme
CSR	corporate social responsibility
Defra	UK Department for Environment, Food and Rural Affairs
DG	Delivery Group
DNA	deoxyribonucleic acid
EPFI	Equator Principles Financial Institution
ESG	environmental, social and governance
EU	European Union
E&WMP	Energy and Water Management Plan
FRAB	Financial Reporting Advisory Board
FSR	Fundamental Service Review programme
FTSE	Financial Times Stock Exchange

G20	Group of Twenty Finance Ministers and Central Bank Governors
GDP	gross domestic product
GHG	greenhouse gas
GRI	Global Reporting Initiative
HMIP	Her Majesty's Inspectorate of Pollution
ICC	International Chamber of Commerce
IFC	International Finance Corporation
IFRS	International Financial Reporting Standards
IT	information technology
KPI	key performance indicators
LPG	liquefied petroleum gas
NFU	National Farmers' Union
MWh	megawatt hours
NGO	non-governmental organization
NO_x	nitrogen oxide
NRA	National Rivers Authority
PFI	Private Finance Initiative
ppm	parts per million
R&D	research and development
rPET	recycled polyethylene terephthalate
SDC	Sustainable Development Committee
SOX	Sarbanes–Oxley Act
SRI	sustainable and responsible investment/socially responsible investment
SSG	Staff Sustainability Group
SWT	Sustainable Workplace Tool
TBL	triple bottom line
UK	United Kingdom
UKCIP	United Kingdom Climate Impacts Programme
UN	United Nations
UN PRI	United Nations Principles for Responsible Investment
US	United States
WSCC	West Sussex County Council
WWF	World Wide Fund for Nature (*formerly* World Wildlife Fund)

one

Introduction to the Accounting for Sustainability Case Studies

Anthony Hopwood, Jeffrey Unerman
and Jessica Fries

We can find our way to a new form of growth which is energy secure, cleaner, quieter, safer and more bio-diverse. And the transition to this form of growth over the next few decades will probably be the most dynamic and innovative in our economic history. It will be something like electricity or railways in earlier periods, or the rise of information technology more recently, but probably still more dynamic and on a larger scale than these radical economic transformations. Put another way, high-carbon growth would kill itself, first from very high prices of hydro-carbons and secondly and more fundamentally from the hostile physical environment it creates. On the other hand, low-carbon growth presents a very attractive and prosperous future. Pessimism and cynicism will be self-fulfilling; we must find a way. (Stern, 2009, p4)

Operating in an environmentally, socially and economically sustainable manner is one of the most urgent challenges facing organizations today. Issues such as climate change, the overconsumption of finite natural resources and the rapidly increasing destruction of the Earth's ecosystems will drive fundamental shifts in society and the economy. It is increasingly important for organizations to understand and respond both to the manner in which these issues will affect their own continuity and long-term success, and to how they can help society as a whole in meeting the challenges faced. Accounting processes and practices have a key role to play in helping organizations develop the more sustainable operations that are a necessary part of this response. Such practices enable the systematic identification and interlinking of the economic, social and environmental costs and benefits of organizational strategies and actions. Accounting can also either help, or potentially hinder, the embedding of these considerations into organizations' decision-making processes. To fulfil its potential in these important roles, accounting practice needs to develop from its traditional focus on the economic to also encompass the social and environmental dimensions of organizational strategies and actions.

As part of a long-standing commitment to sustainable development, His Royal Highness The Prince of Wales has underlined that economic development and human prosperity are reliant on, and fundamentally connected to, the continued health of the Earth's ecosystems. Through the creation of The Prince's Accounting for Sustainability Project (A4S) in 2004, he recognized the key role that accounting can play in ensuring that economic development is sustainable – that it is not achieved at the cost of long-term severe degradation to the environment and/or to social structures and cohesion which, if unchecked, will undermine economic progress. At the launch of A4S, The Prince of Wales emphasized the urgent need to develop appropriate sustainability accounting processes and practices. He stated that such accounting developments were needed 'to help ensure that we are not battling to meet 21st century challenges with, at best, 20th century decision-making and reporting systems'.

A4S addresses these issues by recognizing the importance of integrating sustainability information into mainstream financial and management processes. This leads to more effective business management by more systematically connecting sustainability considerations to management decision-making and organizational action.

The main proposals from the project, which were based on work with over 200 companies, government agencies and other organizations, are explained in Chapter 2 of this book. These recommendations reflect steps to:

- embed sustainability considerations within organizations' strategic and operational decision-making, processes and practices; and
- report all aspects of organizational performance in a connected, concise and consistent manner, reflecting the organization's strategy and the way in which it is managed.

The aim of this book is, through a series of in-depth case studies, to document and probe the ways in which private- and public-sector organizations can apply the guidance developed by A4S and use these principles to embed sustainability into day-to-day decision-making and reporting.

The book also seeks to test and further develop the proposition underlying A4S's work – namely, that a broad and inclusive concept of sustainability can be, and needs to be, integrated into mainstream financial processes. Through the case studies, it seeks both to further develop the tools that can support this integration and to disseminate and share best practice in this area. It does this by analysing the impact of methodologies and tools for integrated or connected sustainability reporting and decision-making on the case study organizations' sustainability performance and on their strategic and operational decision-making.

Six leading companies (Aviva, BT, EDF Energy, HSBC, Novo Nordisk and Sainsbury's) and two UK public-sector bodies (the Environment Agency and West Sussex County Council) have taken part in the case study project, the results from which are reported in this book. The case studies have been researched and written by a team of leading business and management academics from UK and continental European universities who have analysed the extent to which, and how, sustainability information has been embedded within the regular operations of the case study organizations. The case studies seek to support and enhance the work of A4S in moving sustainable decision-making into the mainstream of business practice.

To set the scene for the case studies that are presented in subsequent chapters, the following two sections of this chapter respectively deal with the relevance of sustainable development and climate change in today's world, and with the role and significance of sustainability for organizations, including the business case for action. The subsequent section 'Embedding sustainability considerations into business practice through accounting for sustainability' then outlines the potential role of accounting processes and practices in fostering sustainable development. It also discusses how to embed considerations of sustainability – in the three connected spheres of economy, society and environment – into strategic and operational decision-making and action within organizations. The final section of the chapter 'Summary of the case studies' highlights the key findings from each of the case studies. These findings emphasize how accounting for sustainability processes and practices can be used to help embed sustainability within strategic decision-making and action, thereby addressing the challenges posed by, and realizing the opportunities inherent in, the sustainability agenda.

Sustainability, sustainable development and climate change

A prerequisite for individuals and organizations being able to survive and thrive in the long term is a society that is economically, environmentally and socially

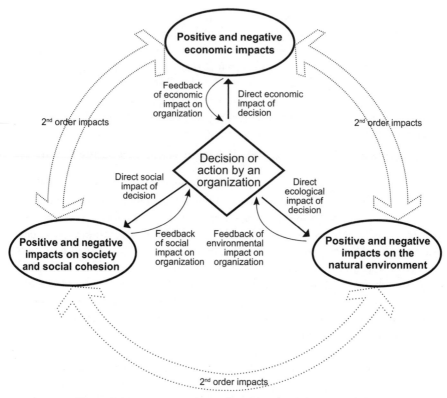

Figure 1.1 Interconnectedness of organizational decisions on the
three spheres of sustainability

Source: Jeffrey Unerman

sustainable. If we ignore the need for durable sustainability in these three key areas, then we risk placing potentially intolerable burdens on ourselves and on future generations. Each of these three areas is necessary because:

- Economic sustainability provides us with future income and resources.
- Environmental sustainability provides a stable ecosphere that supports and protects life, including the provision of food and water.
- Social sustainability provides well-functioning societies that protect and enhance quality of life and safeguard human rights.

Taking the above factors into account, the concept of sustainable development recognizes the vital social role of economic activity and development. But it also seeks to ensure that this economic development is undertaken in a manner that weighs and balances positive economic and social impacts against negative social and environmental ones, taking into account the long-term sustainability of that economic activity and development.

Figure 1.1 shows that these three spheres of sustainability are closely related, as it is increasingly recognized that actions and impacts in one sphere can and do affect sustainability in the other spheres. For example, since the start of the Industrial Revolution, economic development has involved the burning of large amounts of fossil fuels, which we have only relatively recently realized has contributed to environmental unsustainability through its impact on global warming. Conversely, economic deprivation through lack of economic development leads to numerous negative social impacts associated with poverty, including:

- hunger;
- inadequate housing;
- poor education;
- declining physical and psychological health (different aspects of which are associated with affluence); and
- increased human conflict, crime and violence.

Many of these negative social impacts reinforce poverty as they hinder the development of an adequate physical and intellectual infrastructure, which is needed to support economic development.

The implications of climate change

Perhaps the most significant and urgent linkage between the three spheres of sustainability flows from environmental sustainability (or unsustainability) – in particular, climate change. The influential *Stern Review* (Stern, 2006) concluded that while the economic costs of reducing greenhouse gas emissions to environmentally sustainable levels would be high, the costs of dealing with the significant negative effects of global warming if emissions are not reduced to sustainable levels would be many times higher. Many of these costs would be imposed directly on business – for example, through higher costs of raw materials and energy, building obsolescence and damage to fixed assets through changing weather patterns, and changing patterns of consumer demand. Other costs would be imposed indirectly through the necessity of higher levels of taxation to fund increased government expenditure on mitigating the social and environmental consequences of global warming. Thus, in the long term, environmentally unsustainable business practices have the potential to significantly damage the financial sustainability of business. Climate change resulting from environmentally unsustainable practices will also produce significant negative social impacts for most of the world's population (Meadows et al, 2004).

The reason that climate change poses such a significant threat to all three spheres of sustainability is the significant adverse impacts that forecast and probable levels of global warming are almost certain to have on essential matters, such as:

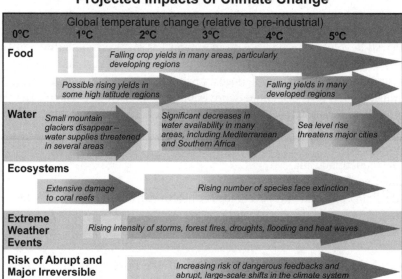

Figure 1.2 Impacts of global warming

Source: Stern Review on the Economics of Climate Change (2006), Crown Copyright

- food production;
- water supplies;
- rising sea levels, making coastal communities unviable;
- extreme weather events, such as storms, droughts, floods and heat waves; and
- the stability of many ecosystems upon which we rely (Stern, 2006).

These impacts from global warming are predicted to increase in severity the greater that long-term average global temperatures rise above pre-industrial levels (see Figure 1.2). The overwhelming scientific consensus, accepted by the international community at intergovernmental level and recognized within the Copenhagen Accord and by more than 500 companies representing the international business community within the Copenhagen Communiqué, is that a rise of more than 2°C in average temperatures will lead to significantly negative and potentially irreversible environmental impacts. As these impacts will not be uniform throughout the world, they are also likely to lead to additional significant social disruption and conflict. Those people who will be worst affected will seek to move to regions that have been less affected, but which will nonetheless already be suffering negative impacts and stress from climate change. Dealing with these major consequences of environmental and social unsustainability will be very expensive, if not impossible, and will thus compro-

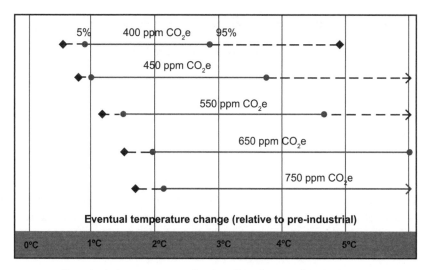

Figure 1.3 Concentrations of carbon dioxide equivalent (CO_2e) and
associated predicted temperature rises

Source: Stern Review on the Economics of Climate Change (2006), Crown Copyright

mise economic sustainability. This will inevitably negatively impact on both businesses and public-sector organizations.

The concentration of greenhouse gases in the atmosphere is widely accepted as a key factor in determining average global temperatures, and these gases are currently rapidly becoming more concentrated. Indeed, they are fast approaching levels of concentration that have a very high risk of leading to irreversible negative climate change, as set out in Figure 1.3. This increasing concentration is due to annual greenhouse gas emissions from human activities – such as industry, transport and agriculture – far exceeding the Earth's finite capacity to absorb and convert these gases. To reduce the significant risks to economic, social and environmental sustainability from climate change, it is therefore necessary to significantly reduce current levels of annual greenhouse gas emissions – of the order of an 80 per cent reduction on 1990 levels by 2050 within developed nations. Achieving this scale of change will require unprecedented technological advances, as well as fundamental changes in the global economic model. Actions to reduce emissions of greenhouse gases are therefore urgently required from all organizations if we are to better ensure a viable long-term natural environment in which companies can thrive economically. Furthermore, as Lord Stern (2009) eloquently argues, making the transition to a low-emissions society will present many economically attractive opportunities that will have the connected impact of enhancing economic, social *and* environmental sustainability.

The role and significance of sustainability for organizations

Drawing on the interconnected sustainability impacts discussed earlier in this chapter, the motivation for organizations to operate in a sustainable manner should be twofold. First, leaders of every organization need to recognize that they have ethical responsibilities to contribute to the creation of a sustainable society and not to harm others. Thus, they should seek to minimize the negative impacts on environmental and social sustainability from their operations and maximize the positive impacts. Second, in addition to this recognition that tackling their organization's negative impact on environmental and social sustainability is a moral necessity, business leaders increasingly need to recognize that it is in the company's own economic self-interest to operate in an environmentally and socially sustainable manner.

Acting responsibly

In governmental policy on sustainable development, some governments (e.g. the UK) regard sustainability in the environmental and social spheres as key outcomes to be targeted by government policy, with a sustainable economy being one of three key enablers for social and environmental sustainability (the other two enablers being responsible use of scientific research and good governance). From this governmental policy perspective, social and environmental sustainability has a higher weighting and priority than economic development in decisions about balancing impacts across the three spheres of environmental, social and economic sustainable development.

However, at the individual organizational level, especially in the private sector, the balancing of impacts across the three spheres will be informed by slightly different considerations to those at governmental level. In weighing all of these impacts, it is important to identify not only the potential positive and negative impacts in each sphere, but also the significance, or materiality, of each impact, both to society and to the organization itself. This is a highly complex process, as every action taken by an individual, a business or a public-sector organization can have numerous and often conflicting impacts within each of the economic, environmental and social spheres, as well as between these spheres (as illustrated in Figure 1.1).

For example, the construction industry has many well-known negative environmental impacts. This is partially due to the high level of greenhouse gases emitted in manufacturing many building products, especially concrete, and in transporting and assembling these products for construction projects. But it is important to weigh many other factors against this negative environmental impact, including:

- social benefits from the provision of additional housing in places where there are housing shortages, especially where social housing is included in a construction project;
- additional social cohesion from well-planned and executed housing projects, and from new commercial property needed to efficiently house businesses that provide employment to local communities;
- environmental benefits from replacing old energy-inefficient homes, offices and factories, and from constructing renewable energy projects (e.g. wind farms);
- negative social and environmental impacts (e.g. the destruction of wildlife habitats) from poorly designed and/or poorly sited construction projects;
- economic and social benefits in the short term from directly employing construction workers and from additional employment in, and business for suppliers to, the construction industry;
- social, environmental and economic benefits from improved transport infrastructure resulting from the construction of new roads, railways and airports;
- additional negative environmental impacts from pollution emitted in incremental passenger and goods journeys resulting from improved transport infrastructure;
- negative and positive social and economic impacts through increased or reduced congestion in local communities around new transport infrastructure (e.g. where a new bypass reduces traffic congestion in a town, but also reduces the number of people visiting the town to use local shops); and
- other (second-order) positive social benefits resulting from the economic benefits described above and negative social impacts resulting from climate change to which the negative environmental impacts contribute.

Balancing this multitude of possible environmental, social and economic impacts, benefits, and risks and opportunities, across and within the environmental, social and economic spheres, is a highly complex task that is increasingly recognized as being among the most significant challenges facing organizations, their managers and society today. The complexity of this task is made even more difficult through the need to weigh the significance of different types and time horizons of outcomes – for example, a longer-term impact on global warming against a more immediate social or economic payback. While some activities clearly lead to 'win–win–win' situations where there is a positive overall environmental, social and economic outcome, many other activities yield overall positive outcomes in one area, while producing overall negative impacts in one or both of the others.

Organizations therefore have a difficult task in deciding strategy and actions to balance their environmental, social and economic sustainability within the boundaries of acceptable behaviour and impacts established by society and science. Such a task represents a new challenge for many businesses.

The parameters within which these decisions need to be taken are identified through governments and intergovernmental agreements, as well as through
accepted ethical standards. Governments have a clear responsibility to set the
parameters of acceptable behaviour and to send clear signals to both individuals
and organizations, whether through establishing a regulatory framework or
putting in place other mechanisms that will deliver sustainable outcomes. In
particular, in the context of the ecological limits of a finite planet, individual
organizations cannot be expected to take responsibility for determining these
parameters; rather, they should recognize the scientific consensus that exists
and seek to factor these limits into their own decision-making. There is then a
need for governments and regulators to assess the cumulative sufficiency of
actions that individual organizations are taking and to adjust the framework
within which organizations operate to balance the outcome of individual actions
with the environmental limits that exist.

For example, governments internationally have agreed that concentrations
of greenhouse gases must not exceed levels that are likely to lead to global
warming of more than 2°C above pre-industrial levels. In balancing different
sustainability impacts, individual organizations need to recognize that limit and
be able to translate it into an assessment of whether their own emission reduction targets are sufficient. At present, at the governmental level, the reduction
pledges made by governments in the run up to the United Nations Climate
Change Conference, Copenhagen 2009 fell short of the levels needed to avoid
dangerous levels of climate change. Similarly, a recent report by the Carbon
Disclosure Project (2010) shows that greenhouse gas emissions reduction
targets set by Financial Times Stock Exchange (FTSE) 100 carbon-intensive
sectors fall far short of reductions required by the UK Climate Change Act.

The business case for embedding sustainability into decision-making

The economic imperative for businesses to act responsibly and embed social
and environmental sustainability considerations into the way in which they
are run, often known as 'the business case for sustainability', is also multifac-
eted. Although in the very short term a business might not suffer many
economic costs from global warming, irrespective of how unsustainably it
operates, this does not hold over the medium or longer term. In addition to
taking into account regulatory costs imposed on polluting organizations by
local and national governments, to remain profitable in the longer term,
businesses need a stable social and ecological environment in which to
operate. A poorly functioning society will impose many costs on many organizations, such as additional costs of security and additional taxation to pay
otherwise avoidable healthcare costs. While some businesses will be able to
identify and make profits from new business opportunities arising from a

poorly functioning society, the overall economic impact for many businesses from operating in a socially degenerating society will be negative. As such, it is in the medium-term economic interests of the business sector overall to operate in a manner that does not contribute to social breakdown and that builds social cohesion.

However, even where this medium- to long-term economic imperative is clear, it can be challenging for individual organizations, which need to demonstrate profitability and growth in the short term, to take action on environmental and social sustainability unless a more immediate and direct business case can be established. There is a rapidly growing body of evidence demonstrating a clear financial rationale for embedding sustainability. This business case will vary according to the individual organization and the sector and markets within which it operates. Areas common to most organizations are summarized below.

Winning and retaining customers

An organization's sustainability credentials are increasingly being integrated within customer purchasing decisions, whether those customers are consumers, businesses or governments. For example, in a 2008 study by the European Commission *Attitudes of European Citizens towards the Environment*, 75 per cent of respondents agreed that they were ready to buy environmentally friendly products even if they cost a little more. This trend is demonstrated by Walmart's announcement in July 2009 of its creation of a sustainability index, initially asking each of its 100,000 suppliers for information on their sustainability performance, and ultimately seeking to provide customers with product information in a simple, convenient, easy-to-understand rating so that they can make consumer choices in a more sustainable way. In major emerging economies, contrary to the expectations of many, this trend is also seen and, in some cases, exceeds that identified in developed nations. A 2008 TNS survey entitled *The Green Life* (TNS, 2009) concluded that the vast majority of respondents from developing nations believe in the threat of global warming (positive responses ranged from 84 to 94 per cent, dependent on country), whereas those from industrialized nations are not yet convinced (only between 49 and 64 per cent believe). Developing nations' respondents also claimed to be willing to pay more for eco-friendly products. Ninety-four per cent of Thai respondents and 83 per cent of Brazilians were willing to pay more for environmental friendliness, compared with 45 per cent of British and 53 per cent of American respondents.

Competitive advantage, innovation and new products

Given the scale of the sustainable development challenges faced, there are huge opportunities for organizations that can develop solutions to address these issues and understand how activities that benefit society can also reinforce corporate strategy and competitive advantage. Research by a range of academics at leading business schools has highlighted the way in which a focus on sustainability can drive innovation and competitive advantage – for example, Professor Michael Porter's work on the link between corporate advantage and corporate social responsibility (Porter and Kramer, 2006) and, more recently, the work by Professor C. K. Prahalad at the Michigan Business School (co-written with Dr R. Nidumolu and M. R. Rangaswami), which underlined this link:

> *Executives behave as though they have to choose between the largely social benefits of developing sustainable products or processes and the financial costs of doing so. But that's simply not true. We've been studying the sustainability initiatives of 30 large corporations for some time. Our research shows that sustainability is a mother lode of organizational and technological innovations that yield both bottom-line and top-line returns.* (Nidumolu et al, 2009, pp3–4)

This type of thinking is demonstrated by General Electric's (GE) 'Ecomagination' initiative – a business strategy designed to drive innovation and the growth of profitable environmental solutions to challenges such as climate change. The resulting products aim to enable GE and its customers to reduce emissions while generating revenue for GE from their sale. 2010 targets include the growth of Ecomagination-related revenue to US$25 billion and a doubling of research and development (R&D) to US$1.5 billion from 2005 levels, in addition to targets relating to the reduction of environmental impacts, such as the 30 per cent reduction in greenhouse gas emissions intensity against a 2004 benchmark achieved in 2009. In financial terms, the 2008 Ecomagination-related R&D spend of US$1.4 billion represented nearly half the company's total R&D spend for the year and 14 per cent of revenues, clearly signalling the significance of these initiatives in terms of strategic direction.

Attracting, motivating and retaining staff

There is a well-established link between an organization's sustainable development performance, employee satisfaction and financial performance. For example, the Towers Perrin Global Workforce Study 2007–2008, involving 40 global companies over three years, found a spread of more than 5 per cent in operating margin and more than 3 per cent in net profit margin between the companies with high employee engagement and those with low engagement (Towers Perrin, 2008). Similarly, Ipsos MORI research published in 2006 (Palmeris, 2006) shows that an organization's sustainability performance will not only improve employee engagement – including aspects of employer advocacy, commitment and motivation – but help to attract and retain employees. For example, for those surveyed in the UK, three-quarters of employees who consider their organization to be paying enough attention to environmental protection and sustainable development exhibit high levels of commitment. In contrast, over half of those working for organizations that they believe possess inadequate policies in these areas demonstrate low levels of commitment.

Managing risk

In addition to reputation risk (discussed below), there is a wide range of sustainability-related risks to which an organization may be subject – for example:

- threats to security of the supply of key inputs and supply chain reliability;
- shortage of skilled labour resulting from changing demographics;
- vulnerability to regulatory change resulting in carbon taxes or tighter environmental permit requirements;
- political risk, particularly when operating in emerging markets; and
- risk of business disruption (e.g. through the projected physical impacts of climate change on site location).

Driving operational efficiencies and cost reduction

Acting in a more environmentally sustainable manner can have direct cost savings – for example, in terms of:

- energy use;
- raw material and other inputs;
- travel costs;
- waste disposal costs; and
- minimizing fines and penalties.

Costs in many of these areas are projected to increase due to increasing global demand and finite limits to supply, as well as from greater environmental taxation, such as the Landfill Tax in the UK. By increasing staff satisfaction, there can also be reduced costs associated with employee turnover and absenteeism, in addition to positive productivity impacts. Indirectly, sustainability can also help to gain support for operational efficiency programmes, breaking down organizational or cross-functional barriers to change. For instance, Marks & Spencer's Plan A – a business-wide action plan to improve sustainability performance – was originally announced as a UK£200 million cost to the business. By 2009, two years into the five-year initiative, it has already been announced as, at worst (from a financial perspective), cost neutral.

Maintaining licence to operate

An organization that can demonstrate a positive impact on the communities and environment within which it operates is more likely to be able to maintain its licence to operate in terms of legal permits and contracts, local community support and broader support from international civil society organizations. Positive outcomes might include:

- the increased ability to obtain planning permission;
- winning government contracts, the terms of which increasingly include requirements related to sustainable development-related performance; and
- reducing local community or international non-governmental organization (NGO) boycotts or campaigns against the company.

Frequently, employees and, in some cases, customers will be drawn from the local community, underlining the need for positive relationships to be established. A deterioration in relationships with communities can have a significant negative impact on profits that can be hard to recover.

Accessing capital

There is a trend towards the integration of environmental, social and governance (ESG) considerations within the finance sector, which has an impact on access to both debt and equity finance. Considerations include:

- improved access to debt financing;
- lower cost of capital through lower perceived risk; and
- the impact of increased shareholder value on the ability to raise capital through debt and equity markets.

Underlining the growing impact of incorporating ESG considerations within the financial markets, 650 institutions are signatories to the United Nations Principles for Responsible Investment (UN PRI). Together, they represent in excess of US$18 trillion in assets and are committed to incorporating ESG within investment decision-making (UN PRI, 2009).

Reputation and brand

One of the most widely recognized benefits from acting more sustainably is the contribution that this can make to an organization's brand and reputation, interconnected with many of the factors described above. Positive brand impact related to sustainable practices can increase an organization's ability to attract and retain all key stakeholders, including customers, employees, governments and investors. Conversely, where a gap between branding and actual performance exists, companies risk the destruction of their brand value. As with risks relating to licence to operate (see above), once an organization's reputation has been adversely affected by perceived negative environmental or social practices, it can be hard to regain the public's trust. This has been experienced by many of the major high street brands, such as Gap and Nike, following negative publicity highlighting human rights abuses in the supply chain.

Embedding sustainability considerations into business practice through accounting for sustainability

Traditional business, financial and accounting practices have tended to focus solely on the financial or economic outcome of business activities. In the commercial sector, these practices have sought to help maximize financial returns in the form of increased profit and shareholder value. More recently, however, a growing recognition of the potentially significant negative social and environmental impacts of human actions (see above) has led many organizations to also consider the social and environmental outcomes of their activities.

Where these outcomes were often previously treated as externalities, without considering their longer-term impact on the organization itself, they are now progressively being brought into decision-making processes. From this perspective, sustainability is seen as an increasingly urgent strategic issue that poses significant challenges to business, the public sector and society as a whole. Creative responses and solutions are required to address these challenges by embedding sustainability considerations within strategic and day-to-day decision-making and action, thereby moving us towards a more sustainable future.

In the context of the widespread and growing recognition that both environmental and social sustainability, alongside economic sustainability, are among the major challenges facing society today, sustainability accounting and reporting practices have developed considerably in recent years. Accounting has a variety of important roles to play in the effective response to the challenges of balancing financial, environmental and social sustainability at the organizational level. It can:

- help organizations to identify their past and potential future environmental and social impacts and benefits, in addition to the historical and forecast financial outcomes from their activities;
- provide forward-looking information to help organizations both formulate and implement strategic solutions to strengthen business performance and respond to the challenges of sustainability;
- support risk management through the identification and analysis of, and response to, sustainability-related risks and opportunities; and

- be used to give an account of an organization's sustainability policies, practices and impacts to a range of third parties to whom the organization is responsible and accountable.

Underlying all of these roles is the potential of accounting to make visible, through both quantitative and qualitative information, a broad range of financial, environmental and social consequences of organizational strategies and actions, and implications of external economic, environmental and social trends for the organization's financial performance. These include not only the consequences that have arisen from past strategy and action, but also possible future consequences based on an organization's strategic plans. Raising the visibility of these consequences can then help to embed issues of sustainability in the day-to-day language and discussions within organizations. This added visibility and embedding through accounting for sustainability can thus raise the profile and status of sustainability management and impacts, both in internal management decision-making and in the external profile of the organization.

For accounting to more fully realize its potential role in this complex arena of sustainability requires commitment and innovative long-term solutions. In recognizing the crucial role of accounting in their sustainability management practices, a growing number of organizations have been committed to developing such imaginative and innovative sustainability accounting and reporting practices.

Often the most visible of these practices are those used to report, to external stakeholders, an organization's economic, social and environmental impacts and its policies and practices aimed at reducing its negative impacts or externalities. In this area of external reporting, many organizations have played an active role in developing social and environmental reporting and assurance guidelines, such as the Global Reporting Initiative's (GRI's) sustainability reporting framework and the AccountAbility 1000 (AA1000) series. Similarly, there is increasing recognition of the importance of explaining performance in relation to environmental and social factors as part of the *Management Discussion and Analysis, Business Review* or *Operating and Financial Review* section of the annual report and accounts, where these factors are material to an organization's performance. The recently released King III report (The King Committee on Governance, 2009) in South Africa, widely recognized as setting best practice in corporate governance, explicitly requires integration of sustainability within reporting as an essential component of good governance. The UK Accounting Standards Board's *Reporting Standard 1: Operating and Financial Review* is seen to represent best practice reporting guidance for companies responding to the UK Companies Act 2006 requirement for the inclusion of matters relating to the environment, employees and social and community issues, to the extent necessary to understand the company's business. A4S's work around connected reporting and development of the Connected Reporting Framework (CRF), described in Chapter 2, builds on these recommendations.

While these guidelines have been used by many organizations to help develop their sustainability reporting, often this has focused on presenting an organization's positive and negative impacts across social, environmental and economic spheres – the 'external' perspective – within a standalone corporate responsibility or sustainability report. Such reporting seldom explicitly links these issues to the organization's own sustainability or provides an explanation of the materiality of social and environmental issues reported upon to the organization's long-term financial viability and success. Similarly, there is little integration and analysis of these issues within the annual report and accounts, even where these would be material to the organization's future performance. In other words, there has been little explicit connection in the reporting of financial sustainability with social and environmental sustainability, or in the materiality of the impacts arising from sustainability issues covered in the reports – either to the organization or to society as a whole.

Unless these issues are explicitly connected, it is difficult for both external and internal users of sustainability and financial reports to fully understand the dynamic interactions between an organization's environmental, social and financial sustainability, and their significance. More explicit connected or integrated reporting, within the annual report and accounts, has the potential to help embed considerations of social and environmental sustainability within strategic and day-to-day management practices by making explicit the financial benefits of greater sustainability and signalling the significance of these issues both to internal and external stakeholders. It can also help these stakeholders, including investors, to better appreciate the financial impacts and benefits of policies and actions aimed at greater economic, environmental and social sustainability.

Furthermore, without explicit connection within an organization's reporting between financial and wider economic, social and environmental impacts, including an indication of the materiality of these impacts, it is easy for a company to convey a false sense of meaningful action on sustainability. Without this explicit connection, its sustainability reporting may focus on incremental changes in socially or environmentally immaterial impacts and present a very different picture than that outlined within the annual report and accounts. There is a real difference between an organization genuinely striving to become sustainable and a company merely employing the rhetoric of sustainability in its external reports without much substance underlying this rhetoric. The former will work to embed an integrated or connected understanding of the environmental, social and economic impacts of its strategies and actions within its decision-making processes and will understand the implications of these external factors on business performance. It should then have the information available to report on its social, environmental and economic performance in an integrated and connected manner, reflecting the governance of these issues and how they relate to results achieved, now and in the future. The latter type of company is unlikely to have information that would enable it to meaningfully report on its sustainability in a connected manner and may be using its external reporting as a form of greenwash.

To help further distinguish between organizations that use external sustainability reporting to reflect their real and meaningful underlying social, environmental and financial sustainability strategies, actions and impacts and organizations for whom external sustainability reporting is effectively a fiction, the sustainability consequences of policies and actions should be made visible inside the organization as well as outside. Organizations that are really serious about addressing issues of sustainability will have invested the resources necessary to develop internal and external sustainability accounting and reporting systems that:

- complement one another;
- connect financial with social and environmental sustainability information; and
- help to embed sustainability considerations within strategic decision-making and day-to-day actions throughout the organization.

While external sustainability reporting is a highly visible activity from which other organizations can readily learn, by their nature the internal sustainability accounting practices developed and used by organizations to aid decision-making and management control are much less visible. There is evidence that sustainability accounting information plays an increasingly important role in management decision-making and control at a variety of different levels in many organizations. However, it is not usually apparent to those outside the organization how sustainability reporting connects, in practice, to strategic decision-making and action. Making these issues visible is part of the aim of the accounting for sustainability case studies in this book.

To help organizations realize some of the above potential benefits from innovative sustainability accounting practices, over the past five years A4S has worked with businesses, investors, public-sector organizations, accounting bodies, academics and NGOs to develop practical guidance and tools for embedding sustainability within decision-making and reporting.

The aim of A4S is to try to move to a position where sustainability is regarded as a more mainstream aspect of organizational functioning, embedded in day-to-day operations and decision-making. Seen in such terms, the way in which accounting and reporting processes affect behaviour and decisions taken within organizations is potentially as important as the way in which the impacts themselves are reflected in the reporting of sustainability. Equally important is recognition of the factors that motivate organizations to engage in meaningful accounting for sustainability and embed these processes and practices within their decision-making.

To avert the significant environmental, social and economic risks from climate change and other threats to sustainable development, described above, and to capitalize on the considerable opportunities from moving to a sustainable economy, it is necessary for organizations of all sizes across all sectors to embed considerations of environmental and social sustainability within their strategic and tactical decision-making, and to transform these decisions into effective action. In developing their response, organizations need to make use of all the tools available to them to help them embed sustainability within all of their discussions, decisions and actions. Accounting provides a variety of such tools. The case studies in this book, which are summarized in the following section, aim to illustrate some of the important roles that accounting and reporting can and do play in helping organizations to become more environmentally, socially and economically sustainable.

Summary of the case studies

Each of the case studies in the subsequent chapters addresses different aspects of accounting for sustainability. In order to help readers who are less familiar with A4S, Chapter 2 contains a summary of the key recommendations and tools resulting from the project's research. In this chapter, Jessica Fries, Karen McCulloch and Will Webster explain the following three aspects of A4S's work:

1   the ten main elements to embed sustainability successfully, based on work with organizations in the food, construction, financial and public sectors;
2   a sustainability decision-making tool or methodology to enable sustainability issues to be taken into account more robustly and consistently in day-to-day decision-making; and
3   the CRF, a new approach to corporate reporting focused on the needs of 'economic' stakeholders (e.g. long-term investors and executive management) that seeks to help organizations report more effectively (both internally and externally) their financial, environmental and social sustainability policies, practices and performance in a connected manner.

The case studies look at how eight organizations have approached the adoption of these principles and tools, setting out both the process followed and key learnings that will help others to better account for sustainability.

Sainsbury's

The first of the case studies, in Chapter 3, examines the application of the A4S decision-making tool at Sainsbury's, one of the UK's largest supermarket chains.

Laura J. Spence and Leonardo Rinaldi examine how the decision-making tool has been applied to help Sainsbury's identify and manage sustainability impacts in their supply chain, along with the main challenges that had to be overcome in doing so. The case study focuses specifically on the application of the decision-making tool in improving economic, social and environmental sustainability at key stages in the sourcing of lamb products. Among the many important issues highlighted in this case study, it was found that the demonstration of commercial advantages in terms of both cost savings and increased income from greater environmental and social sustainability was a key factor in helping to embed sustainability both internally and among suppliers to Sainsbury's. For example, many sheep farmers who operate at very low profit margins were initially reluctant to engage with the sustainability agenda as they thought it was a luxury they could not afford. However, when the connected environmental and financial impacts were clearly explained, the farmers realized that operating in a more environmentally sustainable manner would also produce positive financial outcomes at the level of the individual farm. Thus, they became willing to change their farming practices to a more environmentally sustainable model. In some instances, particularly at the more strategic level within Sainsbury's, quantification of commercial benefits is not always possible. For this type of decision, which relies, to a certain extent, on managerial instinct, clear leadership and effective communication were found to be essential factors in embedding sustainability considerations within decision-making.

EDF Energy

The case study of EDF Energy, a power company that is the UK's largest distributor and supplier of electricity, is presented in Chapter 4. Linda Lewis and David Ferguson analyse how the principles underlying A4S have been used to drive changes in EDF Energy's sustainability decision-making. This is considered to be a core component of EDF Energy's values-driven approach to business performance. As in the Sainsbury's case, the principal role of accounting for sustainability at EDF Energy was seen to be in providing internal information to help embed sustainability considerations within decisions taken at all levels of the organization. The values-driven performance agenda at EDF Energy is focused through the company's adoption and dissemination of five key 'ambitions' as its strategic objectives. These ambitions are in the interrelated areas of:

- safety for all stakeholders;
- providing customer choice, while protecting vulnerable customers;
- fulfilling financial expectations for shareholders;
- meeting its social and environmental commitments; and
- developing its employees while embedding equality and diversity.

To help achieve each of these 'ambitions', EDF Energy sets measurable targets and monitors performance against these by using a combination of practices, including reporting and assurance. The internal information used to evaluate performance in this manner forms the basis of EDF Energy's external sustainability reporting. The case study shows how internal use of the CRF has helped EDF Energy to develop and embed several of its sustainability decision-making practices and has added additional visibility and rigour to the manner in which performance is evaluated for each of the five ambitions. In particular, the case study focuses on the manner in which connected reporting has helped to connect thinking in the areas of EDF Energy's climate and social commitments. As with Sainsbury's, EDF Energy has found that support from senior management and clear communication of the key issues to other levels in the organization are essential factors in the more effective embedding of sustainability within decision-making.

West Sussex County Council

Chapter 5 takes the focus from sustainability decision-making in private-sector consumer-driven organizations to such decision-making in the public sector. It outlines a case study of accounting for sustainability at West Sussex County Council – a large local authority in the south of England. Suzana Grubnic and David Owen trace the 'golden thread' of policies, practices and structures at West Sussex County Council. These are designed to link operational activities and internal decision-making to the council's overarching public commitment to sustainability strategies across the three spheres of economic, social and environmental sustainability. In particular, the case study examines the role of the principles within A4S in providing a connected framework for:

- the council's Corporate Sustainability Programme;
- integrated performance management systems developed to deliver on this programme through setting challenging but achievable targets; and
- a set of tools developed to embed sustainability considerations within operational decisions and actions.

Alongside its financial statements, the council is also committed to publishing annually an external sustainability report consistent with the principles underlying the CRF. A key finding from the West Sussex County Council case study echoes findings from the Sainsbury's and EDF Energy case studies. This states that a clear commitment to sustainability from senior leaders (in this case, both political leaders and senior executives at the council) is an important factor in embedding sustainability throughout the organization's operations. Furthermore, despite this being a public-sector organization, clear communication of a business case linking positive environmental and social outcomes to financial benefits has helped in embedding a connected understanding of sustainability within decisions and actions. However, the long-term nature of many social and environmental initiatives was seen to sometimes conflict with an often short- to medium-term political time horizon among the local authority's elected political leaders, hindering the embedding of the business case for sustainability. This challenge is seen to be exacerbated by a lack of connected sustainability thinking between some central and local government policies, which can hinder the effective realization of several sustainability targets at local authority level.

The Environment Agency

One body that can exert pressure on central government on issues of sustainability is the UK Environment Agency, the subject of the case study in Chapter 6. Ian Thomson and Georgios Georgakopoulos explore the role of accounting for sustainability both in internal operational decision-making and in external connected sustainability reporting at this UK public body. The Environment Agency's main aims are 'to protect and improve the environment and to promote sustainable development'. In fulfilling these aims, it seeks to be an exemplar on sustainability issues for UK public- and private-sector organizations, including in the area of systems and practices in accounting for sustainability. The case study finds that the Environment Agency's own development of accounting for sustainability systems and practices has been integral to its management decision-making and control systems for many years. There is, therefore, a well-developed management accounting system that captures and records considerable detail regarding non-financial environmental impacts alongside more traditional economic cost information. The case study provides examples of how some of the detailed non-financial sustainability information is captured in the Environment Agency's management accounting systems and how this is used in decisions taken at all levels of the organization. Although many of these detailed practices predate A4S, it is felt that the CRF has helped to provide additional legitimacy for what the Environment Agency was doing in this area. Practical challenges are also highlighted in the case study, along with the recognition that although the connected reporting data in the Environment Agency's management information systems is built from the bottom upwards, buy-in and leadership from senior management has been an essential component in seeking to embed sustainability across decision-making at all levels.

Turning to external connected sustainability reporting, the case study explains that, in addition to its own reporting practices, the Environment Agency is active in bodies establishing reporting guidelines for UK public-sector organizations. In this role, the agency states that the CRF has a key part to play in helping organizations to report more effectively on their sustainability strategies, actions and impacts. However, it also believes that the most effective implementation of such reporting in the public sector will require the principles in the CRF to be established within a mandatory reporting standard.

BT

The case study of BT, a global communications company and the largest such company in the UK, develops the theme of external sustainability reporting in Chapter 7. Jeffrey Unerman and Brendan O'Dwyer focus on the CRF at BT and examine the way in which sustainability decisions and impacts drive the company's external connected reporting. This external reporting focus of the BT case study is in contrast to the previous case studies, which have primarily focused on how the principles underlying A4S were used to help develop connected understandings of sustainability in strategic and operational decision-making. For several years BT has, indeed, acted to embed such sustainability considerations within its strategic and operational decision-making processes. It has achieved this by clearly developing and communicating business case reasoning that links the direct and indirect economic benefits of an action with consideration of its social and environmental impacts. This connected thinking on sustainability, which has been embedded within decision-making at all levels in BT, in the context of a values-driven organization, provides many sustainability-related issues that could be integrated with BT's external reporting to demonstrate the connections between the company's strategy, its financial performance and sustainability factors.

The case study explores the manner in which BT attributes risk and materiality to each sustainability issue. This illustrates how decisions are made regarding which issues are reported in BT's detailed sustainability reports and which are then incorporated within the summary sustainability review and throughout the annual report. Focusing on a specific example of one of BT's core corporate responsibility risk areas – supply-chain ethics through BT's Sourcing with Human Dignity Initiative – the case study demonstrates how these issues of risk and materiality play out in articulating and embedding the business case for sustainability in this area within BT's operations. It then leads on to decisions regarding how and what to report about the initiative in BT's external reports. Consistent with the findings from the previous case studies, it is found that leadership direction from senior management and carefully targeted clear communication of the benefits from sustainability are key factors in more successfully embedding sustainability within decision-making at all levels.

HSBC

The relationship between the management of sustainability issues through HSBC's strategy, operations and both internal and external initiatives provides the focus for the case study of HSBC in Chapter 8. Alnoor Bhimani and Kazbi Soonawalla begin by exploring HSBC's adoption of a key sustainability initiative in the banking sector, the Equator Principles, and how HSBC has extended these principles to develop its own sector policies. Through the adoption of the Equator Principles, banks such as HSBC systematically take sustainability risk criteria into account in screening major project finance loan applications, and therefore can exert considerable influence on the sustainability practices of this group of large business customers. This integration of sustainability risk considerations is also incorporated, through HSBC's sector policies, within lending or investment decisions in companies or projects operating in sensitive or high-impact sectors such as forestry.

The case study then looks at the ways in which sustainability, particularly the impacts of climate change, have been integrated within the organization and culture of the bank. This is considered from two perspectives. First, the approach to day-to-day operations is discussed, with examples of how target-setting and the use of information systems can support organizational change. A further example used to illustrate this is drawn from HSBC's services supply chain, where many environmental impacts are managed within a service's outsourcing relationship. As a result of this relationship, HSBC benefits from the contractor's wider experience with other organizations, while at the same time the contractor broadens its own experience. The second perspective explores some of the various initiatives that the group has put in place to encourage change in employee behaviour. Finally, the case study analyses how the focus of issues covered in HSBC's sustainability reporting has evolved over the period from 2000 to 2008, and how external frameworks (such as the Equator Principles and CRF) were increasingly used in the content and structuring of the reports. HSBC first used the CRF in its 2007 *Sustainability Report*; since then it has helped to provide a more coherent picture of the connected nature of sustainability and financial information.

Aviva

The importance of connected thinking and reporting in helping to foster sustainability both within an organization and, much more broadly, in a range of businesses in which the organization invests is explored in Chapter 9. In the case study of Aviva, Martin Brigham, Paraskevi Vicky Kiosse and David Otley examine four key sustainability initiatives related to accounting for sustainability at this global financial services group. These four initiatives are:

1   the implementation of connected reporting, especially around operational environmental impacts;
2   commitments to carbon neutrality in Aviva's operations;
3   fostering sustainability of stakeholder behaviour at different stages of Aviva's value chain, including suppliers and companies in which the various investment funds managed by Aviva hold shares; and
4   extending this last initiative through to enhancing sustainability considerations in Aviva's socially responsible investment products.

Aviva recognizes the importance of good environmental and social governance practices at investee companies when assessing the risk and future performance of these. It has therefore sought to embed a connected understanding of financial, social and environmental factors within the investment appraisal and analysis undertaken by all of its investment funds. Aviva does not only restrict these factors to decisions related specifically to socially responsible investment funds, although such funds will additionally have ethically informed explicit restrictions on the types of companies in which they can invest. The case study also explains Aviva's external sustainability reporting practices, which have applied the guidance in the CRF to direct environmental impacts since 2007. This reporting draws upon extensive quantified records of environmental impacts in many areas of Aviva's operations. A key added dimension from adopting the CRF has been a clearer demonstration of how financial impacts are linked to the environmental impacts of strategies and actions, thereby clarifying the business case for sustainability. The case study concludes with a range of lessons and suggestions drawn from Aviva's experiences to help other organizations embed a connected notion of sustainability within their strategy and actions through accounting for sustainability.

Novo Nordisk

The final case study in Chapter 10 examines accounting for sustainability at the Danish pharmaceutical company Novo Nordisk. Colin Dey and John Burns provide a range of forward-looking illustrations of how the principles underlying A4S might develop to further embed sustainability considerations within organizational strategy and actions. Although, at the time of writing, Novo Nordisk has not formally adopted the CRF, its practices in the area of accounting for sustainability have developed over a long period and are deeply embedded within the DNA of the company. Many of these practices are consistent with the recommendations of A4S; but Novo Nordisk has also developed some practices that go further and deeper. The case study examines Novo Nordisk's 'integrated reporting' and how this reporting has served to embed sustainability within decisions taken at all levels in the company. Since 2004, when a range of sustainability commitments was formally adopted in the company's Articles of Association, Novo Nordisk has published a fully integrated annual report that covers both financial and social and environmental sustainability issues. The report complies with International Financial Reporting Standards, and with the GRI and AA1000 frameworks; but, unlike the CRF, the connection between financial, environmental and social factors, or between these factors and the organization's strategic action, is not made. The case study examines internal management control systems and feedback mechanisms within Novo Nordisk. These are integral to its embedding of accounting for sustainability within the company's broader framework of sustainability management guidelines and systems embodied in the Novo Nordisk 'Way of Management'. Central to these practices and systems has been:

- the evolution of a triple bottom line (TBL) approach to reporting sustain-ability;
- the use of balanced scorecards in the strategic and operational management of sustainability; and
- the application of what are considered to be best-practice Sarbanes–Oxley-style governance and monitoring processes to non-financial sustainability reporting.

In addition, Novo Nordisk has developed a mechanism entitled 'facilitation' to further embed sustainability. This provides effective and detailed feedback through tri-annual in-depth reviews of the sustainability processes and practices of each business unit, conducted by a specialist sustainability team drawn from senior managers. All of these processes and practices are generally supported by staff throughout the company who tend to be committed to the principles underlying sustainability.

Conclusions

Taken together, the findings from the eight case studies provide a broad range of insights that can help many organizations to:

- embed sustainability considerations within organizational decision-making, processes and practices in a way that is compatible with a sustainability agenda;
- improve the effectiveness of their reporting for both external and internal users of this information; and
- demonstrate how a broad and inclusive concept of sustainability can be, and needs to be, integrated into mainstream financial and business processes.

The case studies demonstrate how these organizations have employed specific aspects of A4S's proposals, and in many cases have also adapted and developed the project's recommendations. By drawing on these invaluable lessons, other organizations should be able to address more effectively many of the challenges and risks posed by the sustainability agenda. In doing so, they will realize the many opportunities and benefits potentially offered to innovative organizations in the essential move to a sustainable economy.

References

Carbon Disclosure Project (2010) *FTSE 100 Carbon Chasm*, London

European Commission Directorate General Environment/Eurobarometer 295 (2008) *Attitudes of European Citizens towards the Environment*, Brussels, Belgium

GE (2008a) *2008 Ecomagination Annual Report*, GE, Fairfield, Connecticut, USA

GE (2008b) *2008 Annual Report*, GE, Fairfield, Connecticut, USA

The King Committee on Governance (2009) *King Report on Governance for South Africa and the King Code of Governance Principles (King III)*, Institute of Directors in Southern Africa, South Africa

Marks and Spencer (2009) *Annual Report and Financial Statements 2009*, Marks and Spencer, London, p42

Meadows, D. H., Randers, J., and Meadows, D. L. (2004) *Limits to Growth: The 30 Year Update*, Earthscan Publications, London

Nidumolu, R., Prahalad, C. K. and Rangaswami, M. R. (2009) *Why Sustainability Is Now the Key Driver of Innovation*, Harvard Business Review, Boston, USA, September

Palimeris, M. (2006) *Engaging Employees through Corporate Responsibility*, Ipsos MORI Employee Relationship Management, London, November

Porter, M. E. and Kramer, M. R. (2006) *Strategy and Society: The Link Between Competitive Advantage and Corporate Social Responsibility*, Harvard Business Review, Boston, USA, 1 December

The Prince of Wales's Corporate Leaders Group on Climate Change (2009) *The Copenhagen Communiqué on Climate Change*, www.copenhagencommunique.com

Stern, N. (2006) *Stern Review on the Economics of Climate Change*, Launch Presentation, HM Treasury, London, 30 October 2006, www.hm-treasury.gov.uk/sternreview_index.htm

Stern, N. (2008) *Key Elements of a Global Deal on Climate Change*, London School of Economics and Political Science, London, www.eprints.lse.ac.uk/4874/1/Key_Elements_of_a_Global_Deal_-Final_version_1300_30-4.pdf

Stern, N. (2009), *Managing Climate Change and Overcoming Poverty: Facing the Realities and Building a Global Agreement*, Grantham Research Institute on Climate Change and the Environment, London School of Economics and Political Science, London, 21 September

TNS (2009) *The Green Life*, TNS, New York, 29 April

Towers Perrin (2008) *Closing the Engagement Gap: A Road Map for Driving Superior Business Performance*, Towers Perrin Global Workforce Study 2007–2008, Stamford, Connecticut, USA

United Nations Framework Convention on Climate Change (2009) *Copenhagen Accord*, December 2009

UN PRI (United Nations Principles for Responsible Investment, 2009) *Annual Report of the PRI Initiative 2009*, www.unpri.org/files/PRIAnnualReport09.pdf
Walmart (2009) *Sustainable Product Index: Fact Sheet*, 16 July, www.walmartstores.com/factsnews/newsroom/9277.aspx

two

The Prince's Accounting for Sustainability Project: Creating 21st-Century Decision-Making and Reporting Systems to Respond to 21st-Century Challenges and Opportunities

Jessica Fries, Karen McCulloch
and Will Webster

To help ensure that sustainability (considering what we do not only in terms of ourselves and today, but also of others and tomorrow) is not just talked and worried about, but becomes embedded in organizations' 'DNA'. (His Royal Highness The Prince of Wales)

Introduction

One of the key propositions made by The Prince's Accounting for Sustainability Project (A4S) is that the integration of sustainability into the way in which all organizations operate – within their 'DNA' – is a prerequisite to achieving a prosperous and sustainable economy and society. This is important to organizations, not just from a desire to act responsibly, but also for reasons underlying the business case for the integration of environmental and social factors within strategy and operations, as set out in Chapter 1.

Since it was established by The Prince of Wales in 2004, A4S has focused on developing practical tools and approaches in order to embed sustainability into mainstream decision-making, accounting and reporting. The work of A4S extends beyond a 'traditional' definition of accounting by considering:

- management practices and processes that can support the integration of sustainability into decision-making; and
- the role of information, accounting and reporting in driving behaviour change within organizations.

These are referred to by the project as 'accounting for sustainability'.

Initial work included assessing how the public sector could achieve increased value for money and improved sustainability outcomes through better accounting for sustainability, including an analysis of barriers to action, such as the structure of budgeting processes. Since then, work has focused on three strands:

1 Research and collation of good practice to explore and explain how to embed sustainability into decision-making processes, including a focus on barriers, how these can be overcome and the development of tools to achieve integration.
2 The development of the Connected Reporting Framework (CRF), a new approach to reporting that better reflects the link between financial and sustainability performance, driven by an organization's strategy and the way in which it is managed. Additional guidance was released in 2009 that focused on how to report in a connected way within the annual report and accounts and/or as part of internal management reporting (2009a). During 2010, A4S is collaborating with international financial accounting and sustainability reporting standard setters, as well as key stakeholder groups, to establish a common international framework and governance around integrated and connected reporting.
3 The creation of The Prince's Accounting for Sustainability Forum in 2008, an international group of organizations committed to the integration of sustainability within accounting and reporting. Key members of the forum include 19 international accounting bodies who have signed up to the forum's five principles. These are:
    - promoting better accounting for sustainability;
    - embedding accounting for sustainability within the signatories' own organizations;

- increasing understanding of good sustainability practice;
- sharing learning and experience; and (perhaps most importantly)
- incorporating accounting for sustainability within training and professional education.

To date, A4S has involved the participation of over 200 organizations, including investors, companies, government, accounting firms and institutes, academics and non-governmental organizations (NGOs). This chapter provides a brief summary of some of the key recommendations that A4S has made over the past three years, setting the context for the steps that the eight case study organizations, examined in subsequent chapters, have taken towards embedding sustainability, including how they have applied the project's recommendations in practice. These recommendations comprise:

- the ten main elements to embed sustainability into decision-making;
- an overview of the A4S decision-making tool; and
- an introduction to the concept of connected reporting and the CRF.

BOX 2.1 THE TEN MAIN ELEMENTS TO EMBED SUSTAINABILITY SUCCESSFULLY

The ten main elements comprise:

1 board and senior management commitment;
2 understanding and analysing the key sustainability drivers for the organization;
3 integrating the key sustainability drivers into the organization's strategy;
4 ensuring that sustainability is the responsibility of everyone in the organization (and not just of a specific department);
5 breaking down sustainability targets and objectives for the organization as a whole into targets and objectives that are meaningful for individual subsidiaries, divisions and departments;
6 processes that enable sustainability issues to be taken into account clearly and consistently in day-to-day decision-making;
7 extensive and effective sustainability training;
8 including sustainability targets and objectives in performance appraisal;
9 champions within the organization to promote sustainability and celebrate success;
10 monitoring and reporting sustainability performance.

Source: The Prince's Accounting for Sustainability Project (2007)

The ten main elements to embed sustainability into decision-making

In 2007, A4S set out ten main elements to embed sustainability successfully, summarized in Box 2.1. These recommendations were based on work with over 150 organizations representing a wide range of sectors from financial services and the public sector to construction and food. The case studies set out within this book provide practical examples of how different organizations have sought to apply these and other steps to embed sustainability, the challenges encountered and the outcomes achieved.

These ten elements are underlined by the findings of the case studies, which also provide detail on how they can be implemented in practice.

An overview of the A4S decision-making tool

As highlighted above, one of the most important elements to embed sustainability into organizational practice is systematic integration into decision-making. Given the complexity of different environmental, social and economic factors that need to be taken into account and balanced against one another in determining the sustainability impacts of different decisions, this is one of the most difficult areas in which to achieve successful embedding of sustainability. Challenges include:

- insufficient, or insufficiently robust, qualitative and quantitative information;
- information not easily accessible to those making the decisions;
- lack of clarity of desired outcomes or authorization to act;
- difficulty of determining what the 'right' outcome is;
- functional or intercompany divides, where more sustainable outcomes could be achieved by collaborative working;
- sustainability considerations not articulated in language that is meaningful or translated into terms that seem relevant to the decision-maker;
- longer time horizons over which the consequences of unsustainable actions will be felt – in particular, relative to pressure to meet often very short-term financial targets;
- outcomes not always quantifiable (in financial or non-financial terms); and
- integration perceived as an 'add on'.

The eight case studies covered within this book provide insights into how different organizations have sought to address these challenges through better accounting for sustainability.

One tool, launched in 2007, which can aid integration, is the A4S decision-making methodology to help organizations to ensure, when decisions about products and services are made, that sustainability factors can be taken into account:

- at the same time as, and alongside, more conventional factors, and in a way that enables the financial interrelationship between the two to be apparent;
- in a way that is consistent and robust across the organization; and
- which facilitates review by more senior management and subsequent reporting.

The methodology was developed by Environmental Resources Management in conjunction with, and tailored by, Cadbury Schweppes, Duchy Originals, Sainsbury's and Tesco. Since the launch of the A4S decision-making methodology, the Open University has developed an online continuing professional development programme based on the tool to help general managers, accountants and financial managers to understand and apply it (http://www3.open.ac.uk/study/professionaldevelopment/course/gt048.htm).

An overview of the A4S decision-making methodology

The decision-making methodology is divided into three broad phases:

- phase 1: reviewing the sustainability impacts of the product or service range;
- phase 2: analysing the sustainability impacts of a specific product or service;
- phase 3: reaching a balanced and informed decision as to how the product's or service's sustainability performance can be improved.

The inputs, outcomes and decisions resulting from each phase are summarized in Figure 2.1 and a brief summary of the overall process within each phase, as set out in the 2007 report, is described below. Additional detail, including a tutorial, can be found on the A4S website at www.accountingfor sustainability.com/embedding.

Phase 1: Reviewing the sustainability impacts of the product or service range

The aim of the first phase is to review the whole product or service range in order to understand, in broad terms, the impacts of that range on the environment, economy and society, as well as how external pressures impact on the product or service category across its life cycle. The methodology enables the user to do the following:

- *Identify relevant environmental and social issues.* This involves a high-level desktop review of a product or service and its life cycle in order to identify significant sustainability issues.

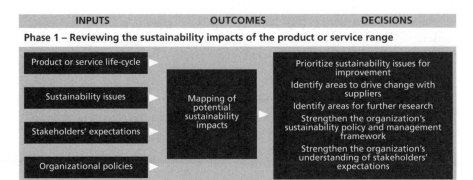

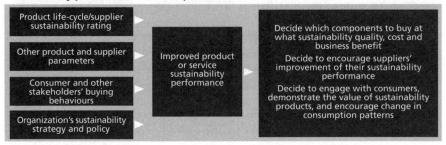

Figure 2.1 An overview of the A4S decision-making tool

Source: The Prince's Accounting for Sustainability Project (2007)

- *Understand and assess stakeholders' expectations.* The relevance of the sustainability issues across the life cycle can then be assessed against stakeholders' expectations.
- *Review current product sustainability standards and overall organizational sustainability policies.* It will be important to assess what the organization's overall strategy and objectives are and how the issues identified from the first two stages impact upon and align with them.

This phase allows the organization to prioritize those sustainability aspects of a product or service range that most critically need to be addressed. This may result in further research or discussion with suppliers.

Phase 2: Analysing the sustainability impacts of a specific product or service

The second phase of the methodology involves a more detailed assessment of a specific product or service life cycle, investigating the impacts and priorities identified in phase 1 in greater depth. It involves discussions with, for example, suppliers, in-house manufacturers and other stakeholders. The analysis is performed across the whole life cycle, from raw material production to manufacturing, distribution, consumer and post-consumer use. As described in Chapter 3, Sainsbury's conducted this phase of the process primarily through a workshop that brought together key suppliers and company representatives from product, technical and other relevant teams.

The methodology enables the user to do the following:

- *Understand the supplier's sustainability context* by:
  - identifying the relevant environmental and social issues and their likely impact on the environment, employees and local community.
- *Review the supplier's sustainability management practices* by:
  - assessing the supplier's sustainability management practices and performance; and
  - identifying areas requiring further improvement to match expected sustainability product or service standards.
- *Develop improvement action plans by*:
  - identifying options available for improving the sustainability performance of the product or service in relation to the significant sustainability issues (e.g. implementing new technology or changing suppliers); and
  - specifying the time frame for these identified improvements.

As a result, either a performance rating is generated to reflect the product's or service's sustainability quality, or an exception report is generated that highlights the products that, and suppliers who, are not meeting their agreed action plans in the time stated.

Phase 3: Reaching a balanced and informed decision as to how the product's or service's sustainability performance can be improved

The third phase involves integrating the newly generated information about the product's or service's sustainability performance rating within the organization's commercial decision-making processes, such as buying, selecting new suppliers and product labelling. It brings together the sustainability information and traditional financial indicators, such as margin, product cost, market share and expenditure.

Sainsbury's application of the decision-making tool

Sainsbury's was one of the companies that helped to develop the decision-making tool and has since applied the methodology to a range of key products and decisions comprising:

- assessing the sustainability of the lamb supply chain;
- assessing sustainability impacts and risks through the life cycle of Sainsbury's bananas (which have been 100 per cent Fairtrade Standard since 2007) to identify potential areas of vulnerability that were 'beyond the Fairtrade Standard';
- informing the sourcing decision between two carrier bag suppliers as part of a wider programme to reduce waste; and
- identifying potential actions that could be implemented to reduce the fungicide levels in citrus fruits that would not, in turn, jeopardize another part of the product's sustainability.

More detail on how Sainsbury's has applied this approach to the lamb supply chain and key learnings from its use, in practice, is covered in Chapter 3.

An introduction to the concept of connected reporting and the Connected Reporting Framework (CRF)

One of the main proposals made by A4S is the need for new approaches to accounting and reporting to reflect the broader and longer-term consequences of decisions taken. Without more complete and comprehensive information, companies, investors and others cannot make the fully informed decisions needed to survive and prosper in the face of the sustainability challenges set out in Chapter 1. The recent financial crisis has highlighted the need for capital market decision-making to reflect longer-term considerations and has called into question the extent to which corporate reporting disclosures highlight systemic risks and value drivers. A shift to a reporting model that supports the information needs of long-term investors, such as pension funds, and reflects the interconnected nature of financial, environmental, social and governance factors, is an essential step towards the creation of a sustainable economy.

The Connected Reporting Framework (CRF), initially developed by A4S in 2007, aims to provide a new approach to corporate reporting and to address the growing dissatisfaction, among both preparers and users, with the incompleteness, length and complexity of many organizations' annual reports and accounts, and sustainability reports. Information reported in a connected manner should identify and explain the connection between the organization's strategic objectives and the:

- industry, market and social context within which the business operates;
- associated risks and opportunities that it faces;
- key resources and relationships on which it depends; and
- governance, reward and remuneration structures in place.

Furthermore, it should explain the connection between delivery of the business's strategy and its financial and non-financial performance. The result of connected or integrated reporting is a more concise, rounded and balanced picture of an organization's overall performance, which reflects the organization's strategy and the way in which it is managed.

One essential element of a connected or integrated report is the organization's sustainability performance. The incorporation of environmental and social factors will help organizations to better identify and respond to sustainability-related opportunities and risks, and better communicate how these factors support delivery of the organization's strategic objectives.

The CRF was developed primarily with the needs of long-term investors and executive management in mind. Its intention was to ensure that reporting should be incorporated within internal management reporting and the annual report and accounts, rather than being reported separately as part of a stand-alone sustainability report. By requiring a company to think and act in a connected manner in order for reporting to be able to demonstrate those connections, the CRF also provides a way of building credibility with a broader set of stakeholders, many of whom increasingly demand the incorporation of material sustainability information within the annual report and accounts. Integration within the annual report and accounts will help to highlight the sustainability of the strategy that the organization is pursuing in financial, environmental and social terms, and that management recognizes and is responding to sustainability issues.

Since its initial release, the CRF has been adopted by a range of companies, including Aviva, BT, EDF Energy, HSBC, Hammerson and Northern Foods. In addition, it has been adapted for use by all public-sector organizations in the UK based on Treasury guidance, due for adoption in 2010, following its pilot by the Environment Agency, West Sussex County Council and a number of other public bodies. New 'how to' guidance, *Connected Reporting: A Practical Guide with Worked Examples* (The Prince's Accounting for Sustainability Project, 2009a), which builds on the 2007 report and reflects consultation with over 100 organizations, was released in 2009. A number of these organizations are covered by the case studies.

A summary of the 2007 guidance

The CRF guidance, set out within the *Accounting for Sustainability Report* (The Prince's Accounting for Sustainability Project, 2007), described the following key elements as fundamental to the framework:

- Sustainability issues need to be clearly linked to an organization's overall strategy.
- Sustainability and more conventional financial information should be presented together in a clear and concise manner so that a more complete and balanced picture of the organization's performance is given.
- There should be consistency in presentation to aid comparability between different years and organizations, with data prepared according to recognized measurement and accounting standards, wherever possible.
- Reported information should be aligned with that used to manage the business.
- The use of the framework should support behavioural change towards more sustainable practices.

The guidance also underlined the importance of strong underlying principles to the credibility of reporting, cross-referencing:

- the International Accounting Standards Board's guidance on the characteristics of financial reporting: understandability, relevance, reliability and comparability; and
- the principles set out within the Global Reporting Initiative's (GRI's) sustainability reporting guidelines.

As mentioned above, core to the suggested CRF is that it provides a framework for reporting strategically important financial and sustainability performance in a way that demonstrates the strong interdependence between the two. This concept is illustrated in Figure 2.2, which shows the interconnected range of activities and sectors that need to be integrated within a connected report.

The guidance then went on to describe five key recommendations that underpinned the CRF, summarized in Box 2.2. Use of the framework was illustrated by:

- a worked example showing how an oil and gas company might apply the recommendations to the five environmental indicators; and
- examples of application, in practice, as part of either internal or external reporting by three companies – Aviva, EDF Energy and HSBC – all of which have continued to develop their application of the CRF and are covered within the case study chapters.

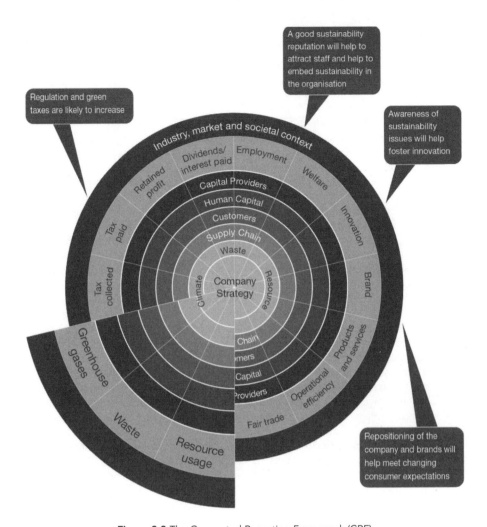

Figure 2.2 The Connected Reporting Framework (CRF)

Source: The Prince's Accounting for Sustainability Project (2007)

Findings from the 2008 consolidated case study into the use of the CRF

During 2008, a consolidated case study was conducted to understand the experience of organizations that had applied the CRF to date and to inform the development of additional guidance. The participants in this consolidated case study came from a wide range of different sectors; but despite this diversity, the issues, benefits and challenges from using the CRF tended to be consistent. In particular, participants noted the following:

BOX 2.2 2007 CONNECTED REPORTING FRAMEWORK
RECOMMENDATIONS

1 *Sustainability and strategy.* It is a critical component of the Connected Reporting Framework (CRF) for the organization to explain how sustainability fits into its operations or business, and to present the information that is material to the organization and its stakeholders in achieving its stated strategy. The framework will highlight this by the connection between sustainability and financial performance and by the use of targets and narrative. The type of information may, of course, change over time as the strategic objectives of the organization change. The provision of targets is particularly important in sustainability areas to ensure and demonstrate that sustainability issues are taken into account when making investment decisions.

2 *Five environmental indicators.* All organizations should report the following environmental indicators: polluting emissions, waste, water usage, energy usage, and significant use of other finite resources. Given the current level of concern about climate change and the environment generally, no organization can afford to ignore these areas. If an organization believes that its impact in one of the five specified areas is not material, then the reasons should be explained. This will avoid concern about possible cherry-picking.

3 *Relevance and flexibility.* In addition to the five indicators noted above, other key sustainability information should be given where the operation or business has material impacts. This will demonstrate that the organization has analysed and is addressing its sustainability impacts across the spectrum. The framework is not prescriptive in this respect in order to avoid the provision of irrelevant and therefore unhelpful and 'cluttering' information and a one-size-fits-all approach.

4 *Industry benchmarks.* To aid performance appraisal, industry benchmarks for the key performance indicators should be included where available. It is hoped that organizations will continue to work with others in their sector or industry to develop these benchmarks.

5 *Beyond the legal core.* An organization should also take into account and, if material, reflect in its reporting the upstream and downstream impacts of its products and services, in addition to its own impacts. Often these are the areas where the greatest sustainability impacts occur and can only be solved by organizations working together with other businesses, investors and government, seeking a more holistic solution rather than one that works solely for one organization.

Source: The Prince's Accounting for Sustainability Project (2007)

- All had a strong desire to link sustainability reporting to financial performance and strategic direction in a connected way.
- Much of the data needed was already available and the additional time needed to collate it, and compile and present the report, was relatively short.

- The CRF helped to identify cost savings by bringing together the analysis of financial and sustainability information.
- Sustainability awareness increased as a result of adopting the CRF, both internally at board and operational level, and externally with investors and customers.
- Use of the CRF drove increased collaboration between different parts of the business – in particular, finance and sustainability teams. Providing a common language and demonstrating the relevance of sustainability led to positive behavioural change and greater integration of sustainability issues within decisions taken.
- Organizations using the CRF wished to see continued development of the framework's scope to include material social impacts, as well as enhanced guidance on the link to overall strategy – an area that most felt they had not yet fully achieved to date.

These findings have been supported by feedback received from other companies that have since adopted this approach to reporting – for example, Paula Widdowson, corporate responsibility director at Northern Foods plc, commented:

> *Since we applied a connected approach to reporting on 'The Northern Way' in our 2008/9 Annual Report, there has been a definite reduction in the number of questions asked by investors. Not only does the reported information pre-empt many questions, but the fact that the data in the annual report is supported by a consolidation of monthly data adds further credibility.*

Additional developments during 2009

In response to feedback received, additional guidance, *Connected Reporting: A Practical Guide with Worked Examples*, was developed through consultation with a range of stakeholders and building on research into the experience of organizations that had sought to report in a connected way (The Prince's Accounting for Sustainability Project, 2009c). The aim of the updated guidance was to provide organizations with a simple approach to making, and reporting on, the connection between strategic objectives, financial performance and environmental and social considerations. Key areas to which the guidance aimed to respond, building on the 2007 recommendations, are summarized as follows:

- *The need for a better link to strategy.* While the 2007 report stated that sustainability issues need to be clearly linked to an organization's overall strategy, it did not define how this link might be demonstrated. There was therefore seen to be a need to provide further guidance on how to demonstrate the relevance of different sustainability factors to an organization's strategic objectives and the links between these different aspects of performance.

- *Principles, not a template.* The worked example referred to above provides a clear basis on which to report, and assists comparability and consistency in presentation. However, many organizations restricted their application to the template which covered the five environmental indicators only, rather than seeking to apply the broader principles and recommendations. This underlined the challenge of implementing strategically focused reporting guidelines that do not lend themselves to use of a standard template. The 2009 guidance sought to underline the need for each organization to think in a connected manner and to use the CRF as a mechanism to support clear communication of this connected thinking.
- *Balance between materiality and comparability.* The CRF's flexibility, seen by many as one of its key attributes, encourages organizations to focus on material sustainability issues, which will differ by sector and individual organization, rather than as a 'tick-box' compliance exercise. This need for flexibility must be balanced against the need for comparability of information, highlighted in the 2007 recommendations. Comparability will only be achieved where reporting is underpinned by common international reporting definitions, metrics and standards that can by applied by organizations in the same sector and, where relevant, across sectors.
- *A 'CRF journey' towards a new reporting model.* Development of the CRF is intended to build on the framework presented in the 2007 report, rather than replace it. Different organizations are at different stages of the journey towards embedding sustainability into their DNA, and A4S therefore presented 'connected or integrated reporting' as a journey. Some organizations will be ready and able to properly integrate sustainability considerations throughout their annual reporting and within internal management reporting. Many others will be starting to make these connections, but may not be able to apply all of the principles of connected reporting across all aspects of performance.

The 2009 update of the CRF provides further detailed guidance on 'what to report' (summarized in Box 2.3) and practical steps suggesting how this might be achieved. In addition, the guidance also contains three worked examples for the food retail, property investment and water/wastewater sectors, developed through industry and investor consultations. The full guidance is available from the A4S website at www.accountingforsustainability.org/reporting.

BOX 2.3 CONNECTED REPORTING: A SUMMARY OF 2009 GUIDANCE ON WHAT TO REPORT

Step 1: Connecting business strategy and sustainability

- *Market context*: an analysis of the environmental and social trends which have a material impact on the sector, market and regulatory context within which the business is operating, where possible in quantitative terms and supported by evidence.
- *Business model*: a description of the implications for the way in which the business operates and generates value in response to identified environmental and social trends.
- *Objectives and strategies, risks, resources and relationships*: the connection between material sustainability impacts and issues, the achievement of the company's objectives, and implications for the strategies it has adopted. The analysis of material sustainability issues should include:
  - principal risks and opportunities, an explanation as to why they are important and an estimate of their impact in either financial or operational terms;
  - assessment of the sustainability of key resources (natural, human and financial) and key relationships (e.g. supplier, customer, employee, regulator, community) upon which the strategy is dependent;
  - reference to the approach followed by management to determine which sustainability factors are material; and
  - a description of the actions being taken by management to effect organizational change, including development, training and incentives.

Step 2: Key performance indicators (KPIs) and actions taken

- The actions taken to address each material sustainability issue, including steps to mitigate key risks or capitalize on opportunities identified, in support of delivery of the business strategy.
- The key performance indicators (KPIs) selected to measure performance, including the accounting policy adopted for each indicator, and the relationship to business performance, if possible quantified in financial terms.
- A description of how management is incentivized to deliver intended outcomes, including the link with governance, remuneration and rewards.

Step 3: The connected performance report

- Clear targets for each KPI, where feasible.
- Actual performance against baselines, prior years, targets and industry or other benchmarks.
- Financial or business performance measures alongside each sustainability KPI to explain the connection to the business's results.
- Commentary on progress towards both targets and intended broader outcomes.

Source: The Prince's Accounting for Sustainability Project (2009a)

Next steps: The creation of an International Integrated Reporting Committee

On 11 September 2009, A4S and the Global Reporting Initiative convened a meeting of investors, standard setters, companies, accounting bodies and UN representatives to discuss the need to integrate financial and sustainability reporting. At the meeting, the group:

- agreed that an international body should be convened to create a generally accepted connected and integrated reporting framework, bringing together those organizations that have responsibility for financial accounting and reporting with those that are widely recognized as leaders in sustainability and other areas of non-financial reporting; and
- called for the G20 to take action to support its creation.

Proposals developed following the meeting were presented at The Prince's Accounting for Sustainability Forum on 17 December 2009 by The Prince of Wales and supported by participants from all stakeholder groups, including financial and sustainability standard setters. The proposals made (2009b) are summarized as follows:

- *Create a new connected and integrated reporting model.* A new, connected and integrated reporting model is needed, one that is capable of providing a more coherent, balanced and complete picture of performance, structured around the organization's strategic objectives, its governance and business model, and integrating both material financial and non-financial information.
- *Establish an accountable governance structure.* Action is now needed to determine how best to create a governance structure to oversee the development of this more concise connected reporting model. This work should consider the role of different organizations, how best to create this International Integrated Reporting Committee, and draw up terms of reference for its work. This would include, in particular, the interface with established institutions, standard setters and others working in this area.

During 2010, A4S is working in collaboration with those organizations that participated in the 17 December meeting, as well as other organizations, to integrate the work of different initiatives. Through this collaboration, more detailed recommendations will be made, including future action required. The findings from the case studies, reported in this book, into how organizations have approached connected reporting and benefited from its adoption provide an important input to this process.

Ultimately, the establishment of an international reporting framework that not only connects financial and sustainability outcomes, but also supports the achievement of a sustainable economy will require support from governments, the finance and accounting community, and wider stakeholder groups. However, its creation will be critical in shifting the focus onto those issues that will determine economic survival in the 21st century.

References

The Prince's Accounting for Sustainability Project (2007) *The Accounting for Sustainability Report*, www.accountingforsustainability.org/media

The Prince's Accounting for Sustainability Project (2009a) *Connected Reporting: A Practical Guide with Worked Examples*, www.accountingforsustainability.org/media

The Prince's Accounting for Sustainability Project (2009b) *Governance and Collaboration: Establishing an 'International Connected Reporting Committee'*, www.accountingforsustainability.org/media

The Prince's Accounting for Sustainability Project (2009c) *Connected Reporting in Practice: A Consolidated Case Study*, www.accountingforsustainability.org/media

three

Sainsbury's: Embedding Sustainability within the Supermarket Supply Chain

Laura J. Spence and Leonardo Rinaldi

Introduction

The multiple food retail sector has long been confronted with sustainability issues, being at the front end of the consumer interface and in a position to have a wide magnifier effect through its supply chains. From standards such as the Temporary Labour Working Group, which led to the Gangmasters (Licensing) Act 2004, to the British Retail Consortium's global standards on technical issues such as food safety, storage, distribution and packaging and the Supermarket Code of Conduct, retailers are subject to substantial reputational risks if they or their suppliers are seen to be wanting in their response to contemporary challenges. Some argue that 'food retailers are by far the most far-reaching organizations in our commercial society' (Sainsbury's chief executive). With a market worth UK£133.3 billion,[1] groceries are the third largest area of expenditure in the UK behind housing and transport. Unsurprisingly, then, the supermarket retail sector is an extremely competitive market.

Sainsbury's has established itself as a front-runner in terms of sustainability in its sector, with a string of awards including being voted the Greenest UK Supermarket in 2008 by the market magazine *The Grocer*. It positions sustain-

Figure 3.1 Sustainability 'from field to fork' at Sainsbury's

Source: Sainsbury's (2009)

ability as having three legs: economic, social and environmental, and relates this directly to the needs and interests of its customers. The organization has identified three areas of impact in terms of sustainability:

1　its own operations;
2　its supplier operations; and
3　customer use of its products.

It is in the second of these, the supply chain, that Sainsbury's has by far the biggest potential impact in terms of sustainability. It is fitting then, that Sainsbury's is pioneering the use of the embedding sustainability in decision-making tool by implementing it in individual product lines and following through on risk assessments of sustainability issues, not just internally, but in its supply chains 'from field to fork'. (see Figure 3.1).

In this chapter we present a case study of the Sainsbury's experience of embedding the decision-making tool developed by The Prince's Accounting for Sustainability Project (A4S) by focusing on a single supply chain. In summary, we find that embedding sustainability in the supply chain works best when:

- It is in keeping with other business developments and links positively to organizational goals and customer satisfaction.
- The complexity of sustainability and difficulty of quantification of sustainability impacts is accepted and 'the best truth' sought.
- The perspective of supply chain partners is actively engaged with.
- Issues around the language of sustainability are acknowledged and addressed according to the requirements of different stakeholders.
- Senior management not only buy into sustainability as a fundamental aspect of the business, but champion it.

The context of the A4S decision-making tool at Sainsbury's

The framework provided by A4S puts forward a prototype of a sustainability decision-making tool to help managers embed sustainability within their day-to-day operations. The objectives of the tool are to ensure that sustainability factors are taken into account when decisions about products and services are made. More specifically, it entails three broad phases. The first phase aims to give a broad overview of the material sustainability issues in order to develop a better understanding of the social, environmental and economic impact of a product or service category over its life cycle. The second phase consists of a more detailed analysis of a specific product or service's sustainability impact over its life cycle, involving its associated suppliers (from raw material production to manufacturing and distribution), consumer and post-consumer use. Finally, the third phase comprises the bringing together of the data generated in the previous phases and its integration within the organization's everyday operations (e.g. selecting new suppliers, buying, costing products and services, distributing and investing).

The adoption of the sustainability decision-making tool is intended to enable organizations to prioritize the sustainability aspects of their products (or services). It is expected that such developments will enhance sales as a result of a better sustainability profile.

The A4S decision-making tool has been used on a number of product lines at Sainsbury's. Applying the tool has complemented the company's existing sustainability-related activities, which it understands to incorporate economic, environmental and social perspectives. At Sainsbury's, sustainability issues come under the remit primarily of the head of corporate responsibility (CR),

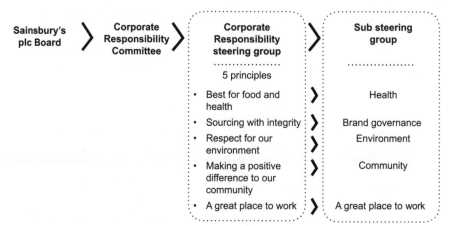

Figure 3.2 Sainsbury's corporate responsibility governance structure

Source: adapted from Sainsbury's (2009)

such that 'sustainability is a big part of our corporate responsibility agenda' (Director of Sainsbury's Brand). It is positioned as part of the Customer Division, with the head of CR reporting directly to the customer director. Hence, the emphasis in terms of CR is on what customers want and expect from Sainsbury's. The head of CR works within a corporate responsibility governance structure that integrates the issues closely with the operational business, as shown in Figure 3.2. Accordingly, operational directors carry responsibility for leading one of the five key CR goals: best for food and health; sourcing with integrity; respect for our environment; making a positive difference to our community; and being a great place to work. So, for example, the group human resources director is responsible for the last of these, working via a topic-specific steering group – in this case, on community. There is also an environmental project manager who is closely involved with the application of the A4S decision-making tool within Sainsbury's and is well versed in the technical aspects of environmental issues.

The 'sourcing with integrity' corporate responsibility values, which are of special interest here since they relate to the supply chain, are led by the Brand Governance Steering Group. These clearly identify the issue of sustainability in the supply chain as one of concern, and potentially risk, for the Sainsbury's brand. Sainsbury's also has an established Code of Conduct for Socially Responsible Sourcing, which it requires suppliers to engage with.

Sainsbury's has been working with the decision-making tool on a variety of product lines, including plastic bags, bananas, oranges and lamb. It is the embedding of the lamb decision-making process which we focus on in this chapter. As with all such things, the A4S decision-making tool is just part of the puzzle within a product supply chain. Sainsbury's was at the time of implementing the tool working to improve the efficiency and sustainability of its supply chain, instigated by a new recruit responsible for agricultural produce. This coming together of new approaches and phases may account for the readiness to embark on the process.

The lamb supply chain and sustainability

The comfortable mental image of frolicking spring lambs on a sunny hillside does not convey the important and complex sustainability issues involved in farming lamb. More widely, agriculture is an important area for sustainability, responsible for 14 per cent of global emissions.[2] Despite representing what we might consider to be essential basic foodstuff, livestock farming generally is said to create a 'long shadow' in terms of its environmental impact,[3] being in the top three most significant contributors to environmental problems.

With social, environmental and financial aspects of sustainability coming into play, the lamb supply chain faces a difficult challenge in balancing the sometimes competing aspects of sustainability evident in triple bottom line accounting. In addition to being socially, economically and politically important (ensuring food security), particular environmental areas of concern arise in relation to land degradation, climate change and air pollution, water shortage, pollution and loss of biodiversity. Despite being commonly less problematic than cow and pig farming, the sustainability issues around sheep farming are many and varied (see Figure 3.3). The issues operate at a number of levels, are not mutually exclusive, and lack clear evidence on what the best preventative policies are.

On the other hand, proponents of sheep farming are quick to point out the way in which British sheep farms, often small family-run ventures, address

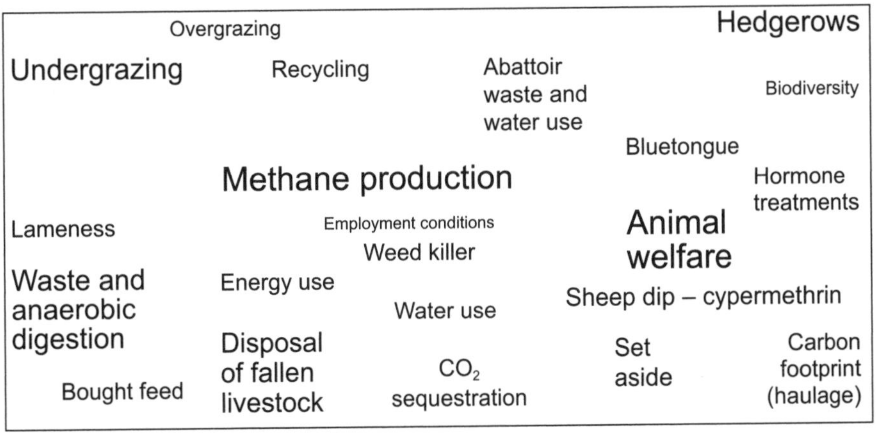

Figure 3.3 Sheep farming sustainability issues word cloud

Source: Laura J. Spence and Leonardo Rinaldi

issues of social sustainability by providing much needed income and employment in rural areas. Farmers are often presented as stewards of the countryside,
taking pride in their natural and traditional methods to rear lambs, which
preserve the British landscape for future generations.

Perhaps most fundamentally, taking the economic aspect of sustainability
into account, the sheep farming sector is not particularly prosperous, with
farmers sometimes selling products at below production cost and farm numbers
unsurprisingly in decline. The economic aspect of sustainability – that is,
economic survival – is of key importance in this case study.

It should not be forgotten that the lamb supply chain consists of far more
than just farmer and supermarket, although this would be problematic enough
with an estimated 7000 farmers supplying lamb to over 500 Sainsbury's supermarkets. While these are the highest-profile participants in the chain, other
intermediaries also have a role to play and any attempt at embedding sustainability within the chain needs to take this into account. Figure 3.4 illustrates a
multi-stage supply chain. At each of these stages, of course, a wide range of
environmental, financial and social sustainability issues on energy use, water
use, transport, animal welfare, employment conditions, economic survival,
packaging and waste disposal are relevant in different measure.

In early 2008 Sainsbury's gathered together its two lamb suppliers, its
agriculture manager, product technologist, buyer and the socially responsible
sourcing manager, and met under the facilitation of an environmental consul-
tancy. The focus was particularly on New Zealand and UK lamb product
sustainability. In May of that year a report on this process was issued that has
helped to shape policy and links to the supplier engagement, which Sainsbury's
is simultaneously developing through farmers' steering groups, set up around
the country with one of its lamb processors, Randall Parker Foods. This ensures
regional representation as there is much variation in production across the
country due to terrain and climate. This is part of Sainsbury's Partnership in
Livestock scheme between Sainsbury's, its supplier (meat processor) and the
farmer. As well as ensuring consistency of supply, these partnerships have
enabled flexible arrangements. For example, where the physical size of lamb
supplied has been impracticably small for UK consumption (e.g. hill farmed
lambs) but no export market can be found, or during the outbreak of foot and
mouth disease,[4] Sainsbury's has maintained the relationship with suppliers and
sought to find creative solutions.

Ultimately, Sainsbury's is seeking to influence the way in which farmers
work to improve their efficiency and other aspects of their sustainability. In the
Sainsbury's Lamb Sustainability Assessment, which was driven by the implementation of the A4S decision-making tool, 'high', 'severe' or 'critical'
vulnerabilities in the generic supply of lamb were identified. It should be noted
that we might also call these vulnerabilities 'risks', but not in strict accounting
terms – rather, in the sense of the vulnerability of the company to be challenged

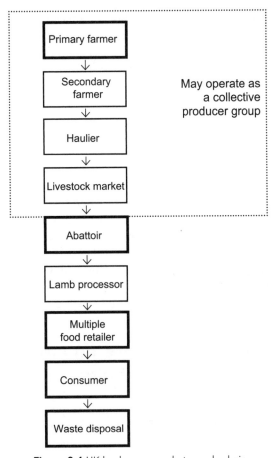

Figure 3.4 UK lamb supermarket supply chain

Source: Laura J. Spence and Leonardo Rinaldi

on a particular point (such as genetically modified organisms in feed). Hence, the term 'vulnerability' is used here, although in much of the chapter the people interviewed indeed used the term 'risk'. The key areas of vulnerability were identified as follows:

- *environmental issues* connected with the use of genetically modified organisms in feed, the impact on local biodiversity, greenhouse gas emissions from energy use throughout the supply chain, abattoir waste and land degradation due to grazing;
- *worker/local community issues* of achieving the minimum living wage despite low incomes from sheep farming, long working hours in excess of 48 hours per week, and workforce well-being issues as evidenced by high stress and suicide rates amongst farmers;

- *supplier livelihood* issues where the sale of products is below cost of production due to unfavourable market dynamics and subsidies; and
- *consumer issues* concerning consumer harm/health due to lack of nutritional labelling, excessive packaging, difficulty of recycling packaging and energy use for consumption.

Some of these issues were quickly addressed by Sainsbury's – for example, in 2008/2009 (reported in its *2009 Corporate Responsibility Report*), it moved its entire fresh meat, fish and poultry summer and barbecue range to recycled polyethylene terephthalate (rPET) trays that can be sent for recycling after use, saving over 10 tonnes of virgin plastic a year, and resolved the on-pack nutritional labelling issue. It is also developing a carbon foot-printing tool for lamb and supporting training for suppliers on working with gangmasters. The carbon foot-printing tool has already been rolled out to all 325 dairy farmers and has received particular recognition, winning the IGD Food Industry Environmental Sustainability Award. Sainsbury's is facilitating the development of online relationships with farmers through its Farm Connections Scheme, which provides computer hardware and software and training to farmers.

Sainsbury's perspective on embedding sustainability

The chief executive of Sainsbury's is clear about how he understands 'sustainability' and where it fits in the business, although acknowledging that it evolves over time, starting out as simply ensuring the availability of safe food. He says: 'My view is that it is all under the banner of quality and that sustainability is just one dimension of quality.' This puts sustainability at the centre of the supermarket business. The head of corporate responsibility put this in context, saying:

> Sustainable, for us, means continuing to be able to supply the products that we wish to supply or that our customers want, now and in the future, and then recognizing that they'll be subject to increasingly constrained external circumstances.

They are frank, however, about the complexity around embedding sustainability in a workable manner within their organization and beyond. Many of those in the business speak of the problem of there being no clear answers to sustainability questions and the difficulties that this brings in getting engagement and commitment. Sainsbury's finds itself asking:

> Where do you draw the line? Which dimensions matter? Because you could have a wide-ranging scorecard and be paralysed in terms of decision-making. So you have to be able to guide your people on real tools

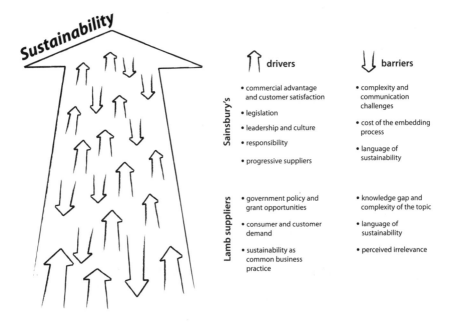

Figure 3.5 Illustration of the drivers and barriers to embedding sustainability within the Sainsbury's lamb supply chain

Source: Laura J. Spence and Leonardo Rinaldi

for making real decisions rather than tying them up in knots. (Head of Corporate Responsibility)

Ultimately, the risk is seen as being financial, with uncompetitive prices and costly burdens on suppliers. Hence, embedding sustainability decision-making within the Sainsbury's supply chain is limited at this stage. Key performance indicators are not yet rolled out to suppliers, although the view is that suppliers will increasingly be required to monitor their business in the same way that Sainsbury's does. As things stand, however, Sainsbury's seeks to encourage suppliers in specific product lines to work towards similar goals in terms of sustainability, and this process is facilitated by the A4S decision-making tool.

While there are substantial motivations to embed sustainability within commercial practices, impediments clearly remain. Drivers and barriers for embedding sustainability in the lamb supply chain at Sainsbury's, summarized in Figure 3.5, are considered in more detail in the following section. Figure 3.5 is illustrative; however, we should point out that we do not intend to suggest that sustainability is an achievable end goal, but rather a direction of intention. There will always be barriers and obstacles, complexities and unexpected consequences in the process. Our task here is to illustrate the position for Sainsbury's at one point of time in its sustainability journey.

Drivers and enablers for embedding sustainability

Responsibility and opportunity for impact

Sainsbury's expresses a sense of responsibility for seeking to make a difference because of the potential impacts that it can have: 'Our position is big enough in the market, we can make a real difference' says the environmental projects manager, going on to point out that this has an impact on Sainsbury's competitors, who may be pressured to follow suit. While Sainsbury's has 17 per cent of the UK supermarket share, in lamb it punches above its weight with 24 per cent; so in terms of making an impact, it is a good product for it to work on.

Commercial advantage and meeting customer needs

The classic definition of sustainability combines the economic, the social and the environmental (see Chapter 1), and this is very much the perspective of Sainsbury's. In all the discussions held with Sainsbury's people, the economic aspect of sustainability was held up as being of crucial importance. This is unsurprising in a commercially successful private-sector business,[5] but challenges the suspicion with which sustainability is often held as simply a cost to the business. However, as the head of corporate responsibility says: 'It has to start with [the] economic, because nothing that's environmentally or socially sustainable can stay that way if it's not also economically sustainable, particularly for a business.'

While the 'sustainability industry' may sometimes couch sustainability as a compromise to competitiveness with associated constraints on trade, the chief executive of Sainsbury's disagrees, saying:

> It's not to say these things don't cost money, it's not to say they're not complex, it's not to say that in the short term they actually make doing business harder. But fundamentally, you're doing all of them because you believe that they enhance the competitiveness of your business.

This comparison with other multiple food retailers is critical in a furiously competitive marketplace, making the relative performance what is important for Sainsbury's. This makes for some tricky decisions:

> There is advantage in going first (in terms of environmental initiatives) if you go in the right direction; but then that's a risk. But these are balanced risks at the end of the day. We need to make sure we have enough information to balance the risk from the sensible business point of view. (Head of Corporate Responsibility)

There is a belief that understanding the challenges of sustainability in food sourcing better than competitors and positioning itself advantageously in terms of the sourcing infrastructure means that Sainsbury's will have access to product to sell when others do not. As the environmental project manager points out: 'We're shopkeepers, we are a bunch of grocers, we need to be satisfying what our customers want, so every decision we make needs to drive down that road.' Non-governmental organizations (e.g. on animal welfare, including the Royal Society for the Prevention of Cruelty to Animals, Compassion in World Farming and Farm Animal Welfare Council) are important in as much as they influence customers and are engaged with where there is an opportunity to address practical implications.

The commercial perspective of embedding sustainability within the lamb supply chain is seen as crucial, requiring a joint approach between supermarket and farmers. The dialogue through the regional farmer steering groups is seen as a mechanism to build trust and acknowledges that, as the agriculture manager says, 'Sainsbury's and farmers need each other.' Farmers need certainty that there will be a market for their lamb at a reasonable price and Sainsbury's needs the certainty that there will be a supply of consistent quality and volume as it requires it. As the agriculture manager goes on to say: 'Sainsbury's has to make money to stay in business, our processor has to make money to stay in business and equally the farmer does' – hence underlining the financial aspect of sustainability concerns, characterizing sustainability as longevity and predictability of supply.

Finally and, perhaps, most importantly from the point of view of commercial motivators for pursuing embedded sustainability are the issues around sustainability integration in order to manage costs. The director of Sainsbury's brand, states:

> The key that unlocks all this is that from an accounting point of view, actually, completely counter-intuitive, is the fact that it doesn't always cost you money to do the right thing for the environment. Actually, it can be more cost-effective because even if some of the elements cost you more to do the right thing environmentally, overall, you manage the supply chain more effectively.

This is evident in the lamb supply chain, where the agriculture manager notes the advantage of supporting farmers to benchmark their energy costs: 'There's a very quick financial win for him to do it and then you've automatically got their buy-in for all the other bits that are a wee bit harder to do.' In a surprising outcome, this might mean that 'the most intensive (sheep) farms actually have the least impact on the environment ... well, that actually means the best managed farms'. Internally too, the cost element gives credibility to sustainability concerns as the head of corporate responsibility identifies in relation to waste management:

> If I'd have said to this business two years ago: 'Let's embark on a programme to reduce our food waste sent to landfill to zero', the first question would have been: 'How much will that cost us to do?' And the

> *reality is, it has saved us nearly UK£10 million a year ... that's sustain-*
> *able; but it hasn't been wearing a hair shirt to say: 'Let's make this*
> *business sustainable.'*

An important caveat should be added to this section, however. While commercial language is at the heart of the Sainsbury's discussion on sustainability, there
remains an awareness at the top of the organization that the complexity and
importance of the consequences of decisions means that the sustainability
choices cannot always be financially quantified. The chief executive, is clear on
this and accepts the ambiguity in good faith – for example, focusing on a specific
instance: 'Could I prove to you that moving to 100 per cent Fair Trade on
bananas has a payback? No, I couldn't prove it. But am I absolutely certain it
does? Yes, absolutely, I don't lose a moment's sleep over it.'

This is an important point for both A4S and those wishing to account for
their sustainability more generally. To get fully embedded sustainability, detailed
quantifiable justification is not always possible, and a little bit of old-fashioned
gut instinct and vision is still needed. This brings us to the next enabling factor
of embedding sustainability around positive leadership and an open culture.

Leadership and culture

It is no coincidence that Sainsbury's focus on sustainability has taken shape since
Justin King, the chief executive, joined the company in 2004. While he describes
there being some sustainability activity when he arrived, it lacked credibility and
was not coordinated. He argues that: 'The thing that the person at the top does,
I think more than anything else, is liberate decision-making and allow people to
move away from having to prove things in quite the same way.' He argues that
the culture of the company as a 'family firm with family values' is in keeping
with a sustainable approach and is natural territory for its customer base.

Legislation

Legislation is clearly a driver for embedding sustainability in the form, for
example, of the European Union Water Framework Directive[6] and the
Framework Directive on the Sustainable Use of Pesticides.[7] These single-issue
perspectives potentially level the playing field in one area, but require
Sainsbury's to balance its other priorities.

Progressive suppliers

Finally, the suppliers themselves, on occasion, can be drivers. The agriculture
manager notes that 'Some farmers push us because they are younger, have been
in other businesses and are more astute businessmen; they challenge us: "Right,
what next, what next? Have you looked at genetics and breeding?"'

Or their needs might be more basic, such as supplying rooms for training and workshops on specific sustainability issues, such as how to work legally and responsibly with gangmasters. Sainsbury's and their lamb processor Randall Parker Foods invest, for example, in the Northumberland Lamb Group to help them reduce costs and work on sustainability via hydroelectric energy production (which also helps against flooding), and planting trees to provide shelter for sheep and carbon sequestration.

The drivers of embedding sustainability at Sainsbury's – responsibility, commercial advantage and customer satisfaction, leadership and culture, legislation and progressive suppliers – are countered by barriers, including the language of sustainability, complexity and communication challenges, and the cost of the embedding process.

Barriers and challenges of embedding sustainability

Lack of voice for, and language of, sustainability

Sustainability-related language includes terms such as 'climate change', 'carbon/water footprint', 'corporate social responsibility (CSR)', 'philanthropy', 'business ethics', 'social justice' and 'security'. We see these topics increasingly debated in the media, researched and taught at business schools and acknowledged as part of the reporting processes in companies through their corporate responsibility or sustainability reports. However, this does not necessarily translate to sustainability being part of the everyday operating language and discussions of the business. This is also true of Sainsbury's. Occasionally, however, this is purposeful. The head of corporate responsibility, for example, coming back again to the cost issue says:

> I try hard not to use the word 'sustainability' in my daily conversations because it can be quite a loaded word for people; it usually implies some kind of additional cost to the business. What we've tried very hard this year to do is actually just have a business conversation with sustainability thinking at the heart of it, but without always using the word 'sustainability'.

There is also simply a knowledge and awareness gap. The agriculture manager notes that she gets 'blank faces' when she mentions carbon foot-printing, but that people nevertheless correctly talk about issues such as reducing energy costs as a sustainability concern since we are all subject to the media and feel we 'should be doing something about the environment'. The director of Sainsbury's brand points out that currently there is not necessarily a 'sustainability voice' at every meeting – that is, someone who ensures that sustainability is *always* part of the discussion. She compares this to the shift to having a customer focus many years ago when someone would be given the responsibility of representing the customer at each meeting, a move which has since been formalized into a report entitled *The Customer Voice*. Given the complexity of sustainability already mentioned, challenges around the language of sustainability are closely related to a knowledge gap on sustainability exacerbated by lack of awareness of what *is* known.

Communicating complex and unresolved sustainability issues

The complexity of sustainability and the myths and sometimes inaccurate perceptions surrounding it are a major challenge for Sainsbury's in communicating about sustainability as part of embedding it. The problem is apparent more or less across the entire supply chain, as well as internally within the organization. Here we focus on communication with Sainsbury's colleagues, customers and suppliers.

Before turning to the communication issue, it is worth briefly relaying some of the trade-offs and confusions about sustainability which Sainsbury's faces. The head of corporate responsibility points out that 'most businesses are only really starting to grapple with the serious trade-offs' and, despite being at the forefront of embedding sustainability, it remains confusing. Variously cited quandaries include carbon footprint versus water use of Spanish strawberries, environmental sustainability versus the livelihoods of farmers in the developing world, battery farmed eggs being the most environmentally sustainable, inconclusive science and, finally, the unanswered question of 'where does the expertise sit?' (Director of Sainsbury's Brand). Targets do not always drive the right behaviour either. To achieve a target of packaging reduction measured by weight, Sainsbury's could simply have temporarily ceased promotions on beer bottles; but it rejected this because it was not in the spirit of the target. Since legislation and taxation in the area is still emerging from the UK and the European Union (EU), choices about which priorities to follow are also hindered. In all of this, the director of Sainsbury's brand notes that all they can do is seek the best truth, then try to communicate it to their colleagues, customers and suppliers.

In order to embed sustainability within Sainsbury's, tailored training to communicate its place in the business is needed at every level of the organization, which is no small task given that there are around 150,000 colleagues. Sainsbury's does this through mechanisms such as the monthly video briefing by the chief executive, which early in 2009 included explanations of Sainsbury's work on its 'no food waste to landfill' initiative, packaging reduction and carrier bags (use of which has dropped by 60 per cent in two years). Hence the importance of:

> ... *engaging with our own people to communicate what we're doing and why we're doing it, broad business communication as well as unique things that we're doing. And then to ask them to play their part, so it's not just this organization is doing 'a', 'b' and 'c', but it's also what part can you play, so it comes back down to some collective responsibility.*
> (Head of Corporate Responsibility)

But there is also the more fundamental expansion of roles, such that, for example, product technologists are trained to assess ethical audits, which would not have been part of their original training.

Customers, as the drivers of the business, are, of course, fundamental in this, and it is the appropriateness for the customer base that, as we have noted, is one of the factors enabling the sustainability focus at Sainsbury's. Yet, as the head of corporate responsibility notes: 'Customers, even aware and articulate customers, will say: "Yes, I only want to buy things that are seasonal and British, but I want to buy them all year round."' In 2009, for the second year running, Sainsbury's supported the National Farmers' Union's (NFU's) Food and Farming Roadshow, which takes the farming facts into the community and, in some instances, into supermarket car parks. The roadshow gives an opportunity to explain to customers how food is produced, with the intention of enabling them to make informed choices and to have confidence in the quality of the food that they eat.

Understandably, for a competitive sector such as multiple food retail, appearing to preach to customers to improve their understanding of sustainability is not an option. As the chief executive says: 'In the end, there's no point pursuing what we believe is the more sustainable agenda if consumers are actually not buying into that and rewarding (other supermarkets) with their custom.' Sainsbury's seeks, instead, to work with customers, still offering customer choice rather than dictating sustainability. Nevertheless, it seems proud, for example, that all its bananas have been fair trade since 2006. The problems really become difficult where customers do not have all the necessary information to make an informed decision and Sainsbury's has to make a choice on their behalf. For example, in agriculture, when balancing animal welfare and carbon footprint, the former is most likely to be seen as essential by the customer, at the cost of the latter, despite the fact that it would surprise many that intensive sheep farming is more environmentally sustainable. Furthermore, there are inconclusive results on whether imported New Zealand lamb might actually carry a lower carbon footprint than that farmed in the UK. In an attempt to resolve this conundrum, Sainsbury's is developing its own tool to measure the impact like-for-like. Communicating these complexities to customers remains a significant challenge.

Dialogue about sustainability with suppliers is facilitated by speaking in terms specifically relevant to the individual sector and building up trust and dialogue. For example, Sainsbury's is developing a carbon foot-printing tool for its lamb supply, which requires a significant level of measuring on farms. In order to achieve this it uses the farmer steering groups established by its lamb processors, Randall Parker Foods and Dunbia. This involves the entire agriculture team (buyers, food technologists, agriculturalists, processors and farmer regional representatives) going to regional meetings on a regular basis. It is not plain sailing by any means, as the agriculture manager, says:

> *At first farmers either say nothing or spend a whole meeting airing their grievances. And they say nothing because they are scared of saying the wrong thing because we're their customer and you have to do three or four meetings of that before you get to: 'Right, what are the key challenges?'*

Improving the efficiency of communication with farmers is what lies behind Sainsbury's drive to develop online relationships through its Farm Connections Scheme, which provides computer hardware, software and training to farmers. Ultimately, the message from the agriculture manager is that working with farmers on sustainability issues is only feasible where it makes sense economically because, as she says, 'I can't afford for any farmer to go out of business.' Farmers also have to be convinced of the business case for sustainability. This is nicely illustrated by an incident from a farmers' steering group relayed by the agriculture manager where: 'One farmer stood up and he said: "It's like this, I can't be green when I'm in the red." And actually what we've demonstrated is you can be good for the environment *and* save yourself money because they all thought it was going to cost them more.'

Thus, in addition to communicating the message successfully, it helps considerably when the content of the message chimes with what suppliers want to hear.

The cost of the embedding process

The process of implementing the A4S decision-making tool is felt to be highly resource intensive at Sainsbury's, especially for the first few product lines where a certain amount of learning about the process itself was also needed. For example, with the focus on the lamb sustainability project, working with the consultants required detailed explanation of lamb rearing and processing that would be second nature to specialists, effectively giving a lesson in 'lamb production for beginners'. The agriculture manager reflects that 'It had to be done, I suppose … they ask lots of questions, but they weren't questions that we hadn't asked ourselves.' Providing the structure and space to do that can, of course, have advantages; but with a large store selling around 30,000 products, resource limitations are clear, although the 1400 products accounting for 50 per cent of sales orientate the approach taken. Learning from earlier experiences, Sainsbury's subsequently set clear boundaries for the meeting on the embedding process (attended by supplier representatives and key personnel within the organization and facilitated by an independent consultant), and considerably narrowed the product focus. For example, in looking at citrus fruit, Sainsbury's worked through the sustainability issues with South African oranges only. A clear recommendation here is to tightly define the scope of the process. Nevertheless, 'In order to get to the level of granularity in real hard facts and data, you have to spend a lot of money to gather the data' (Director of Sainsbury's Brand).

The supplier perspective

Suppliers, on the whole, agree with Sainsbury's understanding of sustainability as being dominated by economic survival, not least since it is the survival of sheep farmers that is more pertinent in this case. Hence, a sustainable sheep sector is one that is profitable and viable to attract future generations of farmers. Randall Parker Foods is concerned that profitability must be included explicitly as a measure of sustainability. Additionally, sustainable approaches to sheep farming are aligned in supplier discussions with traditional farming and 'natural' grass-fed lamb production.

Stewardship of the natural environment is part of this. In some cases it is proposed that sheep farming in the UK upland areas, especially, is extensive by its very nature and operates close to organic standards. The drivers and barriers for embedding sustainability for suppliers have some cross-over with the Sainsbury's perspective. The most pertinent points are briefly discussed here. For suppliers, the drivers include grant opportunities and government policy, sustainability as common business practice, and consumer and customer demand. Barriers include language, perceived irrelevance and knowledge gap and complexity of the topic.

Drivers and enablers for embedding sustainability

Grant opportunities and government policy

For suppliers and, particularly, farmers, environmental protection specifically is guided by the availability of government grants. The procurement director of Randall Parker Foods notes that 'Even the (farmers) [who] perhaps aren't driven by the ethics of lamb production and maintaining the area as well as they can, most of them are … in a stewardship scheme so they're driven financially to do that.'

For example, the UK Department for Environment, Food and Rural Affairs (Defra), through its Environmental Stewardship Scheme[8] and the Tir Gofal[9] in Wales, the Welsh Assembly's agri-environmental programme funded by the Rural Development Plan for Wales (supported, in part, by the EU), directly affect the approach of farmers. The objectives of the Tir Gofal scheme, for instance, are to protect and enhance habitats of importance to wildlife, beauty of the landscape, historical and archaeological features, to provide opportunities for new public access to the countryside, and to help protect and improve the quality of water, soil and air by reducing pollution. Pointing out the financial difficulties faced by sheep farmers in recent years, one industry member notes that 'When your back's against the wall you have to look for ways to take any opportunities that come your way (e.g. environmental stewardship scheme).'

Business as usual for farmers

The argument was repeatedly made that farmers are natural stewards of the environment and because of the nature of their business working with the land:

> They are doing a lot of work for the environment that just goes unrewarded or isn't noticed, just basic farm maintenance from hedge laying, managing the woodlands on the farm, maintaining and enhancing habitats, all these sorts of things they're doing anyway as a by-product. (National Farmers' Union)

One sheep farmer describes how he seeks to use the land in a holistic way to provide for the farm's needs:

> We rely heavily on the plants such as clover which fix the nitrogen so we don't need to put artificial nitrogen on. And then we also have plants called chicory which bring up minerals so it gives the sheep a natural source of minerals and trace elements from the ground. So we're trying to source as much as we can, not only from an environmental, but obviously from our own business point of view, it's more sustainable if we can do that. We're producing everything, so to speak, off the ground.

Consumer and customer demand

Farmers are aware of the increased interest in provenance of food for the British consumer. Farmer representatives such as the NFU seek to highlight the local production and link this to the British countryside via the 'Buy British' slogan. They also feel the influence of the retailer preferences in relation to sustainability through the supply chain, noting that 'power lies with the retailers' (NFU).

Competition between supply chains is also a driver for sustainability. A lamb processor notes:

> I am always aware of trying to look for something that will give us an edge over our competitors... And it's really my role and as a single-species plant – we're so dependent on lamb – to be exploring every avenue there is to produce lamb with perhaps just something else to the story ... and to give confidence to the farmers, to keep in the lamb business.

The supplier perspective can be summarized as follows:

> We are trying to offer Sainsbury's a product that's of high quality, that's traditionally produced, farmed using traditional methods, that has a provenance, a story behind it, for whatever reason and from whatever region. And that they can be confident to be able to explain it to the consumer, we have a card and recipe leaflets and that sort of thing that

they then can actually say: 'This is where it comes from, this is a typical farmer in that area and this is how he produces his lamb.'

Barriers and challenges of embedding sustainability

The barriers and challenges of embedding sustainability within the supply chain mirror Sainsbury's perspective and can be briefly described, though they are powerful in effect. As mentioned previously, suppliers lack the *language* of sustainability and, therefore, the ability to readily communicate about it in terms of both their successes and failings. Some aspects of sustainability may seem *irrelevant* to UK lamb farmers – for example, the focus on water despite the heavy rainfall in a given year. This, of course, reflects a wider *knowledge gap and complexity* of the subject already discussed. Finally, the focus of the British farmer is first and foremost on *short-term economic survival* and this tends to supersede any other element of farming life. In this respect, Sainsbury's work with Randall Parker Foods and Dunbia to clarify purchasing arrangements throughout the year and guarantee a market for traditionally farmed West Country new-season lambs is well received.

Thus, while there are advantages from both Sainsbury's and the supplier's perspectives of further embedding sustainability within business operations, there are also a number of key challenges to overcome in achieving this. We might summarize these as legitimizing the language of sustainability and ensuring its relevance, the difficulty in communicating about it, and the resource implications of implementing a sustainability embedding process. Ultimately, however, none of these challenges is surmountable where the facts about sustainability issues remain unclear. Without understanding the impacts of Sainsbury's product lines, moves to embed sustainability will lack credibility and may actually work in the wrong direction.

The next step for Sainsbury's: The Connected Reporting Framework (CRF)?

Sainsbury's is cautiously pleased with the A4S decision-making tool. As the director of Sainsbury's brand summarizes, the process:

> *... gets you to ask the questions that you would never normally ask because actually you are relying on other people to have asked those questions and you assume that they have. But you can never assume anything ... at the end of the day you have to want to ask yourself those questions. It would be very easy ... to accept things on face value and walk away and sleep at night knowing that actually you've got an answer. I suppose the key thing for me is: have you got the best answer?*

Even with the assistance of the decision-making tool, results are not always clear. The environmental project manager, to whom it falls to analyse much of the detailed data, notes that 'It's built on qualitative (information) which could be anecdotal, you can then end up with ... quite literally some issues as half high vulnerability, half low vulnerability! What do I do with that?'

Within the application of the decision-making tool in the lamb process, the agriculture manager disagreed with the facilitating consultants on the risk of, for example, genetically modified products in small amounts of feed brought in for sheep. She says: 'I thought it low risk, they put it as high risk. We just had to agree to disagree. There was no conclusion on who was right or wrong.' The decision-making tool does not provide the answers, of course: it merely encourages the participants to narrow down the most important issues. Finally, in the context of this book, one respondent noted that: 'You can't use the word "accounting" to describe it because it is based on perception and anecdotes.'

Sainsbury's is well aware of what might be considered the next step, which is to sign up to the Connected Reporting Framework (CRF) and the financial reporting of agreed key performance indicators (KPIs). The head of corporate responsibility says that 'We have no problem with the KPIs; it's just that we report them in a non-financial report, which is the corporate responsibility report, and we don't assign a financial value to them.'

He notes the difficulty of genuinely pinning everything down to a financial value: 'If you're going to be truly honest about your direct operational footprint, you should include everything that makes a difference. Now, not all of those things can be easily measured or valued in this way ... it's the detail of what's inside it that is a bit more of a challenge.'

A clear problem, as has already been alluded to in this chapter, is the need for sector-specific frameworks and sector-based comparison. The Sainsbury's perspective is clearly articulated here:

> Sectors have to agree to report in the same way. It won't be meaningful if you can't really cross and compare, and people don't use the same ways of measuring things... Because the challenges of a retail business are different to those of financial services businesses or a utilities company or whatever ... if you're going to report like this, ultimately you want to create some degree of competitive impetus. (Head of Corporate Responsibility)

This can be related to the investor community directly, especially socially responsible investors, where measures of sustainability do not really have much value unless they are standardized. At the time of writing, A4S is working with those in the sector to develop an illustrative example of the CRF. This is intended to be an example of how a company in the retail sector might report in a connected way, demonstrating how sustainability is fundamentally linked to business performance. It is not intended to be a standardized reporting

Table 3.1 Summary of Sainsbury's embedding sustainability and key learning points

Ten elements to successfully embed sustainability	Sainsbury's response	Key learning points
1. Board and senior management commitment	CE acts as a figurehead for sustainability and takes the senior management with him.	The leader can make an enormous difference, liberating sustainability thinking in an organization.
2. Understanding and analysis of the key sustainability drivers for the organization	Sainsbury's materiality assessment process, informed by stakeholders, resulted in a strategic tool to inform their sustainability priorities. For Sainsbury's, the supply chain is the most significant area, the primary issues being carbon and food security.	This is the starting point of the embedding process. It is a highly complex, organizationally specific task informed by global, national and local issues as well as industry specific ones. A big resource investment is needed to make the right choices at this stage.
3. Integrating the key sustainability drivers into the organization's strategy	Sainsbury's addresses sustainability in terms of 11 key commitments derived from the materiality process, published in the Corporate Responsibility report. The focus is on the most material sustainability issues in the supply chain and those with the highest volume.	Translating key sustainability drivers into organizational strategy requires open commitment and integrated thinking to redirect organizational strategy.
4. Ensuring that sustainability is the responsibility of everyone in the organization	Sainsbury's has established a deeply rooted corporate responsibility governance structure so that sustainability has become part of the organization's procedures at any level of operation. It functions through a board level Corporate Responsibility Committee and is supported by a Corporate Responsibility Steering Group.	Having sustainability as the responsibility of one department is an inadequate approach, it needs to be seen as a trading and operational issue with top level responsibility underpinning the credibility of sustainability as a priority, and organization-wide buy-in.
5. Breaking down sustainability targets and objectives for the organization as a whole into targets and objectives that are meaningful for individual subsidiaries, divisions, departments	The information at the board level is disassembled and allocated to an operating unit. Each bit of information has an owner (or a cluster of owners) at a lower level, who has the responsibility to measure it through the given metric, using it as a system of tracking the progress.	The allocation of measures and the subsequent reporting process has gained Sainsbury's an unprecedented knowledge about the prioritized sustainability issues, whose management has ended up with a more efficient supply chain. Early results also reveal that 'it doesn't always cost you money to do the right thing!'

continued

Table 3.1 continued

Ten elements to successfully embed sustainability	Sainsbury's response	Key learning points
6. Processes that enable sustainability issues to be taken into account clearly and consistently in day-to-day decision-making	Shifting sustainability to an input rather than an output has the consequence that each member of the staff is required to think about the relevant day-to-day operations from the sustainability point of view, rather than collecting sustainability related information (e.g. energy consumption, water usage, carbon emissions) after the products are manufactured and packaged. The surfacing of details in the supply chain through the embedding process has also revealed previously hidden trade-offs.	This is an enormously challenging aspect of accounting for sustainability. Sainsbury's lacks what might be called 'fluency in the language of sustainability' throughout the organization and doesn't always succeed in having a sustainability 'voice' at each meeting.
7. Extensive and effective sustainability training	The culture of sustainability and its increased awareness within and outside Sainsbury's has been promoted by workshops, presentations and ad hoc information provision. Members of selected teams such as Product Technologists are also trained on the Ethical Trade Initiative and how to assess an ethical audit.	Furthering their widespread training on sustainability remains a key challenge for Sainsbury's, but is acknowledged as an essential part of future progress. Without this, understanding of sustainability remains superficial throughout the organization.
8. Including sustainability targets and objectives in performance appraisal	Sustainability Key Performance Indicators are set by the board level Corporate Responsibility Committee in the form of targets for the responsible board member and his or her reports in turn. A performance measurement system then embeds the KPIs in the system and 'wires' the whole organization accordingly.	This is a requirement to underpin the legitimacy of sustainability orientated decision-making for all employees.
9. Champions to promote sustainability and celebrate success	The CE, Director of Sainsbury's Brand, Head of CR and Environmental Project Manager are all champions of CSR. Sustainability related rewards are reported on the website with a high profile.	Champions need to be high profile and multiple. Success should be celebrated but with a plethora of awards, care should be taken with regard to which ones to focus on to distinguish the organization from its competitors.
10. Monitoring and reporting sustainability performance	Each of the 11 key commitments has measurements attached to them and the monitoring and reporting system of sustainability performance happens on a quarterly basis. However, Sainsbury's has stopped short to date of full financial reporting.	Standardization of reporting sustainability performance within sectors is needed.

Source: adapted from The Prince's Accounting for Sustainability Project (2007, pp8–13)

template; however, interest has been expressed by some companies for this work to be extended to include a common core base of connected reporting indicators that link financial and sustainability performance. Each company would augment this core reporting with company-specific indicators and assessment of performance, drawing out points of differentiation relative to competition. Meanwhile, Sainsbury's is intending to run a shadow project of the CRF.

Conclusions

In this concluding section we reflect back on the ten main elements for the successful embedding of sustainability identified in earlier work conducted by A4S and use these to assess the good practice at Sainsbury's and key learning points from their experiences, as shown in Table 3.1. In doing so, we illustrate where other organizations might learn from the successes at Sainsbury's and demonstrate the depth of the commitment needed to fully embed sustainability.

Sainsbury's has begun to address the need to embed sustainability within each of the particular areas noted in the A4S decision-making tool. Nevertheless, working towards sustainability is not a destination, but a journey reflective of new approaches rather than a finite position to be achieved, as represented by Figure 3.5. The Sainsbury's approach has weathered the storm of the economic crisis thus far; but without sustainability being linked to competitiveness and cost reduction, the extent to which it would remain embedded is unclear. Ultimately, sustainability at Sainsbury's is being built onto and within the existing commercially driven business model. Nevertheless, Sainsbury's predicts that the world around us is changing:

> I think that what we will see over the next five years is a much more intelligent engagement with sustainability in the wider sense of the word; I think that's a good thing, but I think that that will cause us to start to raise questions about our lifestyles. (Chief Executive)

Sainsbury's, like everyone else, cannot predict the future; but are having to make commercial decisions today that both contribute to and are influenced by the way in which it believes things will go. Here is the fundamental difficulty with which Sainsbury's, the Accounting for Sustainability Project and we all must struggle. Sustainability is about the future, which at a global and a local level we find hard, even impossible, to predict precisely because there are so many unknown and contingent factors. While Sainsbury's is searching for expertise on the sustainability issues in a given product line, it recognizes clearly that any information it gets is an imperfect truth, yet finds itself in the position of being the arbiter of which is the best truth for the environment, society and the economy, as well as its business. This is a big task indeed.

It is perhaps appropriate to give the last word to the chief executive of Sainsbury's. Despite all the activity outlined in this case study, the sustainability agenda is fast changing; so too are the drivers and barriers. Without consistent, permanent commitment, the momentum built up by any organization would be lost. Justin King summarizes thus: 'I think the point about sustainability, without overplaying the word, is that your commitment to it needs to be sustainable as well.'

Acknowledgements

The assistance of Sainsbury's is greatly appreciated, but this chapter remains the opinion and perspective of the authors. With thanks to the following for their help in gathering the information on which this chapter is based: Judith Batchelar, director of Sainsbury's brand, Sainsbury's; Juliet Davies, procurement director (retail), Randall Parker Foods; Annie Graham, agriculture manager, Sainsbury's; Justin King, chief executive, Sainsbury's; John Mercer, chief livestock adviser, National Farmers' Union; Neil Perkins, sheep farmer, Dinas Island Farm; Jat Sahota, head of corporate responsibility, Sainsbury's; Mary Salmon, environmental project manager, Sainsbury's.

Notes

1   Institute for Grocery Distribution, Figures for calendar year 2007, www.igd.com, accessed 31 October 2009
2   FAO (United Nations Food and Agriculture Organization) (2009) *Anchoring Agriculture within a Copenhagen Agreement*, Policy Brief by the FAO, www.fao.org/docrep/010/a0701e/a0701e00.HTM, accessed 16 September 2009
3   See the detailed report on this produced by the UN: Steinfeld, J., Gerber, P., Wassenaar, T., Rosales, M. and de Haan, C. (2006) *Livestock's Long Shadow*, Livestock, Environment and Development Initiative, Rome
4   For more on the impact of foot and mouth disease on the lamb supply chain, see Bourlakis, M. and Allinson, J. (2003) 'The aftermath of the foot and mouth crisis in agricultural logistics: The case of the UK fat lamb chain', *International Journal of Logistics: Research and Applications*, vol 6, no 4, pp211–228
5   During the period of research in the economically challenging times of 2009, pretax profits announced in May climbed 11.3 per cent from the previous year to UK£543 million
6   See www.ec.europa.eu/environment/water/water-framework/index_en.html, accessed 16 September 2009
7   See www.ec.europa.eu/environment/ppps/home.htm, accessed 16 September 2009
8   See www.naturalengland.gov.uk/ourwork/farming/funding/es/default.aspx, accessed 16 September 2009

9   See www.wales.gov.uk/topics/environmentcountryside/farmingandcountryside/
    farming/agrienvironmentschemes/tirgofal/, accessed 16 September 2009

References

The Prince's Accounting for Sustainability Project (2007) *Accounting for Sustainability Report*, www.accountingforsustainability.org/media
Sainsbury's (2009) *140 Years of Making a Difference: 2009 Corporate Responsibility Report*, J Sainsbury plc, London

four

Using the Connected Reporting Framework as a Driver of Change within EDF Energy

Linda Lewis and David Ferguson

Introduction: EDF Energy

EDF Energy is the UK wholly owned subsidiary of the French group EDF SA. It came into existence in 2003 following the acquisition, in the UK, of London Electricity, South Eastern Electricity and South Western Electricity, London, and Eastern Power Networks and a number of generation assets. More recently, following its acquisition by EDF, British Energy, primarily a generator of nuclear power, has been integrated within EDF Energy. EDF Energy is a vertically integrated energy utility in that it generates and distributes electricity and supplies both gas and electricity to residential and commercial customers. To give some indication of the scope of operations, EDF Energy has four inter-linked business units of operations as well as a shared service centre and has around 20,000 employees. The four business units are Energy Sourcing and Customer Supply, Networks, Existing Nuclear and New Nuclear Build.

The case study

Sustainability means doing business in a way that delivers not just economic profitability but environmental performance and social well-being. Only when all three elements are in balance is the business truly sustainable ... there can be no more important driver guiding everything we do. (EDF Energy, 2007)

The main aim of this case study is to highlight how EDF Energy is attempting to implement its own working definition of sustainability. It is also designed to demonstrate how the Connected Reporting Framework (CRF) has helped the company to evaluate and report on its progress in embedding sustainability as the key driver of business performance. While the case focuses on positive developments and achievements, it also outlines the challenges, as identified by EDF Energy, which it still faces. From an accounting perspective, the internal control and measurement systems are of particular interest. The case study shows how EDF Energy has developed, designed and redesigned performance measures, evaluation and feedback processes. It reflects EDF Energy's acknowledgement that embedding sustainability in business is not just about measurement. By focusing on what seems to work and what needs further work, the company recognizes that if sustainability is to become part of 'business as usual', there is room for improvement in getting this message across to employees at all levels if full engagement by staff is to be achieved.

Background and history of EDF Energy and accounting for sustainability

EDF Energy has its own autonomous approach to accounting for sustainability to reflect the context in which it operates within the UK. The company uses sustainability as both a driver for business performance and as a means of branding in the UK energy market. In relation to EDF Energy 'the brand', there are a variety of initiatives in place that raise the company's profile in that relatively competitive market. These include acting as premier sustainability partner for the 2012 Olympic Games; the involvement of stakeholders – both customers and employees – in the Carbon Challenge to reduce carbon footprints; and working with suppliers via ethical and green procurement initiatives. Although such 'branding' exercises represent how the company wishes to be perceived externally, the company is keen to stress that at the heart of its 'brand' are a set of values that drive the way in which the company carries out its work and underpin the principles of operations. The values are:

- respect for individuals;

- respect for the environment;
- excellent performance;
- social responsibility;
- integrity.

Support for both the value-driven operational approach and the market positioning aspects of branding are evident in the way in which EDF Energy declared 'Our climate commitments' in 2007, followed by 'Our social commitments' in 2008. Both commitments include a series of pledges to take action that go beyond the purely economic objectives of a commercial organization. Sustainability as a driver for business performance is significant, therefore, in that EDF Energy has set itself publicly declared strategic objectives that have a direct influence on the way in which it operates as a business.

EDF Energy and 'five ambitions'

Since the formation of EDF Energy in 2003, sustainability has been a consistent key business driver under the leadership of the chief executive officer (CEO), Vincent de Rivaz. At the time of formation, the company had a corporate responsibility team and encouraged corporate responsibility and economic performance by the incorporation of specific targets within staff incentive schemes. The basis for the targets was performance measured and evaluated against achievement of the following five ambitions that the company set itself in 2004:

- *fit, safe and responsible*, which was EDF Energy's recognition of its health and safety responsibilities for contractors, customers and for the public at large;
- *point of reference*, which was designed to reflect EDF Energy's ranking against other companies in activities associated with corporate social responsibility;
- *shareholder's expectations*, which was recognized as critical for delivering a sustainable business in a highly competitive environment;
- *care for our customers*, which was designed to ensure that customer views were taken into account in determining issues that needed to be addressed and areas in which EDF Energy might need to improve; and
- *employee satisfaction*, which recognized responsibilities towards employees and their value to the company in achieving the ambitions.

Although amended in 2007 (see later section on 'EDF Energy's sustainability journey'), these five ambitions are designed to ensure that EDF Energy's values underpin the company's way of doing business. They are an expression of how EDF Energy is translating sustainability to drive business operations and are designed to enact the company's strategic mission 'to bring sustainable energy solutions home to everyone'. Operationally, they mean that employees know what the company is working to achieve.

From an accounting and reporting perspective, they have required the development of measures, target-setting, monitoring, measurement, reporting and assurance processes to be put in place in order to evaluate progress in performance against the five ambitions. Operationally, the evaluation of progress means management accounting information is instrumental in directing performance towards achieving the strategic objectives. It also provides a basis for EDF Energy to communicate such progress externally.

Attempts to achieve a balanced approach

Although the term 'corporate responsibility' was used in 2003, the meaning of it is synonymous with 'sustainability' in that, as the five ambitions reveal, it represented the balance between the social, environmental and financial objectives that are regarded as important by the company. Corporate responsibility as a term was significant in those early years as it chimed well with EDF Energy's strategy of 'branding' through its commitment to sustainability. This was evident in the way that EDF Energy set itself within the ambition 'point of reference' to be the 'top company amongst its peers' as ranked in the Business in the Community (BITC) corporate responsibility index. This was achieved by 2006 as the company gained the Platinum Award for being in the top ten companies for corporate responsibility. In order to achieve the award, a company has to demonstrate that corporate responsibility is practised through a variety of interrelated activities and in engagement with a range of company stakeholders. In 2009, there was evidence that EDF Energy had made further progress when the company was awarded Platinum Plus Status by the BITC, one of only seven companies to achieve this accolade.

However, during the early years, despite the obvious success of the BITC award, there were concerns within the company that corporate responsibility was still not perceived as a wholly integrated part of business operations amongst employees. This seems to have contributed to 'sustainability' becoming the term used to describe the key business driver of performance in 2005. It not only reflected the company's commitment within the five ambitions, but promoted sustainability as an integrated set of factors to be understood and enacted by employees – literally, that sustainability should be embedded across the company and not regarded as something additional to, or separate from, doing business.

Of significance was a feeling that forms of reporting did not reflect corporate responsibility as integrated or balanced with economic activities. Although the commitment to the five ambitions was made apparent in early reports, senior managers became concerned that the reporting of social and environmental activities did not appear directly connected to the financial performance contained in the annual accounts. Through acknowledgement of these concerns, external reporting had a change of emphasis from 2006 onwards as the company began to refer to sustainability performance.

Difficulties in achieving a balanced approach

Difficulties in getting employees at all levels to recognize the significance of the 'balance' as the way to deliver sound financial performance led EDF Energy to think about actions to better embed sustainability across the organization. The company was clearly demonstrating within the five ambitions that practising responsibility to all stakeholders was regarded as the way to achieve good business performance. However, certain levels of employees, owing to their sphere of work, found it easier to relate to the economic and functional aspects of business performance compared to the broader social and environmental objectives. For example, it is much easier for employees involved in the direct operations of the energy business to see the environmental impact of their activities compared to those involved in some of the 'softer' company operations, such as accounting and marketing. Even so, whatever the type of work, unless there are mechanisms to communicate not only rates of productivity, but reductions in creating waste or energy usage, it can be difficult to engage employees fully in all aspects of sustainability.

As a top-down strategic initiative, therefore, sustainability as reflected by the five ambitions as a driver for sound business performance was better understood and embedded at the senior executive level; but this was not always the case lower down the line at operational levels. The accounting controls of budget-setting and financial constraints seemed to exert a significant influence on performance and seemed more relevant, particularly at middle management levels. In addition, many workers did not seem to perceive how they could contribute to the achievement of the corporate social and environmental objectives in the way that they carried out their 'day job'.

Reflections on how to better achieve the 'balance' at an operational level led to consideration of the forms of internal reporting and whether this balance was reflected adequately within the internal systems of performance evaluation and feedback. A necessary element for seeing if, and to what extent, all three aspects of the strategic objectives are being met is the existence of mechanisms within the company that ensure sustainability is achieved as intended. For 'achievement' to occur, it is also important that sustainability is translated into clearly defined operational targets. One of the main aims of accounting for sustainability at EDF Energy is to use the internal reporting process as a means of driving change, in behaviour and performance, towards the achievement of the objectives. Thus, EDF Energy has recognized the importance of the accounting information system as a means of support for the enactment of sustainability as the driver of business performance.

EDF Energy and the Connected Reporting Framework

The balanced approach aspired to by EDF Energy helps to explain why the company is a participant in the Connected Reporting Framework (CRF). The five ambitions are evidence that, even before participation in the CRF, EDF Energy wanted to ensure there was connectedness between performance in social welfare, environmental and economic activities. Connectedness underpins its strategic objectives, so it is critical that this message is appreciated by employees, at levels beyond those of executive and senior management. It is equally important that employees understand what they can or are required to do to contribute to sustainable business performance. The company recognizes that embedding sustainability across all levels of the organization is necessary if it is to become an accepted and unconscious way of working: 'business as usual' rather than 'business' and 'sustainability'.

Conceptually, therefore, the CRF complements the way of thinking at EDF Energy. By encouraging the company to think about what it wishes to achieve, how this can be best communicated and how performance might be measured and reported, the CRF has been instrumental in addressing some of the issues of translating the five ambitions into measurable working goals for employees. Thus, when the team from The Prince's Accounting for Sustainability Project (A4S) approached EDF Energy in 2007 to promote the CRF project, it was literally 'knocking at an open door'. The approach came at the same time as Mark Bromley, the head of business performance and internal control at EDF Energy, responsible for developing systems for evaluating and reporting performance, was trying to develop a mechanism to report progress against the climate and social commitments referred to above as part of the five ambitions.

The climate and social commitments

Before going on to demonstrate EDF Energy's progress in sustainability and the adoption of the CRF, it is useful to provide some background on its climate and social commitments since these have been significant in providing the basis for the internal reporting processes that attempt to integrate financial impacts, and environmental and social welfare concerns.

EDF Energy formulated the climate commitments in 2006 and launched them publicly in 2007 when it declared its contribution to tackling climate change. The climate commitments are based on a set of pledges in the areas of carbon, customers, employees, and resource and waste management and are identified in Table 4.1. 'Financial impact' is also considered by EDF Energy and is expressed as either investment costs or cost savings associated with achieving the defined targets. The figures in Table 4.1 are derived from the amounts disclosed in EDF Energy's *Sustainability Performance Report* for 2008. For each climate commitment, EDF Energy indicates the self-imposed targets to be

Table 4.1 Climate change commitments

Commitment	Target to be achieved	Investment/savings	Risk assessment
1. Reduction in the intensity of CO_2 emissions from electricity generation	60% by 2020	£12 billion investment in British Energy + investment in renewables	
2. Action to cut CO_2 emissions from offices	30% by 2012	Investment to date £300k. Future investment £2.4m Savings at 2008, £263k	Expansion of building portfolio and energy consuming IT equipment may put the target at risk
3. Action to cut CO_2 emissions from our transport	20% by 2012	Savings at 2008, £900k	
4. Reduce the proportion of CO_2 arising from customers' energy consumption	15% by 2020	Investment in 2008 in CERT contributions £90m	
5. Employee involvement	100% by 2012		
6. Reduce the volume of materials from generation activities sent to landfill	50% by 2012	Investment to 2008 £6.2m Future investments £2.2m	More ash than forecast sent to landfill in 2008 owing to problems with new plant. Demand for ash from cement industry is slowing down, increasing ash going to landfill
7. Reduce street works landfill waste	Eliminate by 2020		Limitations could be imposed on the re-use of excavated materials
8. Reduce volumes of waste produced in energy billing activities	30% by 2020	Investment in 2008 in CERT contributions £90m	
9. Reduce office and depot waste to landfill (in addition increase recycling rate)	Eliminate by 2020 Recycling rate 65% by 2012		Large investment projects from DPRC5 may increase waste

Source: adapted from EDF Energy (2008)

achieved by 2012, and, in some cases, by 2020. The starting point for achievement is 2006. The significance of this baseline implies that the data was available from that time as EDF Energy projects its expected annual rate of progress between 2006 and 2012. This is not surprising. Many of the commitments are based on what the company was already doing internally as the company developed key performance indicators around actions to reflect achievement of the strategic ambition of 'environmental performance'. In

Table 4.2 Social commitments

Commitment	Investment/savings
1. Keep prices competitive and provide enduring support to vulnerable supply customers until 2012.	Investment to date: £9.2 million
2. Lead the industry in protecting vulnerable customers from the adverse effects of power cuts.	
3. Extend health and safety activity to support children, community groups and customers.	Plans to invest £135,000 in 2009
4. Work with suppliers to ensure that they meet the ten principles of the Global Compact to guarantee an ethical supply chain.	
5. By 2012, ensure that 2.5 million young people in the UK will have participated in the Sustainable Schools Programme.	Planned total project costs £2.3 million
6. Attain gold standard from independent experts for the approach to diversity and inclusion.	

Source: adapted from EDF Energy (2008)

addition, as indicated in Table 4.1, EDF Energy identifies any risks that might slow down the rate of progress towards achieving targets.

The social commitments are based on a set of pledges towards customers: continuity of supply, safety, supply chain and employees, as outlined in Table 4.2. Unlike the climate commitments, they are aspirations for improvement (by 2012) rather than explicit quantitative targets. Financial impacts are indicated as either costs to date or as planned investment. As with the climate commitments, these were reported in the 2008 Sustainability Performance Report. It is against EDF Energy's 2008 starting position that the targets for achievement have been set.

The significance of the information in Tables 4.1 and 4.2 is that it has been included in EDF Energy's 2008 *Sustainability Performance Report*, available online to the public. This is the first time that EDF Energy has reported on progress towards achieving the commitments in a way that reflects how the same information is reported and used internally. While some of the detail in the internal reports is not provided externally, the company is open and transparent about the rate of progress being made and the risk that commitments will not be achieved by 2012. In the spirit of the CRF, the connection is being made not only between social, environmental and economic performance, but between internal and external reporting.

EDF Energy's operations

A short summary of the scope of EDF Energy's operations was provided at the beginning of this chapter. It provides an insight into the scale of EDF Energy's task to ensure that sustainability is perceived as the key driver of business performance across the organization. For example, with a target of 100 per cent employee involvement in the climate commitments (see Table 4.1), it has to be appreciated that this now involves around 20,000 people. Equally, while, on the one hand, the vertically integrated nature of operations allows the company to control a series of related activities, on the other, it demonstrates the broad range over which the strategic objectives underpinned by sustainability are to be achieved. The four business units indicate the breadth of the company's operations. Within each of the business units there are the support functions of finance, human resources, marketing and communications. In order to ensure employees in these support functions are also engaged in achievement of sustainability, careful consideration has had to be given to how this might be achieved.

In addition, as a result of the recent acquisition of British Energy and a number of divestments and in-sourcing of activities during the last three years, EDF Energy is also experiencing the physical consequences of merging resources, activities and employees, which further increases the difficulties in fully reporting and embedding sustainability.

EDF Energy's sustainability journey

Going back to its formation in 2003, the company recognized at an early stage that organizational structure and delegation of responsibility was important to deliver against the five ambitions. At EDF Energy, such delegation is achieved by a two-tier system of executives. At the top is the Company Executive Team consisting of directors for a range of identified areas of responsibility; then there is an Executive Management Team of senior leaders for each of EDF Energy's four business units. Although initially the company had a head of corporate responsibility, there was a change of emphasis in 2005 when sustainability was established explicitly as a driver of business performance. In 2006, this led to the development of sustainability manifestos, the formation of a stakeholder panel in order to achieve the ambition for stakeholder engagement, and the creation of a One Planet Ambassador programme amongst employees. The objective of this initiative was to encourage participation and the promotion of sustainability by capturing and building on the personal convictions of employees. In 2008, following the launch of the social commitments, the One Community Ambassador programme was established. At the beginning of 2009, there was a transition to a single employee Ambassador Scheme.

Following developments in 2006 and to add further emphasis to sustainability as a driver of business performance, a director position with specific responsibility for sustainability was created at the company executive level. In addition, in order to ensure that sustainability was enacted across all company operations, a director with responsibility for sustainability was appointed as part of the executive at each of the four business units described above.

2007 is significant in that with the influence of external developments such as concerns about climate change, modifications were made to the five ambitions as the strategic objectives to be achieved by 2012. These became:

- *safe for all*: aspiring to a zero harm safety record;
- *customers' choice*: making EDF Energy first choice for customers, including looking after the vulnerable;
- *shareholder's expectation*: delivering strong financial performance;
- *sustainable performance*: leading in sustainability (including delivery of the climate and social commitments in 2012, while staying on track to deliver the 2020 targets); and
- *high-performing people*: including achieving the gold standard by independent assessors for its approach to diversity and equality and sustaining high levels of staff engagement and performance.

Sustainability as the spirit of the original five ambitions remains; but the profile of particular concerns, such as equality and diversity and the protection of vulnerable customers, has been raised. In some ways the reinterpretation of these five ambitions is an outcome of attempts to better achieve the balance between social, environmental and economic aspects of company operations. The ambitions are more integrated as there is an overlap in the commitments within 'sustainable performance', with some of those expressed in the other ambitions. Take, for example, employee engagement and looking after vulnerable customers, which have been set as commitment targets for achievement (see Tables 4.1 and 4.2). By learning from the experiences since 2003, it is a better articulation to all stakeholders, including employees, of what specific areas of sustainability the company will work towards for the next five years.

Progressing the delivery of sustainability

To deliver sustainability, the company set up three management groupings with clearly defined lines of responsibility. The first grouping is the Company Sustainable Development Committee (SDC), a sub-committee of the EDF Energy Board, comprising the Executive Team of EDF Energy and chaired by the chief executive officer. The second is the Corporate Responsibility and Environment Panel (CRE Panel), which is headed by the chief officer of people, organization and brand performance (previously headed by the director, sustainable future), and consists of senior managers from the corporate centre and each of the four business units. This group is responsible to the SDC and for strategy, as it determines policy and direction for operational levels to deliver sustainability objectives. As a result, the panel reviews operational progress against those commitments. It also takes account of operational recommendations and future planning considerations.

The third grouping is a Delivery Group (DG) responsible for sustainability at the operational level. It is chaired by the head of business performance and internal control who also sits on the CRE Panel. Heads of sustainability from the business units and representatives from shared services and the corporate functions sit on the DG.

The DG plays a significant role in the company as it has to coordinate and deliver aspects of sustainability performance. Equally, it has to ensure that communication occurs across all functions as the basis for reporting and guiding actions – in other words, that the objectives of sustainability are perceived as relevant across functions and not just for achievement by a sustainability team. Thus, measurement and communication are key functions for the DG.

Measurement through the development of appropriate key performance indicators is crucial for setting targets as a means of directing operational managers. It is also important for enabling performance against commitments to be evaluated. The corporate function with responsibility for developing quantitative performance criteria, and represented on the DG, is that of business performance. As a function, it represents a team that coordinates the reporting, the data-gathering and the assurance processes. The head of business performance and internal control agreed to participate in the CRF as his team was grappling with developing measurement criteria and reporting processes for the climate and social commitments. His title and responsibilities are a further demonstration of sustainability as a key business driver at EDF Energy.

Progressing measurement and internal reporting processes

From the descriptions of developments from 2005 to 2007, it is clear that EDF Energy has undertaken a series of actions to address the concern that there was a perceived lack of integration between corporate responsibility and financial performance and to ensure that sustainability is better established as a driver of business performance. The significance of sustainable performance as a strategic objective for the delivery of the company's social and climate commitments means that two forms of reports are prepared by the Business Performance Team. One is a report of progress to demonstrate if the company 'is on track to meeting the strategic objectives'. It is based on achievement against the social and climate commitment targets by the business units and involves the production of quarterly progress performance reports. As well as the CRE Panel, the reports are put before the SDC.

These progress reports are 'easy-to-read-at-a-glance' pages in which progress on each of the commitments (see Tables 4.1 and 4.2) is indicated based on a traffic light system. Green (a diamond shape) means that the company is on track to meet the 2012 target. Amber (a circle) signifies that the company is 'middling'– although the rate of progress may be slower than planned to date: the target is still achievable by 2012. Red (a square) signifies that the company

Table **4.3** Climate commitment performance and progress

Climate commitment	Sponsor	Key performance indicator (KPI)	Actual 2008	'Target' 2009	Latest view	Current status
We will cut our CO_2 emissions from offices and depots by 30% by 2012	Named director	Kilo tonnes CO_2	22.1	20.1	22.5	■

Source: EDF Energy (2009a)

is currently not on track to meet the target by 2012. Where progress is indicated as 'red', some narrative is provided which indicates why progress has been affected and the initiatives or interventions that might be necessary to advance progress and ensure achievement by 2012, or to identify the risks of non-achievement. By way of example, Table 4.3 provides an example of how progress in achieving one of the commitments was communicated for the third quarter of 2009.

The narrative to accompany the example in Table 4.3 explains why overall consumption of energy has risen rather than fallen – increased server usage, new buildings and increased building usage being offered as an explanation, even though efficiency initiatives remain on track to deliver around 6 kilo tonnes of carbon dioxide (CO_2) reduction. Identification of a 'sponsor' is to indicate which Company Executive Team member has the line of responsibility for the commitment identified and who will take sponsorship (ownership) of the initiative(s) that will ensure that eventual delivery of the commitment will take place.

The other form of report produced by the Business Performance Team is designed for the DG as it is much more focused on the operational performance that has contributed to the state of progress in achieving the commitment targets. The report is also a performance progress report against each of the commitment targets. This report provides more detail on the variety of initiatives that contribute to achieving the commitment as well as identifying any risks and detrimental influences that have or may impact upon progress. As a result, it reports on progress in relation to each of the initiatives as part of a decision tree process for determining the red, amber and green status of progress in achieving the commitment target, as shown in Table 4.3. It also provides a basis for the narrative explanations when progress is designated as 'red'.

By way of example, Table 4.4 demonstrates how progress would be reported to the DG by summarizing the information criteria.

This allows the DG to see if operations are proceeding as planned on an annual basis towards achieving the commitment by 2012. Missing from Table 4.4 is the information that would accompany it, in which the same criteria are identified by way of progress in the total package of initiatives put in place to

Table 4.4 *Commitment Progress Report* (extract) provided
to delivery group

Delivery indicator (how the commitment is delivered – e.g. reduction in energy consumption)	Key performance indicator (KPI)	KPI performance (annually by target, forecast and actual from 2006–2012)	Commitment, risks and detrimental influences	Total financial impact (annually by sum of initiatives)	Commentary

Source: EDF Energy (2009b)

deliver the commitment. In this way a red, amber or green status is determined for each initiative. It informs the functional managers and heads of sustainability for the four business units of the effectiveness of the initiatives and where performance needs to be improved.

Progress in sustainability at EDF Energy

Although much progress has been made, EDF Energy is open in saying that its 'sustainability journey' since 2003 is still a 'work in progress'. Progress has been made in communicating the five ambitions, and in designing and developing measurement and reporting processes for evaluation against objectives and for reporting on that progress. However, problems and issues have arisen both in the appropriateness of the measures adopted or in gaining full commitment from all levels of employees. For example, as part of the climate commitments, tensions have arisen in trying to encourage staff to waste less or to recycle more where employees perceive that this slows down their ability to 'do the day job'. Additionally, some of the sustainability commitments seem so far removed from what employees feel that they do in the organization that they fail to appreciate how they, as individuals, can make a contribution or how these commitments are integrated within business operations. Some of these issues have been dealt with. Others still exist and help to explain why EDF Energy would itself admit that it is still in the process of development in relation to the effectiveness of some of the measurement processes, in translating the ambitions into meaningful targets for employees, and in embedding sustainability within the company across all staff levels.

Self-reflection is an important part of the progress made within EDF Energy. Part of a process of review has been to work with a PhD student sponsored by EDF SA who has undertaken a thorough analysis of the way in which the company enacts sustainability and its achievements so far. As a result, he has been able to identify four drivers of sustainability performance and five inhibitors of speedy progress to achievement, as shown in Table 4.5.

Interestingly, the 'drivers' appear to be structural and controllable top down. Some of these, such as executive commitment, have existed from the time

Table 4.5 Drivers of sustainability performance and inhibitors
of 'speedy progress'

Drivers of sustainability performance	Inhibitors of 'speedy progress'
1. Chief executive/senior commitment and leadership 2. Sustainability commitments and targets 3. Internal performance reporting 4. Changes/additions to governance/ organizational structures	1. 'This is an iterative process and we are learning from doing … all this takes time.' 2. 'We develop some solutions to implement, but then other unexpected effects stop them from taking place.' 3. 'We still experience problems in the definitions of operational measures for strategic sustainability targets.' 4. 'Some of the big things we want to do, it's just that our customers are not demanding it.' 5. 'Sustainability is really complex and we can only do some of the basic things.'

Source: David Ferguson, Cranfield Management School

sustainability became a business driver at EDF Energy. Significantly, the 'inhibitors' reflect the attitudes and perceptions of employees, but also some of the practical problems of implementation which EDF Energy is trying to overcome. Both have led or will lead to changes in the way that sustainability is enacted. For example, identification of problems in the definitions of operational measures has led to modifications and considerations of their appropriateness in performance evaluation.

Such modifications are also a good example of external concerns and pressures that make certain issues more critical than others. Although it has defined and raised the profile of these social welfare aspects of sustainability, 'unexpected effects' are, indeed, a potential inhibitor to 'speedy achievement', as identified in Table 4.5, if they lead to an amendment of commitments. For example, it may slow down the process if appropriate new or amended monitoring and measurements need to be developed. These events act as a driver for change and clearly prioritize certain issues (in this case, specific social welfare aspirations) more than others. Another good example of 'unexpected effects' is the increased urgency to deal with climate change, which prompted the development of 'Our climate commitments', declared in 2007. While allowing EDF Energy to better articulate its environmental ambitions, internally and externally, it takes time to put measurement systems in place to evaluate performance against the nine pledges that comprise these commitments. Also, and more significantly, it takes time to ensure that the underlying activities are taking place and that staff are fully aware of what is necessary and required of them.

Table 4.5 identifies the commitment and support at executive level as a key driver of sustainability performance; but EDF Energy is aware of the importance of staff at all levels and how they work and support achievement against the five ambitions. The company has had to think carefully about how it communicates 'sustainability' to employees at different levels in a way that seems relevant to what they do in the company: in other words, to consider how it can embed sustainability across the organization such that it is an accepted but unconscious way of doing business on the part of employees. Ignoring this issue would lead to potential failures to achieve the five ambitions.

EDF Energy is equally aware that attempting to avoid such failure has implications for monitoring and collating information as part of the measurement and evaluation processes. Unless employees see the relevance of what is being measured, they may not fully cooperate in providing reliable, timely and accurate information. The more serious implication of this is that it could potentially damage EDF Energy's credibility. For example, EDF Energy has produced *Sustainability Performance Reports* for 2007 and 2008. The 2007 report describes performance against the five ambitions established in 2003; the 2008 report indicates progress against the amended ambitions, and, in particular, against the climate and social commitments. Before being made available, there is an extensive assurance process for ensuring that information is accurate. While the nature of information made public may not be in the same format as that of internally produced reports, it is important that any claims about performance can be verified. It is also important for linking what goes on operationally with the branding strategy and external face of EDF Energy. With the recent 2008 *Sustainability Performance Report*, EDF Energy achieved the Global Reporting Initiative grade 'A+' rating. This aim would have been seriously undermined if unreliable information was generated or there was a suggestion that operating procedures, particularly for environmental performance or social welfare activities, were not taking place.

Sustainability and the CRF

Integrating the key sustainability drivers within an organization's strategy and developing and providing sustainability information that is strategically important fits well with the approaches adopted at EDF Energy. Adoption of the CRF has been a useful intellectual exercise and has introduced some rigorous thinking about ways of evaluating performance against strategic objectives. The suggestion from heads of sustainability within the business units is that 'The CRF influence on measurement mechanisms and reporting has made issues visible to managers at the operational level that were previously not visible.'

This was achieved by rethinking ways of breaking down performance against the climate and social commitments at operational levels into measurable targets that operational managers could realistically control and achieve. Equally, operational managers had to think of ways in which they could break down their own objectives into the actual work tasks that were undertaken by employees. This involved considerations about the impact of employee tasks on the commitments and how to get employees 'on board' to conduct those tasks in ways directed towards achieving the commitments. Feedback to the employees about their contribution and what form it would take was also considered an important issue to be dealt with as a means of encouraging continued effort towards achievement.

Apart from influencing ways of translating strategic objectives down to operations, the CRF has introduced rigour into the internal reporting processes for evaluation – for example, the processes for identifying, measuring, evaluating and reporting progress towards achievement of the climate and social commitments by 2012. Participation in the CRF has encouraged EDF Energy to develop ways of communicating performance in simple, easy-to-read internal reports that reflect such progress. The tangible outcomes of this were evident from the work of the Business Performance Team described above in preparing progress against commitment reports to present to the SDC and to the DG. Table 4.6 provides an extract of a performance update report on 'Our climate and social commitments', presented at a meeting of the Sustainable Development Committee in November 2009. One additional feature of this 'at-a-glance' report is that the star shapes featured are also indicated in green, as with the diamond shape that represents 'on track', to signify that the end-of-year target has been exceeded.

The description provided above of the reports and the determination of progress towards climate and social commitments makes the process sound unproblematic. For the Business Performance Team, however, a continual process of review and reflection on the reliability of the underlying information takes place. The difficult part of the process for the Business Performance Team is to combine the traffic light status of each of the initiatives into determining the state of progress towards the commitment target to be achieved. This is where problems are still being experienced. Although the initiatives are colour coded, it is not simply a case of one colour outweighing the rest to become the traffic light status on progress towards achievement. In reaching their determination of that status, consideration is given to the nature of the 'commitments, risks and detrimental influences'. At the same time, the team has found it necessary to reflect on the suitability of the initiatives that have been identified to contribute to achievement and the reliability of information that has been collated to assess their progress. This indicates that although reporting on progress has become systematized, the Business Performance Team is still defining and refining the information that is used to derive the progress reports and thinking about the suitability of the underlying measures that it requires. Such information is very often derived from middle managers who do not fully relate to sustainability as the driver of business performance.

Reliability of the evaluation processes is important as EDF Energy drives actions and operations within the company towards achieving strategic objectives. However, a more critical reason for reliability in the information being collated within the company relates to the concept of connectedness within the

CRF: in particular, that the information in the internal reports would be connected and linked with that provided in the external reports on the implementation of corporate strategy. As EDF Energy becomes more confident in the processes of evaluation and reporting internally, it is beginning to use the progress reports as a basis for reporting externally on how it is achieving its ambition of sustainable performance. The intention is to provide more of such reports in relation to other aspects of sustainable business performance in future years. This makes the need for the commitment to sustainability at all levels even more of a necessity as the outcomes of initiatives and measurement systems need to be properly evaluated and taken seriously.

Conclusions

To conclude, EDF Energy describes its 'sustainability journey' as a work in progress. Yet, in a short period of time, EDF Energy has made considerable progress to ensure that sustainability as a key business driver is aligned with internal monitoring, evaluation and reporting processes. It has also made progress in making tangible connections between internal and external reporting as a way of evaluating performance against the five strategic ambitions to its stakeholders. This is even more apparent in information disclosed in EDF Energy's *Sustainability Performance Report 2008* (see Table 4.7), where the company has disclosed how it is performing against the five ambitions; significantly, it has disclosed how performance has changed between 2007 and 2008 (where possible). The CRF has been instrumental in much of this progress. Admittedly, there are some issues still to be addressed; but many might be seen as part of a development process at EDF Energy as it attempts to enhance the reliability of measurement and data collation in the company. Some of these issues go back to the observation that employees need to feel they can contribute to the achievement of the five ambitions and to recognize the relevance of them in their working environment. Ideally, this requires employees to feel committed to all aspects of sustainability, which brings the key issue back to the need for EDF Energy to embed sustainability across the business.

Part of the exercise of 'embeddedness' is the regular monitoring of progress in relation to the five strategic ambitions and consideration of how to communicate that progress effectively to employees at all levels. One aspect of the 'success' in the internal reporting system is that if any deviation from planned rates of achievement is identified, action is taken to put progress back on track. This is a consequence of having clearly defined goals and the desire to use sustainability as a driver of business performance. Significantly, however, the reporting process is also useful as a learning mechanism as it allows senior managers to reflect on the appropriateness of the commitments in the light of market and societal conditions.

Table 4.6 Extract from update report on progress in climate and social change commitments

		RY Actual	RY target	End of Year Objective	End of Year Status
OCC c1	We will reduce the intensity of CO_2 emissions from generation production by 60% by 2020	785 tonnes CO_2/GWh	807 tonnes CO_2/GWh	807 tonnes CO_2/GWh	◆
OCC c2	We will cut CO_2 emissions from our offices and depots by 30% by 2012	20.0 kt CO_2	21.1 kt CO_2	21.1 kt CO_2	◆
OCC c3	We will cut CO_2 emissions from our transport by 20% by 2012	26.1 kt CO_2	27.1 kt CO_2	27.1 kt CO_2	◆
OCC c4	We will reduce the proportion of CO_2 arising from our customers' energy consumption by 15% by 2020	6.05 tonnes/ prod. acc.	5.90 tonnes/ prod. acc.	5.90 tonnes/ prod. acc.	●
OCC c5	We will have 100% employee involvement by 2012	42%	44%	44%	●
OCC c6	We will reduce the volume of materials (ash) sent to landfill by 50% by 2012	475 kt	416 kt	416 kt	■
OCC c7	We will eliminate waste sent to landfill from street works by 2020	7% to landfill	40% to landfill	40% to landfill	★
OCC c8	We will reduce the volume of waste from energy billing by 30% by 2020	Orchard on track	Orchard on track	Orchard on track	◆
OCC c9	We will send no office or depot waste to landfill by 2020	31.5%	35.0%	35.0%	★
OSC c1	We will commit to keeping our prices competitive and will provide enduring support for our most vulnerable supply customers until 2012	158,110 customer accounts	150,000 customer accounts	150,000 customer accounts	★
OSC c2	We will lead the industry in protecting vulnerable customers from the adverse effects of power cuts	5,068 packages of assistance	3,000 packages of assistance	3,000 packages of assistance	★
OSC c3	We will extend our health and safety activity to support children, community groups and our customers	287,773 participating children	282,000 participating children	282,000 participating children	◆
		12,572 CO detectors	11,500 CO detectors	11,500 CO detectors	◆
OSC c4	We will work with all our suppliers to ensure they meet the ten principles of the Global Compact to guarantee an ethical supply chain track	project on track	project on track	project on track	◆
OSC c5	By 2012, 2.5 million young people in the UK will have participated in our Sustainable Schools Programme, learning about the sustainable use of energy	498,488 pupils engaged	259,650 pupils engaged	259,650 pupils engaged	★
OSC c6	By 2012, we will have attained gold standard from independent experts for our approach to diversity and inclusion. We will also have increased opportunities for our employees to develop and improve a range of skills including basic life skills	project slightly behind	DIAG attendance ensured	DIAG attendance ensured	●

Source: EDF Energy (2009c)

Quantifed benefits to date [2006 to 2009]	Top Short Term Risk to Delivery
	Failure to deliver renewable assets results in higher carbon generation mix leading to OCC1 not being delivered in the short term
£M 0.5	Increasing demand from business expansion, both in terms of space and IT equipment results in higher energy usage leading to OCC2 not being achieved
£M 0.9	Existing fleet size is maintained or increased resulting in higher CO_2 emissions leading to OCC3 not being achieved
	Our initiatives fail to deliver sufficient change in customer behaviour and / or our energy purchases are not sufficiently low carbon resulting in customer CO_2 not reducing and OCC4 not being delivered
	Employees do not participate in community investment activity, reducing our ability to support the delivery of OCC5
	Sale of processed ash into the construction industry is affected by the economic downturn resulting in increased landfill requirements and impacts our ability to meet OCC6
	Inability to comply with appropriate highways authority specifications on the usage of alternative reinstatement materials results in more waste going to landfill leading to OCC7 not being achieved
	Project Orchard is delayed and / or does not deliver / facilitate a move towards online billing resulting in OCC8 not being achieved
	Increasing waste from non-integration activity and /or decreasing recycling rates result in increased waste to landfill affecting our ability to meet OCC9
	As a result of the economic downturn Energy Assist customer number increased beyond the level we can afford impacting the ability to meet OSC1
	Other priorities result in resources not being focused on the distribution of packages of assistance leading to OSC2 not being delivered
	Changes in school priorities (e.g. change to curricula) and / or loss of team members results in a lack of engagement and OSC3 not being achieved
	Product defects or failures result in the objectives of OSC3 not being met
	Lack of C* approval by Corporate PfB for this project results in a delay in the development of the Supplier questionnaire and associated risk matrix jeopardising delivery of OSC4
	Registration targets are not met resulting in lower than anticipated pupil engagement leading to non delivery of OSC5
	Company restructuring results in a refocusing of Diversity and Inclusion commitment and strategy leading to a delay in delivery of OSC6

Table 4.7 EDF Energy's *Sustainability Performance Report 2008* (extract)

AMBITION	MEASURE	KPI	2008	2007
Safe for All	Days of zero harm	Days	259	n/a
	Lost time incident rates	/100,000 hr	0.33	0.39
Shareholder's	Profit before tax	£M	189	342
Expectation	Turnover	£M	6,616	5,744
Customers'	Preference rate	%	82.8	82.6
Choice	Customer product accounts	millions	5.6	5.5
	Networks customer satisfaction	%	64.7	69.5
	Distribution customer interruptions	Number per customer per year	194	191
	Distribution customer minutes lost	Minutes per customer per year	224	204
Sustainable	CO_2 from power stations	Millions tonnes	21.9	21.5
Performance	CO_2 from buildings	'000 tonnes	22.1	22.5
	CO_2 from transport	'000 tonnes	25.4	26.8
	CO_2 per customer account	tonnes	6.1	6.1
	Employee involvement	Index %	39.2	25.2
	Ash to landfill	'000 tonnes	673	701
	Street-works waste to landfill	%	18.6	35.4
	Managed building waste to landfill	%	37.9	47.1
	Eligible customers on social tariff	No.	126,723	
	Packages of support to vulnerable customers	No.	632	
	Children educated in electrical safety	No.	112,980	
	Children registered on Sustainable Schools' programme	No.	53,698	
High	Employee engagement survey	% engaged	63.7	65.6
Performing People	No. of employees	Headcount	13,406	13,158

Not described in this case study are the extensive attempts that have been undertaken by EDF Energy to communicate the nature and the significance of the five ambitions to employees. Yet, there is still some ground to cover in convincing people who are working to deadlines and under pressure from budget constraints and targets to generate revenues that they should equally be working towards the company's social and climate commitments, as articulated in the sustainable performance ambition. EDF Energy is not unaware of the need for sustainability being in the 'heart and minds' of employees if the five ambitions are to be fully realized. The company is addressing this challenge through a variety of initiatives and incentives to embed sustainability within the company, but acknowledges that it is a slow process.

Acknowledgements

We are grateful to the staff at EDF Energy who readily and willingly agreed to give their time to be interviewed as part of this case study. In particular, we would like to thank Mark Bromley, the head of business performance and internal control, for his help and support throughout.

References

EDF Energy (2007) *Sustainability Performance Report 2007*, EDF Energy, www.edfenergy.com/sustainability/performance-report/archive-reports/index.shtml
EDF Energy (2008) *Sustainability Performance Report 2008*, EDF Energy, www.edfenergy.com/sustainability/performance-report/index.shtml
EDF Energy (2009a) *EDF Energy Progress Report*, Performance Quarter 3, EDF Energy, London
EDF Energy (2009b) *EDF Energy Commitment Progress Report*, EDF Energy, London
EDF Energy (2009c) *Report to Sustainable Development Committee*, November, EDF Energy, London

five

A Golden Thread for Embedding Sustainability in a Local Government Context: The Case of West Sussex County Council

Suzana Grubnic and David Owen

Introduction

The Prince's Accounting for Sustainability Project (A4S) is viewed by various key players, both elected members and senior officials, at West Sussex County Council (WSCC) as simply presenting the right framework at the right time. As a public-sector organization, the onus is on the council to drive forward the three pillars of sustainability – that is, economic prosperity, social inclusion and a protected local environment. A general well-being duty is enshrined in the Local Government Act 2000 and has been more recently reaffirmed in the Local Government White Paper *Strong and Prosperous Communities* published in 2006. Efforts towards preserving the natural environment are in the process of being mainstreamed throughout the council's operations, rather than being the sole responsibility of a separate environmental department. Key to mainstreaming environmental protection has been a general diffusion of the notion that there is a business case for preserving natural resources and economic benefit in mitigating the impact of climate change. Additionally, while currently not as well developed as the environmental dimension, social sustainability is also increasingly featuring in council decision-making practices, with particular initial emphasis on employment issues, such as training and education and equal opportunities, as part of a wider move towards pursuing a sustainable community strategy.

Chapter overview

The focus of this chapter is on the internal operations of WSCC and, in particular, the mind-sets and activities of key players that are helping to embed sustainability throughout the organization. The chapter is organized into four further sections. The following section provides a background of the local government context and offers a brief overview of the council and surrounding area. Next, the chapter presents the perspectives of council officials and a prominent cabinet member on the embedding of sustainability and provides detail on the establishment of a 'golden thread' linking council strategies to the day-to-day working activities of employees. The penultimate section describes policies, performance structures and specific tools that have been developed in order to underpin this golden thread and assesses their role in promoting sustainable development throughout council operations. Particular attention is focused here on the recently developed Corporate Sustainability Programme (and associated performance system: Perform), which provides strategic direction in the form of a demanding set of targets covering a five-year period (2009 to 2013) and addressing a wide range of social and environmental issues, as well as establishing a commitment to produce an annual sustainability report based on A4S's Connected Reporting Framework (CRF). Additionally, we consider key supporting measurement tools established to monitor staff behaviour (the Sustainable Workplace Tool), inform project appraisal (the Sustainability Appraisal) and promote reduction in carbon dioxide emissions (the Carbon Model). The case study also outlines efforts or intentions by the council to influence suppliers, local residents and other public-sector organizations in the area. Finally, the chapter reflects on the course taken by WSCC and offers insights into future developments.

Background: Local government and West Sussex County Council

Local government in England

Local government leadership

Local government authorities, arguably, are perhaps the only institutions with the responsibility of meeting the needs of all sectors in the community. Responsibility extends from providing environmental services (e.g. local transport planning and waste management), to facilitating social inclusion (e.g. provision of care and education), to promoting the stability of the economic business community. Leadership is assumed to be naturally vested in them given that they are noted as having a long and proud tradition of developing innovative solutions to local problems (DTLR, 1998, section 8.4). Leadership of services within an area is recognized in the mandate for local authorities to formulate strategies with the police, probation services and healthcare organizations, as well as with private and voluntary organizations. Local authorities have a legal duty to prepare a sustainable community strategy and, further, a requirement to produce a local area agreement. The former is a longer-term plan setting out the strategic vision for an area, while the latter specifies a single set of priorities for local partners. Furthermore, local authorities are employers of significant numbers of staff and hold power in procuring products as wide-ranging as food for schools to cement used in the maintenance of roads.

National government steering

In line with principles of universalism and equality, central government steers local authority organizations along with other public-sector organizations. On sustainable development, the UK government outlined in *Securing the Future: The UK Government Sustainable Development Strategy* (Defra, 2005) its vision of living within environmental limits: ensuring a strong, healthy and just society; achieving a sustainable economy; promoting good governance; and using sound science responsibly. More recently, and in contrast to other national states, the government has passed legislation requiring greenhouse gas emissions to be reduced by 80 per cent by 2050 against a 1990 baseline. This initiative has cascaded down to local government and three national indicators have been set relating to progress on climate change in *The New Performance Framework for Local Authorities and Local Authority Partnerships: Single Set of National Indicators* (DCLG, 2007). Specifically, the indicators include NI185 on carbon dioxide reduction from local authority operations, NI186 on per capita reduction in carbon dioxide emissions in the local authority areas, and NI188 on planning to adapt to climate change. Performance on the indicators is to be

assessed by the Audit Commission as part of the new Comprehensive Area
Assessment (CAA). The CAA replaces the former Comprehensive Performance
Assessment (CPA) and came into effect in April 2009.

Central government steering is further evident in the distribution of grants
in four separate blocks (dedicated schools grant; grants for specific services;
formal grants; and area-based grants) and in the efficiency drive announced
during the 2004 Comprehensive Spending Review. Following an independent
review by Sir Peter Gershon, local authorities were initially expected to achieve
an efficiency target of 2.5 per cent a year until 2008. The target was raised in
the 2007 Comprehensive Spending Review to 3 per cent and an additional
provision made that all gains must be cash releasing.

From April 2010, local authorities will be required to comply with the CRC
Energy Efficiency Scheme (CRC), as will all organizations exceeding the quali-
fication threshold of 6000MWh of half-hourly metered electricity. The CRC
scheme requires the purchase of allowances at the end of the year during the
first year of operation and upfront payments in subsequent years based on
expected energy use. Furthermore, organizations participating in the scheme
will be expected to monitor and report energy use to a CRC administrator. A
league table revealing the relative performance of all organizations covered by
the CRC is to be published by the UK Environment Agency at the end of each
year and is intended to promote protection of, and improvements in, performance by individual participants, including local authorities.

Support agencies

In addition to audit and inspection, the Audit Commission in England provides
support to local authorities in the form of general guidance publications. Local
authorities also have access to both government-sponsored and other agencies
established for the purposes of developing local government capacity and
dissemination of best practice. As an example of the latter, Forum for the
Future has produced a Sustainability Standard – a matrix of progressive actions
– that enables a local authority to rate performance in four key areas. The four
key areas relate to what are regarded as drivers for ensuring sustainable development and include high-level commitment from senior management and
members; ownership and understanding of sustainable development in practical
terms by all management levels and staff; integration of sustainable development into council priorities and processes; and provision of leadership and
discharge of accountability to the community. Advice is also available from the
Carbon Trust, Improvement and Development Agency, Local Government
Association and Regional Government Agency, amongst others. The Global
Reporting Initiative (GRI) issued a *Sector Supplement for Public Agencies* in
2005 and the Chartered Institute of Public Finance and Accountancy (CIPFA)
published a sustainability reporting framework for public services in 2006. More

recently, HM Treasury has published an *Exposure Draft* of proposed developments in the *Government Financial Reporting Manual* (HM Treasury, 2009) and invited comments on proposals relating to sustainability reporting. Significantly, and in line with the CRF, the *Exposure Draft* puts forward the requirement for organizations to report, within the annual report and accounts, in absolute volume or consumption terms, together with information on related financial costs, against sustainability targets for greenhouse gas emissions, waste minimization and management, and use of finite resources.

West Sussex County Council

West Sussex County Council is managed by an elected cabinet and executive board and is Conservative party controlled. Located in south-east England, it serves a population of 760,000 and is responsible for providing 80 per cent of local government services (WSCC, 2009a). The services include highways, schools, children and adult services, early years, libraries, community safety, fire and rescue, adult education, youth services, planning, countryside management, waste management, rights of way, emergency planning, archives and records, the registration service and trading standards (WSCC, 2005). In environmental terms the county exhibits a varied landscape, although half of the county occupies three nationally designated Areas of Outstanding Natural Beauty (AONBs). Socially, there are affluent areas in rural West Sussex with high standards of living and, at the other extreme, relative deprivation and high health inequalities, particularly amongst residents along the coastal strip and in the north of the county. The council employs in the region of 23,000 employees (6880 full-time equivalents) and has a gross spending requirement of almost UK£1.3 billion per annum (WSCC, 2009b). A Fundamental Service Review initiated in 2006 has, to date, resulted in UK£40 million in savings (WSCC, 2009b).

Embedding sustainability within
the county council

Chief executive and member championing of sustainability

In a drive to improve the council's corporate sustainability performance, both the chief executive and cabinet member for finance and resources have provided commitment to, and championed the process of, embedding sustainability throughout the council's operations. Commitment was partly attributed to their professional backgrounds and prior experience of environmental development issues:

> *I went from being director of environment to chief executive, Louise*
> *Goldsmith went from being cabinet member for environment to cabinet*
> *member for finance, which has meant there has been a bit more under-*
> *standing and simply more commitment, I think, to make some of these*
> *things work in practice.* (Chief Executive)

The cabinet member for finance and resources explained that the shift in role
from environment and economy to her present position has had a welcome
advantage in helping to mainstream sustainability within internal operations:

> *It wasn't that I didn't want to do the other job; I was asked if I'd take on*
> *the [finance] portfolio and it was a huge wrench because I did love what*
> *I did. On the other hand, there are ways of influencing matters when*
> *you've got a finance portfolio, which is why sustainability comes with me*
> *into County Hall... So here is a way that I can help effect change through*
> *the finance portfolio. Properties are mine, staff are mine, all in my portfo-*
> *lio now. It's a very good position to be in to help drive things ... most of*
> *the big procurement contracts go through my portfolio. So it allows me to*
> *ask green questions.* (Cabinet Member for Finance and Resources)

In staffing terms, she has oversight for 1228 full-time equivalents, in comparison to 74 previously, and a gross budget of UK£20.9 million compared to UK£7
million for environment and economy (WSCC, 2009b). The championing of
sustainability has been further aided in that she enjoys a close working relationship with the replacement portfolio holder for environment and economy.

Developing a sustainability strategy

The principles and guidance of A4S are perceived by the chief executive as a
holistic framework for achieving sustainability and as a means of connecting
environmental considerations to the economic and financial operations of an
organization:

> *It seemed to us that the whole project and the reporting framework were*
> *going to provide impetus for a coherent and holistic approach to what our*
> *footprint was environmentally across a whole range of issues. So this*
> *seemed to offer the way forward for us to make a single commitment that*
> *would have multiple impacts, if you like ... a single corporate commit-*
> *ment to achieving greater sustainability and reducing our environmental*
> *footprint. We have used the project, the framework and the reporting as*
> *the means of checking we were doing it.* (Chief Executive)

For assessment and benchmarking purposes on the sustainability 'journey', the
Sustainability Standard developed by Forum for the Future's network of 30
local authorities was considered as working 'hand in hand' with A4S. In line

with recommendations of both projects, for example, the chief executive and cabinet member for finance and resources indicated that resources had been dedicated for the long haul of ensuring that sustainability is an integral part of council activities and, further, stated aspirations for the council to act as 'community leader' to residents and businesses of West Sussex. In the context of the former, after only achieving a 'weak to fair' rating in 2006 on the Sustainability Standard, WSCC endorsed an ambition to be considered excellent by 2011/2012. Progress towards this aim is apparent in subsequent improvement to a 'fair to good' rating, with movement towards the good end of the latter category achieved in 2008/2009.

Consistent with both the ethos of A4S and the aim to achieve a better rating on Forum for the Future's Sustainability Standard, the chief executive explained that a standalone sustainability strategy did not exist, but, instead, that sustainable development underlies all strategies of the council:

> *In a sense, we have tried to avoid having a sustainability strategy as such because in large complicated organizations like ours, having a strategy for anything normally means that if you're not directly involved in the delivery of that strategy, you don't necessarily adapt what you're doing to those aims. What we have tried to do is have sustainability underpinning all the strategies, be it the schools' building strategy, the transport strategy, the economic strategy or all the other things that we're responsible for.* (Chief Executive)

He went on to note that 'What we want to create is a set of values, I think, that are common to different places where people work in the organization, and respect for both the organization's impacts and our policy impacts on sustainability is definitely a strong part of that.'

In pursuing this ambition the intention is for the Chief Executive's Board and Strategic Management Group to take on responsibility for sustainability rather than for them to rely upon one individual. Following a restructuring of the Chief Executive's Board in April 2008, the post of strategic director for environment and development no longer exists, and strategic direction for sustainable development falls within the work remit of the executive directors for adults and children, customers and communities and business services.

Meeting the challenges

A perceived challenge to the championing of sustainability by the chief executive and cabinet member for finance and resources within the council has been the extent to which sustainability considerations can be outside their direct control. As an example, both recounted delays in a Private Finance Initiative (PFI) for the investment, maintenance and operation of street lighting stock, as the UK Department for Transport took time to accept their specification for higher environmental standards on light fittings. On inviting bids for funding, the Department for Transport had not specified the need for energy efficiency, although the council held the view that an energy-neutral solution at least was required. As another example, the chief executive argued that improving environmental outcomes was just as legitimate as improving educational or economic outcomes. The Comprehensive Performance Assessment, however, by weighting education four times more than the environment in the service assessment, does not appear to give the same message. For her part, the cabinet member for finance and resources simply noted that the Audit Commission could be 'a little more encouraging of sustainable behaviour ... it would be quite nice if that was given quite high ratings'.

Lack of funding, coupled with the requirement to achieve efficiency savings, was also viewed by both the chief executive and cabinet member as imposing challenges in the pursuit of sustainable development. The chief executive, for example, drew attention to an overall cut in budgets of about one third:

> We have to reduce spending by 10 per cent in the next 18 months and another 10 per cent in the two years after that, having reduced it by 10 per cent in the last three years. So in four years' time, we'll have reduced expenditure basically by about 30 per cent across the board.

However, despite admitting that it would be easy to put sustainability to one side under such pressures, the chief executive maintained that this was not the case at WSCC. As an example of taking both an economic and environmental position, the cabinet member for finance and resources has committed significant resources to an Energy and Water Management Plan (E&WMP), including the creation of an invest-to-save fund. The upfront investment by the council was matched by Salix, an independent company funded by the Carbon Trust: 'I'm putting a huge amount of faith in this Salix venture, UK£250,000 investment... I think that you can then really start showing some substantial savings, then people will think this is such a great idea' (Cabinet Member for Finance and Resources).

In addition to protecting the council against future increases in costs by utility companies and reducing liability under the government's Carbon Reduction Commitment, the E&WMP was conceived as taking steps to reduce energy and water as part of wider measures to manage carbon dioxide emissions.

Notwithstanding the council's clear desire not to let financial 'imperatives' distract from pursuing sustainable development objectives, the cabinet member for finance and resources acknowledged that 'at the moment everybody's thinking about surviving and budget and costs, and it has pushed things to the side a bit', while the chief executive admitted that 'we do have to significantly reduce head count'.

A major resource that might be drawn upon by the council in seeking to maintain its focus on sustainable development in a highly adverse economic climate lies in the support of the local population. As the chief executive put it:

> There is a very strong tradition of stewardship on a number of environmental issues across the county. And I think that the population at large do expect us both in what we do as an organization and in the sort of policies we pursue to be taking full account of environmental and sustainability issues.

Championing of sustainability to the local population was in the remit of the cabinet member for finance and resources, who particularly drew attention to their support in terms of issues such as recycling and waste management initiatives, but, significantly, went on to note potential limits to pursuing a sustainability agenda in that 'I think if you said your council tax would go up UK£1 a month because we're doing some very green project, I'm not sure whether they'd actually vote for that at the moment.'

The Sustainability Group and the establishment of a golden thread

Charged with day-to-day responsibility for championing sustainability in the council and directing efforts towards integrating and translating sustainable development into practical terms for everyday activities is a small designated specialist unit – the Sustainability Group – variously described by people whom we spoke to as 'sustainability champions' and 'the conscience of the organization'. Significantly, their remit goes beyond consideration of environmental protection alone:

> A lot of people go on about sustainability; they take the three core areas now: social, environmental and economic impacts. But what we're trying to do is take those three areas and then that is surrounded by finance. So we can do sustainability, but where's the finance people? And they're the main people you need to take forward sustainability. (Sustainability Group Manager)

Notwithstanding the commitment to promoting sustainability in the fullest sense of the term, as the chief executive readily acknowledged, to date 'the social aspects, the community and cohesion aspects of sustainability have been sort of second runners in this'. The problem as he saw it here simply lies in the fact that there is less consensus on what the council is trying to achieve in these areas compared to major environmental challenges such as climate change, while robust measurement processes are also far less developed. He went on to add:

'Where I'd like to see us get to is measuring the impact on social issues and social cohesion and communities in the same sort of way as we're able to in an audit of environmental impacts.'

Some progress towards incorporating the social dimension in council decision-making processes, particularly with regard to the human factor, is, however, apparent in references made by the sustainability group manager to the development of workforce skills in the local economy featuring as part of the sustainability appraisal process in awarding contracts and the growing need to engage with customers on equality issues. Also of significance in this context is the prevalence of quantified targets addressing issues such as occupational health and safety, training and education, and diversity and equal opportunity appearing within the five-year Corporate Sustainability Programme.

For mainstreaming purposes, the sustainability group manager has worked to embed the view that decision-making on the environment is not a nicety, but makes good financial sense. For example, a decision to invest in home composters would serve to reduce waste sent to landfill and, importantly, result in a saving of UK£40 per tonne that would otherwise be spent on landfill taxes. The group manager responsible for finance emphasized that the council spent UK£10 million alone on landfill taxes annually and that the rate would increase from UK£40 to £72 per tonne in the next few years. Given the financial slant, the sustainability group manager argued that sustainability needed to be at the core of business decision-making as an integral part of a long-term cost-benefit analysis process. Examples of financial benefits included increasing business efficiency through a reduction in operating costs, increasing productivity in the use of natural resources, and reducing environmental liabilities such as payments under the new CRC.

The specialist Sustainability Group itself has been deliberately kept to four team members (based within the Policy and Partnership Directorate), while at the same time the intention is to increase the number of people taking responsibility for sustainability issues as part of their overall portfolio as sustainability considerations become more integrated within operational units. For the purposes of securing integration, the Sustainability Group sought to establish a 'golden thread' of sustainability running throughout the organization, from strategies set by cabinet members through to individuals responsible for planning and delivering services. One manager explained how the idea of a golden thread applied to her unit in the following terms:

> Our team have got their own business plan where we've got objectives around improving the way we actually deliver [services]. And sustainability is also part of that as well. It's making sure that because it's one of the corporate strategies, sustainability will be fed down through everybody's personal development review in some way, shape or form. (Service Manager, Training)

In order to further strengthen the golden thread, one sustainability officer explained how it was her role to reinforce objectives and targets contained in business plans by discussing projects with responsible parties, feeding into their achievement and discussing resource needs. In addition to the efforts of the Sustainability Group, a majority of operational units have a Staff Sustainability Group (SSG) member charged with motivating efforts and feeding back to the Sustainability Group on progress. This has the advantage of ensuring a sustainability presence throughout most parts of the council, with the intention of this eventually being rolled out to ensure coverage of all parts of the council's activities. A major problem here, however, acknowledged by a member of the Sustainability Group, arises in the dual nature of the role of SSG member, in itself a voluntary position, which gives rise to the tricky question of how far can sustainability issues be prioritized against other (arguably more core) aspects of their job specification. Somewhat worryingly, one SSG member outlined the problems faced in the following terms: 'I'm under pressure not to spend that long on it [sustainability issues] personally. I get told: "It's not your core work", so if we get busy with [other work priorities] it will be the sustainability stuff that I won't be able to do. And that pressure, I think, is on everybody.' Exacerbating the problem in this individual's view is the fact that there isn't a designated budget for the Staff Sustainability Group members.

Some further tension underpinning the 'missionary' efforts of the Sustainability Group is apparent in the somewhat fraught relationship between the wider 'business' approach to sustainability now being promoted and a natural, more avowedly moral, disposition towards the environment exhibited by some SSG members. A sustainability officer, for example, noted:

> It's a fine line sometimes, this communication business of engaging new audiences without losing the one that you already had and that were [sic] your strongest advocates. But I do think it's changing generally; there's more recognition of the broader implications of doing this, it's not just about tree-hugging and saving the planet, which is, I think, where it was pigeon-holed to be. And it is moving into sustainability and there are broad benefits and people are recognizing that.

The Sustainability Group maintained that its position on sustainable development was not designed to alienate the SSG members; rather, it was perceived to be more beneficial to attempt wider organizational buy-in and in the process convince the SSG members that their approach was the right way forward.

Support for embedding environmental management practices within economic decision-making was offered both directly and indirectly by the group. For example, in terms of direct support, the climate change officer indicated that it was within his remit to empower individual members of staff, including officials within schools, to achieve an annual 10 per cent reduction in energy and water use as contained in the E&WMP. He particularly drew atten-

tion to the fact that the E&WMP coincided with the CRC period and that the
government mandate helped him in his role:

> One of the really interesting aspects of this project is to say that there are
> two bits to it. The first one is our buildings: how are we going to deal
> with that? The second is the schools: how are we going to empower them
> to achieve what we believe they need to achieve. So from that perspective
> we're putting our customers [client departments] at the top of the tree
> here, and we're saying this is the challenge, this is what we're going to
> try and do, and we're going to support you to achieve what you need to
> do, however best you see fit. (Climate Change Officer)

On the issue of indirect support, members of the Sustainability Group
worked with the Business Services Directorate to identify savings as part of
the Fundamental Service Review (FSR) programme. As part of the FSR
Accommodation Strategy, for example, measures were implemented, such as
replacing water coolers with filters on taps and, more radically, the rational-
ization of office space by introducing open-plan offices and flexible work
stations for those who require a desk for less than 30 per cent of their working
time. As an example of joint working within the council, one of the sustainability officers recounted how she had worked with the service manager for
training to incorporate sustainability within both the purchasing and procurement training modules, including consideration of whole-life costing issues.
Given the purchasing power of the council, this has potential to release significant savings, not necessarily in the shorter term, but over the duration of
contracts. As the service manager herself told us, this is but one example of a
wider policy decision to incorporate sustainability issues within all relevant
training modules rather than running a designated specialist module that few
might attend.

   Given the encouraging developments internally in promoting sustainable
development, the Sustainability Group saw great scope for engaging residents
by effectively acting as community leaders: 'and I think this becomes a very
effective way for us to show community leadership because … if we're serious
in all the things we say about climate change and so on, isn't it beholden on us
to get our house in order' (Group Manager, Customers and Communities
Finance)?

   In addition:

> If we just take one issue like landfill, this county council has now reduced
> its landfill internally by 33 per cent, which is similar to the kind of thing
> we're asking our customers to do. We'll also reduce energy by so and so,
> which is something we're asking our customers to do. (Sustainability
> Group Manager)

Following the introduction of the Comprehensive Area Assessment and the need to demonstrate partnership in working with public-sector organizations in the locality, leading sustainability beyond the council was likewise seen as a possibility:

> *If we can take this kind of financial reporting and transparency and show what we're actually paying over in costs from a tax perspective and landfill and all that kind of thing, then I think that would bring people more on board. And I think this is a vehicle for doing that kind of thing.*
> (Sustainability Group Manager)

Policies, performance structures and tools

Performance programme and governance

For the purposes of clarifying the meaning of sustainable development within the council and promoting steps along the journey, as well as ensuring compliance, a Corporate Sustainability Programme (CSP) has been produced and performance structures formalized. The CSP replaced the former Sustainability Action Plan and contains targets for the 2009 to 2013 time period. While environmental objectives on reducing water and energy were carried forward, the new programme incorporates further objectives relating to social issues such as diversity, communications and employee satisfaction. In total, the new programme has 50 objectives contained in ten separate subsections relating to the council's commitment, ownership and understanding, performance, leadership in the community, people, environment, finances, suppliers, anti-corruption record, and communication and dialogue (see Table 5.1).

The sustainability group manager described the programme as a crossing of elements from Forum for the Future's Sustainability Standard with those from the Global Reporting Initiative, together with best practice observed in corporate sustainability reports published in the last ten years by other public- and private-sector organizations. For each objective, there is a lead person responsible for overseeing achievement, an annual metric, baseline figure and an annual target that covers the five-year period. Table 5.2 shows an extract from the programme relating to 'our environment'. The word 'our' has been incorporated in order to signal joint ownership amongst the workforce and induce a sense of individual duty towards realization. It is also reflective of the broad consultation exercise that was conducted across the council during production of the CSP and prior to approval by the cabinet.

Securing compliance towards achieving objectives contained in the CSP was attributed, in part, to the new performance system entitled Perform. Progress on targets is available each quarter and, following release, named leads are required to provide a red, amber or green status, commentary and a predic-

Table 5.1 Corporate Sustainability Programme 2009–2013:

Sub-sections and objectives

Our Commitment
Improving our high level and strategic commitment to delivering sustainability

---

CC1	Increase Members' ability to deliver corporate sustainability
CC2	Ensure a robust policy framework is in place to ensure delivery of the 'Corporate Sustainability Programme' (CSP)
CC3	Achieve 'Excellent' level of the Sustainability Standard
CC4	Increase the sustainability of projects

Our Ownership and Understanding
Improving the ability of our management and staff to incorporate sustainability into their work

---

OU1	Increase support for management and staff on sustainability issues and understanding how they can be incorporated into their work

---

Our Performance
Ensuring we have the ability to measure the integration of sustainability into our corporate practices

---

P1	Increase the delivery of the CSP through integration into the corporate performance management framework
P2	Increase transparency of delivery of the CSP through public reporting
P3	Maintain political accountability for delivery of the CSP

Our Leadership in the Community
Sharing our knowledge in delivering sustainability in the community

---

CL1	Increase the number of staff engaged in the County Council community volunteering schemes
CL2	Increase the sustainability of local businesses
CL3	Increase the number of staff travelling to work by sustainable modes of transport

---

Our People
Investing in our people to create a more diverse, knowledgeable, equal and safer workplace

---

EPWP1	Maintain an acceptable rate of turnover
EPWP2	Increase rate of employee satisfaction
EPWP3	Reduce rate of employee days lost
EPWP4	Reduce the number of 'Health and Safety' incidents reported
EPWP5	Increase number of staff receiving annual PDRs
EPWP6	Increase the 'Skills Level' of WSCC staff
EPWP7	Increase proportion of women represented as 'top earners' in the organization
EPWP8	Increase the proportion of black and minority ethnic groups represented as 'top earners' in the organization
EPWP9	Increase proportion of employees with a disability as 'top earners' in the organization
EPWP10	Increase the number of employees from black and minority ethnic groups to reflect the community of West Sussex
EPWP11	Increase the number of employees from disabled groups to reflect the community of West Sussex
EPWP12	Increase the number of employees from the lesbian/gay/bisexual/transvestite community to reflect the community of West Sussex
EPWP13	Reduce reports of bullying and harassment

Table 5.1 continued

Our Environment
Reducing our impact on the environment

EP1	Reduce the amount of non-hazardous waste being sent to landfill
EP2	Reduce the amount of hazardous waste being sent to landfill
EP3	Reduce the amount of highway waste being sent to landfill
EP4	Reduce the amount of energy consumed by County Council buildings
EP5	Increase energy saved in County Council buildings due to conservation and efficiency improvements
EP6	Incorporate the use of renewable energy in all new (or refurbished) County Council buildings over £2 million
EP7	Reduce the amount of energy consumed by schools
EP8	Reduce the amount of water consumed by County Council buildings
EP9	Reduce the amount of water consumed by school buildings
EP10	Increase the number of property construction/refurbishment schemes achieving BREEAM 'Very Good' rating
EP11	Increase the sustainability of schools
EP12	Improve the overall sustainability of staff behaviour and the workplaces they occupy
EP13	Reduce carbon dioxide emissions from the transport fleet
EP14	Reduce NOx emissions from the transport fleet
EP15	Reduce corporate business mileage by casual, essential and lease car users
EP16	Reduce the carbon dioxide equivalent emissions from activities directly controlled by the Council
EP17	Influence schools to reduce their carbon dioxide equivalent emissions
EP18	Reduce vulnerability to climate change of the Council's infrastructure

---

Our Finances
Learning to understand our financial exposure through non-sustainable practices

---

EC1	Ensure the *A4S 'Connected Framework'* is used to report on the Council's financial performance

---

Our Suppliers
Ensure our suppliers meet or exceed our own level of corporate sustainability

---

PR1	Increase the amount of food sourced locally
PR2	Increase the sustainability of procurement activities
PR3	Increase the sustainability of capital expenditure projects

---

Our Anti-Corruption Record
Ensuring we maintain a high level of honesty in our business dealings

---

CAF1	Ensure all incidents of reported corruption and fraud are investigated

---

Our Communication and Dialogue
Ensuring our Members, managers, staff, suppliers, business partners and customers are aware of corporate sustainability issues and how they can change behaviour to become more sustainable

---

CP1	Increase the awareness of corporate sustainability amongst members/managers/staff/suppliers/business partners/customers
CP2	Increase the Council's sharing of good practice in delivering corporate sustainability
CP3	Increase the number of externally recognized 'Awards' received in delivering the objectives in the CSP

Source: West Sussex County Council (2009c)

tion on end-of-year results. An extract from the system for the first four objectives on 'our environment' is presented in Table 5.3.

Members of the Sustainability Group explained that, for the first time, every single business plan across the organization was also going to be entered into Perform. Since objectives contained in the CSP feature in business plans, a 'red' outcome indicates that it is not only sustainability objectives that are not being achieved, but overall business plans as well. This was viewed by the members of the Sustainability Group as 'integrating sustainability into day jobs':

> *You'll have named contacts on there, and all these targets will link up with individual business plans; so if I'm named in here as being responsible for this it will link through to my business plan to say you're supposed to be delivering that. So from that perspective there is no sense in which this is additional. This is not additional. This is what you do; so from that perspective again it's totally enmeshed in what we're actually there to deliver.* (Climate Change Officer)

> *It's getting scrutiny, then, not just because it's a corporate sustainability programme target, but also in terms of how our general day-to-day business is being done, and we're achieving our targets from the management level. So we're getting that kind of management buy-in as well.* (Sustainability Officer)

Compliance was also sought by the Sustainability Group in a review of governance arrangements, the sustainability group manager acknowledging here that simply having a policy in place is insufficient in terms of delivering results: 'If you haven't got the right governance structures, with all the will in the world you'll never be able to deliver a Corporate Sustainability Programme because you'll have no authority behind it.'

The current governance structure comprises the cabinet and Chief Executive's Board, Corporate Sustainability Group and Staff Sustainability Group. Additionally, at the request of the cabinet, the Strategic Environment Services Select Committee has agreed to provide scrutiny and overview of the CSP on a six-monthly basis. The governance structure is illustrated in Figure 5.1.

As well as their role in questioning lack of performance, parties in the governance structure were perceived by the Sustainability Group more generally as a supportive resource. The chief executive and Corporate Sustainability Group, for example, can help by trying to 'unpick problems', coordinating across the organization and, potentially, providing financial assistance. Additionally, individual cabinet members act as 'political sponsors' for individual projects.

Table 5.2 Extract from Corporate Sustainability Programme 2009–2013

Our environment Aspect	Reducing our impact on the environment Objective	Annual Metric	Baseline	Target 09–10	Target 10–11	Target 11–12	Target 12–13
Materials	EP 1. Reduce the amount of non-hazardous waste being sent to landfill.	Percentage of non-hazardous waste sent to landfill.	95% (2007/08)	70%	65%	60%	55%
	EP 2. Reduce the amount of hazardous waste being sent to landfill.	Percentage of hazardous waste sent to landfill.	To be established by June 2009	tbc	tbc	tbc	tbc
	EP 3. Reduce the amount of highway waste being sent to landfill.	Percentage of highway waste sent to landfill.	50% (2006/07)	15%	Zero%	Zero%	Zero%
Energy	EP 4. Reduce the amount of energy consumed by County Council buildings.	Percentage reduction in energy use.	37 861 MWh per annum (2007/08)	34 075 MWh per annum (10% reduction on baseline)	30 667 MWh per annum (19% reduction on baseline)	27 600 MWh per annum (27% reduction on baseline)	24 840 MWh per annum (35% reduction on baseline)
	EP 5. Increase energy saved in County Council buildings due to conservation and efficiency improvements.	Total energy saved due to conservation and efficiency improvements.	To be established as part of the 'Energy and Water Management Project'	tbc	tbc	tbc	tbc
	EP 6. Incorporate the use of renewable energy in all new (or refurbished) County Council buildings over £2 million.	Percentage of new (or refurbished) County Council buildings costing over £2 million that have incorporated renewable energy.	64% (2008/09)	60%	65%	70%	75%
	EP 7. Reduce the amount of energy consumed by schools.	Percentage reduction in energy use.	116 754 MWh per annum (2007/08)	105 079 MWh per annum (10% reduction on baseline)	94 571 MWh per annum (19% reduction on baseline)	85 114 MWh per annum (27% reduction on baseline)	76 603 MWh per annum (35% reduction on baseline)

continued

Table 5.2 continued

Our environment Aspect	Reducing our impact on the environment Objective	Annual Metric	Baseline	Target 09–10	Target 10–11	Target 11–12	Target 12–13
Water	EP 8. Reduce the amount of water consumed by County Council buildings.	Percentage reduction in water use.	198 080 cubic metres per annum (2007/08)	178 272 cubic metres per annum (10% reduction on baseline)	160 445 cubic metres per annum (19% reduction on baseline)	144 400 cubic metres per annum (27% reduction on baseline)	129 960 cubic metres per annum (35% reduction on baseline)
	EP 9. Reduce the amount of water consumed by school buildings.	Percentage reduction in water use.	372 031 cubic metres per annum (2007/08)	334 828 cubic metres per annum (10% reduction on baseline)	301 345 cubic metres per annum (19% reduction on baseline)	271 210 cubic metres per annum (27% reduction on baseline)	244 089 cubic metres per annum (35% reduction on baseline)
Buildings	EP 10. Increase the number of property construction/refurbishment schemes achieving BREEAM 'Very Good' rating.	Percentage of property construction/refurbishment schemes achieving BREEAM 'Very Good' rating on completion.	10% (2007/08)	100%	100%	100%	100%
	EP 11. Increase the sustainability of schools.	Number of schools with Eco-Schools 'Green Flag' Award.	Number of Green Flag Schools registered in March 09	Baseline + 5	Baseline + 10	Baseline + 15	Baseline + 20
	EP 12. Improve the overall sustainability of staff behaviour and the workspaces they occupy.	Number of services that have achieved an 'excellent' rating of the Sustainable Workplace Tool.	1 (2007/08)	3	8	10	12

Our environment Aspect	Reducing our impact on the environment Objective	Annual Metric	Baseline	Target 09-10	Target 10-11	Target 11-12	Target 12-13
Transport	EP 13. Reduce carbon dioxide emissions from the transport fleet.	Reduction of carbon dioxide emissions from transport fleet.	1 043 986 grammes of CO_2 per annum	918 708 grammes of CO_2 per annum	850 000 grammes of CO_2 per annum	825 000 grammes of CO_2 per annum	800 000 grammes of CO_2 per annum
	EP14. Reduce NO_x emissions from the transport fleet.	Reduction of NO_x emissions from transport fleet.	4.01 tonnes per annum (2008)	3.9 tonnes per annum	3.8 tonnes per annum	3.7 tonnes per annum	3.6 tonnes per annum
	EP 15. Reduce corporate business mileage by casual, essential and lease car users.	Reduction of business mileage recorded on SAP business mileage reports. (2007/08)	7,164,493 miles per annum (2007/08)	7,000,000 miles per annum	6,965,000 miles per annum	6,930,175 miles per annum	6,895,500 miles per annum
Emissions	EP 16. Reduce the carbon dioxide equivalent emissions from activities directly controlled by the Council.	Reduction of carbon dioxide emissions.	27,632 tonnes CO_2 per annum (2007/08)	24,562 tonnes per annum (10% reduction on baseline)	21,492 tonnes per annum (19% reduction on baseline)	18,421 tonnes per annum (27% reduction on baseline)	15,351 tonnes per annum (35% reduction on baseline)
	EP 17. Influence schools to reduce their carbon dioxide equivalent emissions.	Reduction of carbon dioxide emissions.	28,618 tonnes CO_2 per annum (2007/08)	25,438 tonnes per annum (10% reduction on baseline)	22,258 tonnes per annum (19% reduction on baseline)	19,078 tonnes per annum (27% reduction on baseline)	15,899 tonnes per annum (35% reduction on baseline)
Climate Change	EP 18. Reduce vulnerability to climate change of the Council's infrastructure.	Reduction in the amount of infrastructure vulnerable to climate change as gauged by 'Level achieved' of the UKCIP 'Adaptation Wizard'.	Level 0 (achieved 2008)	Level 1	Level 2	Level 3	Level 4

Explanatory Note: For EP4, EP7, EP8, EP9, EP14, EP15, EP16 and EP17 the individual year targets state the emission or usage target after the reduction, rather than the quantity by which the emissions or usage is to be reduced.
Source: West Sussex County Council (2009c)

Table 5.3 Extract from *Perform: Quarterly Results Relating to Corporate Sustainability Programme*

		Objective	Metric	End of year target	Quarter 1 result ▲ ⇔ ✖	Comments *Please give a brief account of any progress made or problems encountered.*	Predicted End of Year result *(please put appropriate symbol in box)* ▲ ⇔ ✖
EP	1	Reduce the amount of non-hazardous waste being sent to landfill.	Percentage of non-hazardous waste sent to landfill.	70%	▲	Proceeding to plan	▲
EP	2	Reduce the amount of hazardous waste being sent to landfill.	Percentage of hazardous waste sent to landfill.	tbc	▲	Proceeding to plan	▲
EP	3	Reduce the amount of highway waste being sent to landfill.	Percentage of highway waste sent to landfill.	85%	▲	Waste diverted from landfill – 91% in quarter 1	▲
EP	4	Reduce the amount of energy consumed by County Council buildings.	Percentage reduction in energy use.	34 075 MWh per annum (10% reduction on baseline)	⇔	Policy for energy and water management being developed and partnerships formed with schools and PSB partners. SALIX invest to save fund in place and contributing to projects. Team roles identified, Energy and Data Manager in post August 2009, a paper, agreed by Head of Capital & Asset Management, to recruit 2 new Sustainability Management posts whose remit is to identify spend to save projects, manage the financial innovation stream and ensure skills development across the county will go to Head of Resources and Performance July 2009, it is hoped to get these posts in place by end of 2009.	▲

Source: Sustainability Group, West Sussex County Council

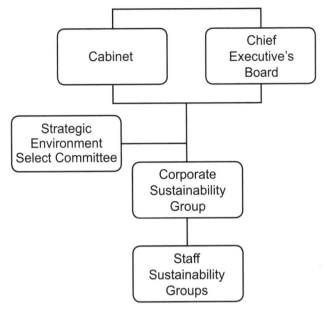

Figure 5.1 Governance structure

Source: Sustainability Group, West Sussex County Council

The use of tools in the sustainable development journey

Sustainable Workplace Tool

Developed and introduced in 2006, the purpose of the Sustainable Workplace Tool (SWT) is to improve the overall sustainability of staff behaviour throughout the council. In the main, the tool is intended to reduce environmental impacts and, in so doing, contribute to financial savings, although there is also some inclusion of social issues within the tool. Sustainability impacts have been identified for six main areas – notably, waste, energy, procurement, water, people and transport – while within two of these areas social concerns are addressed. Within procurement, for example, sourcing of local products is encouraged and in the people section, the principle of treating all staff equally is highlighted and the strengthening of community life through volunteering promoted. Data from the SWT is captured as part of the Corporate Sustainability Programme 2009–2013 and feeds into the performance management system.

The purpose of the SWT is to be achieved through a combination of a web-based questionnaire and the coordination efforts of SSG members. The questionnaire contains questions on more sustainable behaviour in a given area and a listing of why behaviours are encouraged. For example, on waste (see Table 5.4), improved sustainable performance can be achieved by setting

Table 5.4 Extract from Sustainable Workplace Tool

Waste		Yes	Partly	No	N/A	Why
Reuse	Do people reuse any paper printed on one side for scrap or note pads?	○	○	○		
	Are envelopes re-used for internal mail?	○	○	○		
	Are folders, plastic pockets and files reused?	○	○	○		
	Do you advertise unwanted office furniture before disposing of it?	○	○	○		
Recycle	Do you recycle the following products:	○	○	○		
	White office paper	○	○	○		Paper can be recycled up to five times, substantially reducing the impacts associated with the production of virgin paper. Each tonne of paper recycled saves 15 average-sized trees, as well as their surrounding habitat and wildlife.
	Plastic bottles	○	○	○		Nearly 3 million tonnes of waste plastic is produced in the UK each year of which only 7% is recycled. Recycling just one plastic bottle saves enough energy to power a 60W light bulb for six hours.
	Glass	○	○	○		In the UK, we use over 6 billion glass containers each year weighing over 2 million tonnes. We currently recycle about a quarter of this. In Europe the average recycling rate is 50% with some recycling over 80%.
	Aluminium cans	○	○	○		It takes 20 times less energy to make a recycled aluminium can than it does to make just one new one. If all the aluminium cans sold in the UK were recycled, there would be 12 million fewer full dustbins each year.
	Newspapers and magazines	○	○	○		
	Plastic magazine wrappers	○	○	○		
	Stamps	○	○	○		Lots of charities collect stamps to sell on to raise funds. Some examples are St Wilfrid's Hospice or RSPB Albatross appeal.
	Printer cartridges	○	○	○		An average new cartridge requires approximately one pint of oil to produce.
	Fax cartridges	○	○	○		
	Office electrical equipment	○	○	○		
	Cardboard	○	○	○		
	Office Furniture	○	○	○		

Question			
If you do recycle are there sufficient recycling bins?	○	○	○
Are these bins located in suitable places?	○	○	○
Do cleaning staff empty the recycling bins?	○	○	○
Are bins clearly labelled so people know what they can and can't put in them?	○	○	○
Reduce Can your printers print double sided?	○	○	○
Are peoples computers defaulted to double sided printing?	○	○	○
Can your photocopiers print double sided?	○	○	○
Are people using this double sided printing option?	○	○	○
Are staff aware of how much paper they use?	○	○	○
Do people cancel unwanted publications/journals?	○	○	○
Are distribution lists used, so that only one or two copies are necessary?	○	○	○
Do people subscribe to online or electronic publications, rather than receiving hard copies?	○	○	○
Do fax machines produce unwanted header or footer report sheets?	○	○	○
Do you use distribution envelopes?	○	○	○
Do you use plastic cups for water (excluding a small number for visitors)?	○	○	○
Are agendas displayed at meetings rather than everyone having to print a copy?	○	○	○
Do people use the online directory rather than ordering a paper version?	○	○	○
Do you format any papers to minimize the amount of paper to be used?	○	○	○

A survey in October 2005 showed that WSCC procures 930 trees worth of paper per year; that's 1.5 trees per person, or the height of 13 Big Bens if the paper was stacked up as A4 reams! Small measures can help a lot to reduce this huge amount.

The photocopier and desktop printer are the greatest users of paper. Setting this equipment to double sided printing can help reduce the amount of paper you use.

Source: Sustainability Group, West Sussex County Council, 2009

computer default positions to double-sided printing, the reuse of envelopes for internal mail and the recycling of printer cartridges. Concerning the latter, the fact is stated that new cartridges require approximately 1 pint of oil to produce. Where appropriate, rather than stating relevant facts, sustainable behaviour is encouraged by raising awareness and promoting the use of centrally developed initiatives. On the issue of travel, for example, the tool informs staff of the 10 per cent commuter challenge, encourages car-sharing through a centrally available website, and reminds staff that pool cars, as well as dedicated bicycles, are available for business purposes. In order to encourage greater energy efficiency still, the tool highlights the availability of telephone conferencing for the purposes of communicating with internal colleagues and that there are comprehensive guidelines for working from home. The SSG member takes responsibility for completing the questionnaire for an area or team, reviewing activities once overall progress is summarized against each of the topic areas in the web-based tool and for sustaining changed practices. With respect to the latter, one SSG member mentioned sending emails at the end of each day, reminding colleagues to switch off computers before leaving for home. Completing the questionnaire results in a score ranging from 0 to 100 being recorded, with ongoing improvement sought by requiring areas or teams to show a 5 per cent increment the next year regardless of whether a poor result (less than 20 per cent) is obtained or an excellent score (more than 80 percent) is achieved.

Notwithstanding its undoubted success in encouraging environmentally (and socially) responsible behaviour on the part of council staff, much remains to be done in terms of clarifying the nature of the environmental and financial linkages assumed by the SWT. The sustainability group manager, for example, acknowledged that savings generated are not currently known, but rather that this is an aspiration. More generally, he noted that data collection was an issue which required some investment:

> Our Sustainable Workplace Tool [is] a very good idea, but it's never been able to get the data into it for people to use, to have specific financial outputs; but it will. It's like cutting back on printing, that kind of stuff, use of printing from PCs. Hopefully with the new systems that come in over the next couple of years, it will register how much is printed to your PC or how much photocopying you did, and therefore the person [who is] responsible for the Sustainable Workplace Tool will then know, same for energy, same for water. (Sustainability Group Manager)

Further challenges relate to a ceiling being reached through group and individual behaviour in some areas (e.g. the Emergency Planning Unit in Policy and Performance and the Training Team in the Business Improvement Directorate both have excellent scores), and the problem of certain key drivers influencing the overall score being beyond the control of affected individuals and units.

Comments offered by a couple of interviewees are instructive in this latter regard:

> We're finding it increasingly difficult to actually improve now because we've done what we can within our own teams, and now it's up to energy improvement. We can't do any more ... we switch our printers off, we switch the lights off. It's now down to getting new windows or insulation and things like that which are not within our direct control.
>
> We score very high because of the way our whole team is very conscious about sustainability, recycling and all that sort of thing... The only thing we can't affect is the building that we're in, an old prefabricated building with single-glazed windows, and that's where we lose energy, for example. And those are the things that are actually causing our score not to get to 100, and the decision from the council's perspective is it's not a building they're going to upgrade anyway.

Sustainability Appraisal

> I've always maintained, concerning sustainability, that it's not that you necessarily make different decisions, but that you take the decisions in full awareness of what their impacts are. I think our decision-making now is pretty sophisticated. I think it would be very rare now for us to miss any of those sorts of impacts. (Chief Executive)

While the SWT has an individual behavioural focus, the Sustainability Appraisal tool seeks to improve the integration of sustainability within future projects initiated and delivered by the council. The approach of sustainability appraisal is consistent with the council's view of sustainable development itself:

> Sustainable development encourages us to look at a problem, need or challenge from a number of different angles to lead to an outcome that will be positive all round. This way of thinking will bring success with issues being properly prioritized. It is only through having an all-round (or 360 degree) view that we will start to look at problems and challenges in new ways and come up with innovative, long-term solutions. (WSCC, 2007, p5)

For the purposes of establishing a golden thread, the four main themes of the Sustainability Appraisal are based on the Sustainable Community Strategy for West Sussex 2008–2020. Projects that go through the process, therefore, incorporate thinking about contributing positively toward a 'better place to live', 'opportunity for all', 'better health for all' and 'staying and feeling safe'. The tool can also be applied to other aspects of the council's activities – for instance, committee reports and business plans.

The Sustainability Appraisal is applied at the inception stage of project development following reasoning that it is here that modifications can more easily be introduced and, as a result, sustainable outcomes are more likely to be achieved. 360 degree thinking is promoted through two main stages. First, project managers are required to work through a web-based tool on how the proposal will affect the four areas identified in the Sustainable Community Strategy. For example, under 'a better place to live', there is a section on environment and natural resources and an objective of reducing emissions of carbon dioxide and other greenhouse gases. The project manager with in-depth knowledge of the proposal is required to think about the objective in relation to the specific project under consideration, grade the project if the objective is applicable, and explain his or her reasoning for the response in an open-ended box. In total, the project manager is required to work through the 35 objectives listed in Table 5.5. Once the tool is completed, a summary sheet is produced and results shown according to the same traffic light system employed in the Perform performance system referred to earlier. Should a 'red' result be generated, the project manager is prompted to re-evaluate the proposal with a view to contributing positively to more of the sustainability appraisal objectives and widening the scope of the project. At the second stage, sustainability appraisals are submitted to the Sustainability Group for review and feedback. A dialogue is entered into on how the proposal may be further improved based upon knowledge of the Sustainability Group and their experience of prior projects. For example, in the case of the PFI project on street lighting, a specification was made to improve the workforce skills of the local economy and, similarly, a recommendation to include apprenticeships in procurement projects may be advised. An additional requirement of the Sustainability Appraisal is to identify suitable metrics and targets through which to track achievement of objectives.

The Carbon Model

The Carbon Model is in the process of development and offers an opportunity for reviewing service provision in order to reduce carbon dioxide emissions attributable to the council. Consistent with the aims of A4S, the model connects financial imperatives with the need to secure both environmental and social well-being. The climate change officer reflected upon his work: 'It's great that [I'm] trying to reduce carbon dioxide emissions; however, there absolutely has to be a financial business case behind it, and there absolutely has to be a social gain associated with it.'

A key driver for the development of the model was identified as the rising wholesale price of energy. Over a six-year period between 2002/2003 and 2008/2009, and excluding energy usage for street-lighting, transport and contractor work, total expenditure on utilities more than doubled. Additional drivers include the need for upfront payment to the Environment Agency on

Table 5.5 Sustainability Appraisal: Sustainability objectives

---

Better place to live: Environment and natural resources

Reduce emissions of carbon dioxide and other green house gases
Increase the proportion of energy needs being met by renewable resources
Minimise the risk to people and property from flooding
Promote sustainable use of water
Improve the quality of inland and/or coastal waters
Improve air quality
Reduce household waste and/or commercial and industrial waste
Increase waste recovery and recycling
Encourage sustainable patterns of travel and the use of sustainable modes of transport

---

Better place to live: Local distinctiveness and communities

Increase the range and affordability of good quality housing for all social groups
Maintain the character of the local area and reflecting local distinctiveness
Help people to participate within their community and build their sense of pride and well-being
Encourage public participation in decision-making and the democratic process
Support access to services for rural populations
Maintain and enhancing the quality and accessibility of public spaces and streetscapes
Maintain and enhancing sites of importance to biodiversity (including green corridors)
Protect and enhancing sites, features and landscapes of historical, cultural and/or geological groups

---

Opportunity for all

Improve learning, qualifications and skills of young people/adults/hard to reach groups
Encourage/facilitate participation in voluntary and community sector activities
Increase employment in hard to reach groups
Create well-paid and long-term employment opportunities for local people
Reduce poverty and social exclusion in those areas most affected
Promoting growth in new business key sectors and industries
Promote use of local resources, goods and products
Improving economic performance in disadvantaged areas
Encouraging a diverse range of visitors and enhance the visitor experience

---

Better health for all

Reduce the inequalities of health outcomes experienced in some communities
Support preventative strategies/measures to improving health (including mental health)
Improve access and education for healthier lifestyle choices
Support/be accessible to those with mental health problems
Encouraging older people to remain active within the community or in employment

---

Staying and feeling safe

Reduce actual levels of crime
Reduce rates of reoffending
Reduce the fear of crime and improving the perception of community safety among the public
Reduce the number of road traffic accidents and improving road safety

---

Source: Sustainability Group, West Sussex County Council, 2009

the CRC, an inflation-adjusted climate change levy, and national indicators on climate change adaptation and mitigation. A presentation by Lord Nicholas Stern to council employees and other delegates in 2008 reiterated the environmental effects of emitting greenhouse gases into the atmosphere and consequences for social development.

The Carbon Model is premised on the idea that processes are required in the delivery of a service and each process has a process owner with responsibility for their part of the service. Furthermore, the Carbon Model classifies energy use into one of four main categories that looks beyond that relating to accommodation or built estate. For example, for road maintenance, referred to as network management, a map of processes was visualized and the service classified according to workstream: customer, service delivery, back office, strategic activity and responding to external requests. For each workstream, a senior person with an overview of the service assigns energy use relating to the four main categories: location, transport, off-grid fuels and contractor works. For network management, data is available on the former two in the form of energy bills for buildings (location) and mileage travelled and fuel consumption (transport) from within the council. Data for the latter two was obtained from one of the council's largest contractors involved in repairing and maintaining the roads. Following on, a report can be generated identifying total carbon emissions in tonnes, carbon emissions from each of the four energy uses and, for network management, carbon emissions per mile of road serviced.

As a general strength of the Carbon Model, the climate change officer noted: 'Once you've got finance and carbon both pushing in the same direction, people are a lot more amenable to actually reducing what they see as being the worst carbon offender in their process.'

Given that the Carbon Model is part of the E&WMP, and that the plan was approved by both the Chief Executive's Board and cabinet members, it also benefits from having both a business (senior officer) and political (cabinet member) sponsor:

> Our business sponsor is, in fact, the executive director for business services, and through our Chief Executive's Board, they highlight the need for resources, they highlight the need for progress, or if we come up against a certain problem then that gets addressed. (Climate Change Officer)

While cost codes are available centrally for transport, the climate change officer inferred that work remains to be done in order to establish cost codes for other forms of energy use, which represents a substantial challenge in view of the size of the organization and complexity of operations.

Following experimentation with the model and initial application to different services, the climate change officer indicated two useful developments. First, through analysis of energy consumption for network management, more than 80 per cent of emissions were attributed to contractor works and this transparency was viewed as a means of incorporating suppliers in the sustainable development journey: 'This is, in fact, an opportunity for us to say you're [supplier] paying loads for that, we're paying loads for that, let's work together to actually bring down our collective prices and carbon.'

Second, the Carbon Model has revealed scope for changing services in order to benefit the local population. For example, at the request of a service manager, an analysis was performed on the provision of services to gypsy sites. It was found that the greatest emission of carbon dioxide is by far related to the use of off-grid fuel. Caravans designed for summer inhabitation were being heated by the gypsies in winter using twin bar heaters. A need was recognized for a heating solution and options mooted such as insulation and low carbon heating.

Reporting externally on sustainability performance

Impacts resulting from the employment of the sustainability performance tools described above, as well as broader sustainability initiatives undertaken by the council, are reflected in the *Sustainability Report*, which adopts the Connected Reporting Framework and is published alongside the *Financial Report and Accounts*. The report is intended to inform local taxpayers of progress made by the council and, significantly, engender changes in supplier behaviour and that of public-sector partners in an attempt to lead by example. Targets met under water and energy usage in the *Sustainability Report 2008/2009*, for example, are attributed, in part, to good housekeeping (as promoted by the SWT), the Accommodation Strategy and the PFI contract for street lighting (see Table 5.6) and may encourage similar actions or stances by other organizations.

Furthermore, reference is made to future works, notably the E&WMP in the 2008/2009 report, and indirect impacts arising from initiatives designed to influence community and supplier behaviour are highlighted. As an additional benefit, inclusion of sustainability expenditure in the report highlights to the council future costs and risks and thereby prompts further actions towards minimizing both. The report, as a whole, provides a 'flavour' of initiatives taken on emissions, waste, water, energy use and transport (elements of the Connected Reporting Framework), rather than a listing of all initiatives.

Conclusions

It is clear that WSCC has made significant progress over recent years towards embedding sustainability considerations throughout its operations. Notably, a number of policies, performance structures and measurement tools have been established that seek to establish a 'golden thread' linking organizational strategies at the top of the council hierarchy to day-to-day work activities of

Table 5.6 Extract from *Sustainability Report 2008/2009*

KEY INDICATOR	Financial performance				Direct county council impacts: non-financial indicators	Targets and narrative	Indirect impacts: customer/supplier indicators	Sector benchmark information
	05/06 £'000	06/07 £'000	07/08 £'000	08/09 £'000				
WATER Operating expenditure	1,034	1,058	1,345	1,372		Water consumption for the County Council fell by 24 per cent between 2004/05 and 2008/09, with much of this reduction achieved in the past year. The target for 2009/10 is a further 10 per cent reduction.	Messages to the public throughout the year have focused on preparedness for flooding and on what they can do to save water. In the communities of Oving and Fishbourne, which have taken part in the Greening Campaign supported by West Sussex County Council, an estimated saving of 158,000 litres of water was achieved, with 215 households taking part.	The Environment Agency's Watermark
*Sustainability expenditure	0	23	6	0		Greater vigilance about water use, good housekeeping and the Accommodation Strategy, which has consolidated a number of smaller offices into the main office hubs, have all contributed to meeting this target.		
* Includes cost of Water Summit (NB although no expenditure shows in 2008/09, sustainability spending on water will have been incurred through the general sustainability section)						The focus of work this year has been on initiating the Energy and Water Management Plan (EWMP) Project which will set out how water reduction will be achieved in future years. In February 2009 the County Council hosted a Water Summit for council Members and other stakeholders on the topic of climate change and water management, within the context of a growing West Sussex population.		

KEY INDICATOR	Financial performance	Direct county council impacts: non-financial indicators	Targets and narrative	Indirect impacts: customer/supplier indicators	Sector benchmark information
ENERGY USE Operating expenditure *Includes the cost of gas, electricity and fuel oil* Including estimated Climate Change Levy payment of: *Sustainability expenditure * Includes cost of energy management and renewable energy	6,630 7,382 9,723 11,635 351 n/a n/a 132 124		The Council's energy consumption in 2008/09 showed a 26.4 per cent reduction since 2004/05, exceeding the reduction target of 15 per cent. For 2009/10 the target will be to reduce the energy consumption of the County Council by a further 10 per cent and to increase the energy saved due to conservation and efficiency measures. Large reductions in energy consumption have been achieved as a result of the Accommodation Strategy. The focus of work this year has been on initiating the Energy and Water Management Plan (EWMP) Project. From this three projects have already been identified to bring about energy reductions in Council buildings, including draught-proofing, improving insulation and the installation of a building energy management system on one site. The EWMP will enable annual targets for energy savings from such improvements to be established and monitored. In addition, the Council is procuring a PFI contract for street lighting, which is expected to be signed during 2009. Even though demand for lighting is likely to rise over the duration of the contract, our aim is to achieve at least an energy neutral outcome through use of the latest technology, e.g. dimming equipment.	This year the West Sussex Sustainable Business Partnership (WSSBP), in a joint project with East Sussex County Council and Ecosys Environmental Management, undertook 22 energy efficiency audits for businesses in Sussex. The project identified 315 energy efficiency related actions. WSSBP is able to provide ongoing support to help the businesses implement more of these identified actions The communities of Oving, Parklands and Fishbourne, took part in the Greening Campaign and saved an estimated 134 tonnes of carbon dioxide through the actions they pledged to take to save energy. In all, 321 households took part in the campaign.	Display Energy Certificates for buildings with a total useful floor area greater than 1000m^2

Source: West Sussex County Council (2009d)

administrative and frontline employees. The success of these various initiatives is evidenced in the number of officials we spoke to referring to a 'cultural shift' having taken place. Central to achieving such a shift has been the political will of key cabinet members, together with the personal commitment of key council officials in pushing the sustainability agenda. Changes in governance structures introduced in recent years have been designed to provide a supportive environment for further embedding sustainability within mainstream council activities. Finally, acceptance of sustainability as an overarching organizational goal has been further encouraged by explicitly promoting a 'business case' and linking sustainability and beneficial financial outcomes.

Notwithstanding the considerable progress made, there are a number of internal and external constraints to be overcome should WSCC wish to fully grasp the challenge of pursuing sustainable development. Internally, there is inevitably some work remaining to do in terms of convincing all departments and personnel of the relevance of sustainability to their day-to-day operations. Considerable progress might be made here if a closer link were established between individual action and scores obtained on the workplace tool. Currently, certain key elements influencing the overall score are outside the control of affected individuals. Furthermore, the status of Staff Sustainability Group representatives could usefully be enhanced and efforts made to address the 'disconnect' between their core operational role and their (voluntary) sustainability brief. As one sustainability officer noted, formalizing the latter through making it part of the job profile would serve to alleviate some of the problems here. Finally, much remains to be done in terms of developing information systems. Initially, the issue of the further development of cost codes for the Carbon Model has to be addressed, and, more generally, much remains to be done on the social indicators side, particularly in the areas of social cohesion and communities.

Even more challenging are a number of external factors, largely outside the council's control, inhibiting the further promotion of sustainability. One immediate problem here lies in the Audit Commission's assessment procedures, which, it is suggested, downplay sustainability objectives in what is perceived as the pursuit of a 'tick box' scoring approach. However, this may change with the move to an area assessment and encouragement to work in partnership with other local public-sector organizations. Even more challenging is the problem of balancing economic priorities, and associated demands for cost-cutting, with longer-term sustainability objectives that may not offer much in the way of a short-term payback. Furthermore, community support cannot be assumed once the council moves beyond win–win situations and pursuit of sustainability objectives potentially leads to higher council tax bills. Underlying all of these individual tensions is a fundamental problem, as highlighted by the cabinet member we interviewed, which lies in the unavoidable contrast between the long-term time horizons central to the sustainability agenda and the short-term political 'imperatives' that underpin much council activity.

Acknowledgements

Interviews were held with the West Sussex County Council chief executive; three members of the specialist Sustainability Group; six further officials holding managerial responsibility in the areas of economic development, training, accommodation strategy, procurement, emergency management and communications; and the cabinet member for finance and resources. Additionally, an earlier roundtable discussion was held with two members of the Sustainability Group and a group manager from the Customer and Community's Finance Team.

References

DCLG (2007) *The New Performance Framework for Local Authorities and Local Authority Partnerships: Single Set of National Indicators*, DCLG, Wetherby

Defra (UK Department for Environment, Food and Rural Affairs) (2005) *Securing the Future: The UK Government Sustainable Development Strategy*, Defra, London

DTLR (Department for Transport, Local Government and the Regions) (1998) *Modern Local Government – In Touch with the People*, DTLR, London

HM Treasury (2009) *Government Financial Reporting Manual (FReM) Exposure Draft No: (09)07 Exposure Draft of Proposed Amendments to the FReM Sustainability Reporting*, HM Treasury, London (28 August 2009)

WSCC (West Sussex County Council) (2005) *The County Strategy 2005–2009*, WSCC, West Sussex

WSCC (2007) *Sustainability Report 2007*, WSCC, West Sussex

WSCC (2009a) *With You, For You: A Strategy for West Sussex 2009–2013*, WSCC, West Sussex

WSCC (2009b) *2009/10 Facts and Figures*, WSCC, West Sussex

WSCC (2009c) *Corporate Sustainability Programme 2009-2013*, WSCC, West Sussex

WSCC (2009d) *Sustainability Report 2008/2009*, WSCC, West Sussex

six

Building from the Bottom, Inspired from the Top: Accounting for Sustainability and the Environment Agency

Ian Thomson and Georgios Georgakopoulos

Introduction

If you were looking for a good example of accounting for sustainability in the UK, a sensible place to start would be the Environment Agency. As well as being responsible for the licensing, regulation and enforcement of environmental protection legislation in England and Wales, it is tasked with transforming businesses and public-sector organizations into more sustainable operations. There are high levels of expertise in sustainable development and environmental protection across the organization, including board members and accounting staff. The Environment Agency has been awarded UK Greenest Organization 2009, won many awards for its environmental practices, including the pension fund, and has published a number of reports on environmental reporting.

Unlike many large multinational corporations, there is no glossy sustainability report, dripping with good intentions, carefully worded mission statements, full of self-praise, high on narrative, low on evidence, with selected stories of good practice. Instead, the Environment Agency includes a four-page sustainability accounting and reporting appendix in its *Annual Report and Accounts*, detailing key environmental performance data and the financial costs associated with these impacts. It would be misleading to assume that these four pages within the *Annual Report* are the total extent of the accounting for sustainability work undertaken in the Environment Agency. Digging deeper into the website uncovers a number of important initiatives, potential best practice operations and valuable lessons for other organizations attempting to account for their sustainability impacts. Some of these practices have been part of the Environment Agency's management systems since its inception in 1996 and some even predate the Environment Agency, having been part of the organizations that were merged to create the Environment Agency (e.g. environment reporting from the National Rivers Authority since 1987).[1]

The Environment Agency's environmental accounting practices have been built carefully from the bottom, underpinned by careful, robust data collection, management and reporting at all relevant organizational levels, and focus on negative environmental impacts. It concentrates on the rather unglamorous, but critical, end of the accounting cycle and is working systematically to solve a number of problems (e.g. working with suppliers to provide physical details, breakdown of costs on invoices, capturing resource use in expense forms or department returns, educating staff in their environmental impact, and maintaining commitment to reducing their negative environmental impact). Senior managers and board members appreciate the need for alignment between organizational outcomes, activities, culture, performance measurement, resource use and costs. Paul Leinster, chief executive, summed this up as 'wanting to maximize the environmental outcomes per pound of funding'.

The next section of this chapter provides background information on the Environment Agency. This is followed by an overview of the Environment Agency's environmental management systems and strategy and its approach to accounting for sustainability. A more detailed description and evaluation of how it accounts for and manages staff travel-related impacts follows, together with examples of other environmental accounting and performance measurement. A discussion of the impact of The Prince's Accounting for Sustainability Project (A4S) in the context of the Environment Agency is provided and the chapter concludes with observations on the key lessons that can be learned from the Environment Agency's environmental accounting practices and its pilot implementation of the HM Treasury guidance, adapted for use from the Connected Reporting Framework (CRF).

The Environment Agency:
Background information

The Environment Agency is an executive non-departmental public body responsible to the secretary of state for environment, food and rural affairs and an assembly-sponsored public body responsible to the National Assembly for Wales. Its principal aims are to protect and improve the environment and to promote the sustainable development of England and Wales. It is also responsible for protecting communities from flooding risks, managing water resources and enforcing and monitoring the carbon reduction commitments arising from the Climate Change Act 2008. The Environment Agency plays a central role in delivering the environmental priorities of central government and the Welsh Assembly.[2]

The Environment Agency currently employs 13,500 employees with an annual budget of more than UK£1.1 billion a year, of which around 60 per cent comes from government. The remainder of its finance mainly comes from various charging schemes. Details of its main functions[3] are as follows:

- protecting people from flood;
- working with industry to protect the environment and human health;
- concentrating effort on higher-risk businesses: those that run potentially hazardous operations or with unsatisfactory performance;
- helping business use resources more efficiently;
- taking action against those who do not take their environmental responsibilities seriously, including court action and fines;
- looking after wildlife – around 400 projects are completed every year to improve the habitat of threatened species;
- helping people to get the most out of their environment;
- working with farmers to build their role as guardians of the environment, tackling pollution that cannot be seen, as well as adding to the beauty of the countryside;
- helping to improve the quality of inner-city areas and parks by restoring rivers and lakes; and
- influencing and working with government, industry and local authorities to make the environment a priority.

The Environment Agency is currently finalizing its strategy for 2010 to 2015, but has as its vision 'a better place for people and for wildlife', which contains five themes, four of which focus on environmental outcomes.

The Environment Agency's head office is split between Bristol and London. Head office functions include the determination of national policies and ensuring that policies are carried out consistently across the country, taking into account the environmental, social and economic differences in each region. In

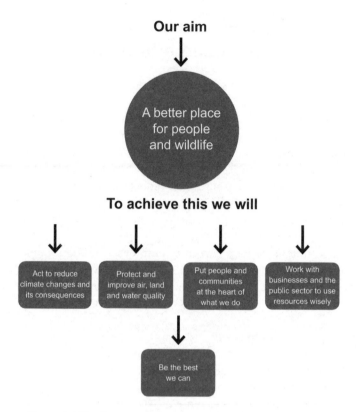

Figure 6.1 The Environment Agency's strategic vision 2010–2015

Source: extracted from Environment Agency (2009a)

the head office there are a number of support functions, such as finance, resources, environmental management and operations. The Environment Agency operates a number of national services and is subdivided into eight regional offices (Southern, Thames, South-West, Midlands, Anglian, Wales, North-West and North-East), which are the responsibility of a regional director. These regional offices support the area offices and coordinate their activities. There are 22 area offices across England and Wales. The people who work in these offices are responsible for the day-to-day management of the area, ensuring that local community needs are met and responding to emergencies and incidents.

Environmental management and strategy

Environmental management and environmental management systems are an integral part of the management systems and were described from the interviews conducted for the purposes of this project as being part of the Environment Agency's DNA. Central to its identity and culture is minimizing the environmental impact of its operations. Since 1996 the Environment Agency has sought to be an exemplar organization in this regard. Internal environment management and environmental management systems are not bolted on, ad hoc, fragmented or decoupled, but are fundamental to the way in which the Environment Agency has been managed. Prior to its involvement in the public-sector sustainability reporting project, led by HM Treasury, the Environment Agency had a robust, extensive environmental management system in place that regularly gathered and internally reported on a much wider set of social and environmental impacts than contained in its 2008 and 2009 sustainability accounting and reporting appendices. Since 2002 the Environment Agency has been fully accredited for all its activities throughout England and Wales under the international environmental and quality management system standards ISO14001:1996 and ISO9001:2000.

The Environment Agency has undertaken a number of environmental accounting initiatives since 1996 and has a number of key staff with specific responsibilities in this area. For example, it has an Environmental Finance Team. This team has two main functions. There is the environmental finance side, which is outward looking and seeks to engage and influence through the Environment Agency's pension fund, general networking, research projects and involvement in standard-setting processes. One active area of interest is on corporate environmental disclosures, where a number of reports have been published with plans to further extend this type of research.[4] Environment Agency staff are involved in promoting and establishing environmental accounting standards for use in UK public-sector organizations. In particular, they are involved with the Financial Reporting Advisory Board (FRAB), which establishes standardized accounting and reporting practices for public-sector organizations. Within this team is an objective to drive and encourage more public-sector environmental management and accountability. There is a strong feeling within the Environment Agency that it is rather hypocritical to be such a strong advocate of environment disclosures from the private sector, yet not subject the public sector, which is a significant consumer of resources and producer of pollution, to similar pressures. The selection of the CRF by the FRAB for initial piloting in the public sector with a view to adopting a version of it as part of its accounting regulation was the reason the Environment Agency became more actively involved with A4S.

The other function within the Environmental Finance Team is environmental management accounting, which is inward looking. This team integrates the Environment Agency's financial and environmental performance data throughout its financial systems and reports, both internally and externally. The Environmental Finance Team utilizes the techniques, concepts and skills of accountancy to report, verify and highlight the agency's environmental impacts.

The Environmental Finance Team also recognizes the importance of promoting the cost savings associated with reducing its negative environmental impacts in driving change.

The Environment Agency has had a well-established set of environment accounting initiatives for many years and has been developing systems and engaging with others to drive change in this area. For example, on its webpages[5] it describes its environmental accounting philosophy, techniques and a number of important outcomes. The Environmental Finance Team has considerable experience in this field and is aware of the challenges ahead, as well as the weaknesses in the current systems. However, it does not perceive these weaknesses negatively, but as part of the programme to develop further the current system in an evolutionary fashion. The Environment Agency is clear that what it is doing in some ways falls short of fully accounting for sustainability, but rather is accounting and reporting on some of its negative environmental impacts. It does not claim to have solved the problems of accounting for sustainability, but has a long-term system for solving these problems in a pragmatic, systematic fashion. The finance and operations staff have a clear idea of what they could and should be doing in the future. This critical reflection on current practices and awareness of how things can be further developed is an important element of the successes achieved so far.

Environmental accounting: A systems approach

The Environment Agency describes its approach to developing environmental accounting as simple, using a standard systems approach: plan, do, check and act. Its environmental accounting system has evolved through the application of basic accounting principles, concepts and techniques to the problem of reducing environmental impacts. It has been building its environmental accounting systems since 1997 using a basic development strategy, which involved:[6]

- the integration of data requirements into management systems (including corporate planning, management accounts, financial accounts, environmental monitoring, health and safety, and business planning);
- monitoring and reporting of in-year performance to management (using management accounts and environmental monitoring);
- the production of a year-end performance report (utilizing a wide range of existing processes);
- ensuring that the output is as robust as possible by independent auditing, verification and internal review;
- working with suppliers to provide environmental data in electronic form which allows the matching of environmentally significant cost and usage information;

- publishing environmental accounting disclosures (budgets are published in the Environment Agency's Corporate Plan, detailed year-end performance in the *Environmental Report*, summary information in the *Annual Report and Accounts* and *Annual Review*);
- integrating processes within existing financial systems in order to reduce implementation costs and gain the support of staff for the environmental accounting activities; and
- reviewing environmentally significant expenditure categories to ensure that they cover both environmentally significant activities and areas of significant spend, and match a prioritized aspects register with a list of expenditure categories.

The Environment Agency's website lists a number of key benefits from the development and operation of its simple systematic application of basic accounting techniques to environmental management, and these include:

- the tracking of UK£60 million of internal environmentally significant expenditure;
- providing information on the costs and savings associated with the implementation of environmental management systems;
- demonstrating cost savings and reduced resource use over four years in case studies on energy, water and business mileage;
- developing its *Annual Environmental Report*, which has been short-listed twice for the Association of Chartered Certified Accountants (ACCA) Environmental Reporting Awards;
- learning valuable lessons and developing tools that enable it to work in partnership with a wide range of groups, including accounting bodies, financial institutions, government bodies and expert working groups, nationally and internationally, on the further development of environmental accounting;
- tracking the UK£1.5 million savings from local environmental improvement initiatives and reduced consumption of over 16 million kilowatt hours of electricity;
- tracking the 39 per cent reduction in carbon dioxide (CO_2) emissions from buildings' energy use over the last five years; and
- identifying the 46 per cent cut in printing costs in the last five years.

The following section provides a more detailed description of how this general approach to environmental management and accounting is operationalized in the Environment Agency, initially in relation to staff travel, with a subsequent discussion of some other examples.

Connected actions, connected reporting, carbon reduction, staff mileage, key performance indicators (KPIs) and corporate scorecards

While the Environment Agency demonstrates a high level of connectedness in its accounting system in a number of areas (waste, energy, water and resource use), it also has a high level of connectedness between strategic objectives, operational decision-making, performance measurement, accounting systems, and organizational routines and practices. A good example of its systematic approach can be found in relation to staff travel, an activity with clearly identifiable social and environmental consequences, where changes in practices can generate measurable financial, social and environmental benefits. This involves an overall commitment to reduce carbon emissions within the Environment Agency, which is then translated into reduction targets for each directorate and subsequently into reduction targets for each area and department. One important aspect of how the Environment Agency sets these targets is to ensure that there is total buy-in to any target. Paul Leinster, chief executive, stated that he 'would rather have a target, which was slightly lower or slightly less tough and somebody who was absolutely committed to going to get that, than a target which they knew they couldn't reach'.

During the planning stage each director commits to achieving their targets, which include internal environmental targets on water, waste, power, resources and staff mileage. This was referred to by Bob Branson, head of financial management, as 'eight shakes of hands'. The regional targets for mileage are subsequently allocated out to the areas, then down to individual teams. Individual teams will have a mileage reduction target and eventually every individual will have a target mileage, although within teams they can barter those with other team members.

In order to help achieve these targets, senior finance staff, in conjunction with the director of operations, developed a staff travel decision protocol to contribute to the achievement of the Environment Agency's carbon emissions reduction targets, as illustrated in Figure 6.2. This protocol is considered to be highly effective and embedded throughout the organization. At the core of this protocol is a framework of choices.

The default position of this protocol is that staff should not need to travel to fulfil their function. The first consideration is whether the task can be done by telecommunications, email, video conferencing or telemetry. If it cannot be done remotely, then public transport would be the preferred option. If it is not possible to avoid driving, then efforts should be made to car share. If the journey is under 70 miles (113km) and no lease cars are available, then use of a personal car is still an option, but only as a last resort. If the journey is over 100 miles

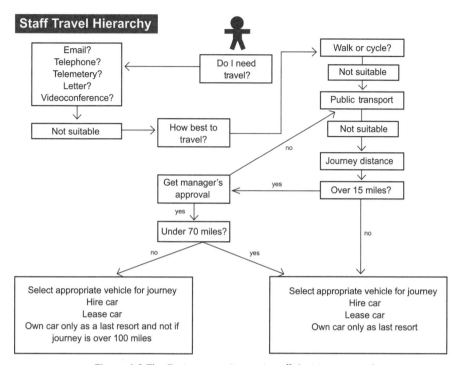

Figure 6.2 The Environment Agency's staff decision protocol

Source: Ian Thomson and Georgios Georgakopoulos

(161km), then rental cars are preferred. The Environment Agency makes extensive use of leased cars as this allows it to have a pool of the most fuel efficient vehicles with the lowest emissions that are fit for purpose. The use of leased cars allows the Environment Agency to keep its fleet as up to date as possible and provides it with a degree of flexibility in case of technology changes. For example, it has a number of hybrid cars used by regular users and a mix of lique-fied petroleum gas (LPG) and conventional fuel vans. The Environment Agency attempts to enable staff to reduce travel-related emissions by providing them with the right kit.

As mentioned earlier, if the journey is over 70 miles (113km), then staff should use hired cars. The Environment Agency has contracts with hire companies that allow them to match the most fuel-efficient cars for each journey. This creates greater flexibility in staff travel compared to purchasing its own vehicles and being trapped with a potentially out-of-date fleet of vehicles with a five- to six-year replacement cycle. There is also a requirement that if a member of staff is going to use their own car for a journey of over 15 miles (24km), then this requires approval from their line manager.

There appears to be a link between reducing staff travel and reducing cost in the Environment Agency's travel protocol; however, this breaks down when the public transport option involves train travel. Train travel is regarded as the preferred travel option; but in the current rail pricing regime it is often the most expensive option. This creates a dilemma in that the desired mode of travel is the worst financial option. However, a decision was made centrally in the Environment Agency to avoid creating incentives against train travel. Even though it costs more to travel by train, train travel is classified as beneficial to the organization, partially justified by the fact that employees can work on the train, whereas they can't in a car.

Integration of financial and non-financial measures of performance

Within the Environment Agency it was considered that financial figures were not always the best way to motivate behavioural change in its employees. Non-financial measures more directly related to operations and operational decision-making were considered more effective. Once a decision protocol has been centrally evaluated and approved, then at an operational level it is not always necessary to use financial measures or to directly consider the financial consequences at the time of the operational decision. For example, targets are set to reduce staff mileages, not just the cost of staff travel.

After the decision regarding the travel choice by an individual employee, then the details of the costs and relevant staff mileage are captured in the financial ledger. Each employee has to fill in an expense claim which specifies the mode of travel and mileage. The Environment Agency has a system that pulls the mileage out of its financial systems in order to report it every month and account for individual employee mileage. This system required some investment in staff time, training and information technology (IT) systems; but it allowed the necessary information to be captured in the financial systems.

Once the non-financial data is input into the system, selected indicators are collated and reported alongside the financial out-turns for departments, teams and areas, and compared with the key performance reduction targets. League tables of selected indicators, based on the Environment Agency's current priorities, are also prepared, enabling internal benchmarking to take place. For example, each region and head office can compare how many miles per staff member were used against their targets and compare staff mileage with performance data from other regions, areas or teams. Managers and directors benchmark this information in order to identify best practice and methods of reducing their staff travel while still achieving their other operational targets. The league tables encourage collaborative internal competition to learn about alternative methods and innovations. Solutions tend to evolve as a consequence of measuring and comparative performance analysis.

Selected environmental indicators form part of the directors' corporate scorecards, which are discussed quarterly at board meetings where each direc-

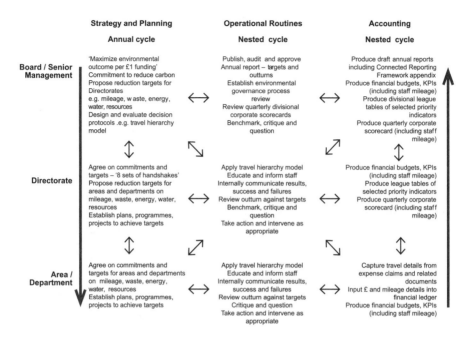

	Strategy and Planning **Annual cycle**	**Operational Routines** **Nested cycle**	**Accounting** **Nested cycle**
Board / Senior Management	'Maximize environmental outcome per £1 funding' Commitment to reduce carbon Propose reduction targets for Directorates e.g. mileage, waste, energy, water, resources Design and evaluate decision protocols .e.g. travel hierarchy model	Publish, audit and approve Annual report – targets and outturns Establish environmental governance process review Review quarterly divisional corporate scorecards Benchmark, critique and question	Produce draft annual reports including Connected Reporting Framework appendix Produce financial budgets, KPIs (including staff mileage) Produce divisional league tables of selected priority indicators Produce quarterly corporate scorecard (including staff mileage)
Directorate	Agree on commitments and targets – '8 sets of handshakes' Propose reduction targets for areas and departments on mileage, waste, energy, water, resources Establish plans, programmes, projects to achieve targets	Apply travel hierarchy model Educate and inform staff Internally communicate results, success and failures Review outturn against targets Benchmark, critique and question Take action and intervene as appropriate	Produce financial budgets, KPIs (including staff mileage) Produce league tables of selected priority indicators Produce quarterly corporate scorecard (including staff mileage)
Area / Department	Agree on commitments and targets for areas and departments on mileage, waste, energy, water, resources Establish plans, programmes, projects to achieve targets	Apply travel hierarchy model Educate and inform staff Internally communicate results, success and failures Review outturn against targets Critique and question Take action and intervene as appropriate	Capture travel details from expense claims and related documents Input £ and mileage details into financial ledger Produce financial budgets, KPIs (including staff mileage)

Figure 6.3 The Environment Agency's staff mileage system overview

Source: Ian Thomson and Georgios Georgakopoulos

tor has to provide an account of their performance. Staff mileage currently forms part of these scorecards. The Environment Agency has been reporting the costs associated with staff mileage for between six and seven years, and on the non-financial performance indicators at a regional, team and individual level for at least the last five years. With the introduction of the sustainability accounting and reporting appendix in the recent *Annual Report*, costs and indicators on staff mileage are now included in the Environment Agency's carbon emissions reporting.

The system in place in the Environment Agency means that the staff mileage reported in the *Annual Report* can be disaggregated into regions, areas, departments, teams, individual members of staff and individual journeys. Therefore, the data is reliable, verifiable and auditable, with full traceability.

What appears to make the Environment Agency's management of staff travel effective is the combination of a set of simple ideas and techniques. It has constructed a system that motivates, inspires, enables, empowers, rewards, monitors, disciplines, educates and simplifies the attainment of a simple objective, which is to reduce the environmental impacts of essential staff travel.

Evaluation of the Environment Agency's approach to staff travel and other examples

None of the individual techniques or accounting methods that the Environment Agency utilizes in relation to staff travel is earth-shattering, unique or novel. However, its approach does seem to work effectively. It has taken a number of well-established techniques and assembled them in a systematic and coherent fashion that eliminates most of the perverse incentives to act in an environmentally damaging way. Its systems reward, recognize better environmental performance and make the better environmental practices the simplest and easiest option for staff to adopt. We argue that what makes the Environment Agency's approach different is the linkages and careful orchestration of these techniques from different management disciplines and expertises. There is coherence throughout the organization in relation to reducing staff travel, as shown in Figure 6.3. This includes strategic intent, operational routines, investment in appropriate technologies, information systems and procurement policies. This coherence also extends to board and top management support and commitment, identity and culture, as well as management systems, decision support protocols, performance measurement and reward systems. This is further supported by the alignment of organizational learning systems, financial systems, cooperative benchmarking, environmental visibility and transparency within the organization and environmentally aware staff. In addition, particularly within the Environmental Finance Team, there is a commitment and realization of the need for persistence and considerable efforts to make the basic systems work properly, rather than on high-profile externally facing initiatives. This approach is not restricted to staff travel.

Similar approaches to capture relevant non-financial information in the financial systems exist for water and energy. This has involved a considerable amount of work with suppliers in order to provide a breakdown of meter readings for specific departments and buildings. While this has proved successful with energy suppliers, it has not been universally successful with other utilities. The Environment Agency does track water usage through its financial system. While it endeavoured to get the water companies to provide this level of disaggregated detail on their invoices and to build the necessary data fields into its financial systems, unfortunately, due to the way in which the majority of water bills are produced, it has been unable to capture non-financial data on water through this route. Information on water consumption is collected through meter readings by local staff and this data is used to allocate costs and usage to buildings and departments, leading to a reduction in the water use throughout the Environment Agency. For example, waterless urinals started to appear in buildings when toilet systems needed replacement. It was claimed that this change was a result of water usage being measured, reported and internally benchmarked.

Waste is more problematic in that it is difficult to establish a reliable physical measure. There are different waste streams (such as volume, weight, toxicity, organic matter and recyclability) and a range of different waste contractors. This requires the Environment Agency to weigh and measure its waste prior to it being collected by waste contractors. These measurements are used to allocate the physical quantities of waste to individual offices.

The Environment Agency places high importance on thinking through and designing systems of data collection in ways that facilitate the maximum use of the data. The capture of relevant, reliable, consistent data at the lowest possible level is a key element in the Environment Agency's approach, which enables the management of the environmental impacts of its operations.

Another good example of the agency's approach can be observed in the building of its new head office, which demonstrates, in a practical manner, what can be done by using simple techniques cost-effectively and not throwing resources at small isolated, high-profile 'demonstration' projects.

The agency's new head office, Bristol 2010, is currently under construction. This new corporate office recently achieved a score of 85.06 per cent from the Building Research Establishment: the highest score ever awarded. No UK office building has achieved such a high rating under either BREEAM 2006 or BREEAM 2008, making this the 'greenest' office in the UK. This building has not cost any more than a conventional build. The approach was not to make it an exemplar environment building by throwing money at it. It was a brownfield development with modern office facilities, commercially viable with the highest environmental standards and a good place in which to work.

Technologies used in the building range from rainwater harvesting, intelligent lighting systems and ground-source heat pumps. Environmental impact during construction was reduced through the use of recycled materials and careful management of energy and resources on site. Paul Leinster, chief executive, commented:

> This achievement demonstrates how organizations can work with developers to build exceptional offices which meet their needs while reducing their impact on the environment. By relocating to a more efficient building, the Environment Agency will save around 10 per cent every year on operational and energy costs, an estimated UK£180,000 saving per year.

The Environment Agency is using Bristol 2010 as an example of how to develop office buildings that reduce their environmental impact, while saving resources and costs.

The Environment Agency's efforts in becoming an exemplar organization in minimizing its environmental impacts and communicating its externalities in a connected manner does not stop with the above examples. Work is undertaken to measure and set environmental targets and to report on the carbon and environmental impacts of its supply chain and on sustainable products that go into its flood defence schemes. The Environment Agency has a fund set aside for environmental innovations, such as ground heat pumps or wind turbines in buildings. Teams can bid for these funds, which then become test programmes, and outcomes are monitored in order to see if there is any merit in the wider implementation throughout the organization. The Environment Agency has initiatives under way in developing life-cycle costing methods, incorporating requirements in supply and building contracts to capture and record physical data measures, as well as supplying carbon calculators to suppliers.

The one area of challenge for the Environment Agency in accounting for its environmental impact is that a lot of its work is contracted out. A substantial amount of spending is on flood defence work. Flood defence work is outsourced to large construction companies and involves pouring vast amounts of concrete, wood and steel over the countryside. Getting hold of reliable information from third-party suppliers down the supply chain is quite a challenge. The Environment Agency's National Capital Programme Team is trying to develop systems that capture data on these environmental impacts, as well as incorporating environment mitigation requirements in its contract specifications.

The Environment Agency is also concerned with future developments in its environmental systems to incorporate embedded energy and water in its procurement, as well as identifying any off-shored carbon and other environmental impacts.

The Prince's Accounting for Sustainability Project (A4S), the Connected Reporting Framework (CRF) and the Environment Agency

In the case of the Environment Agency, the CRF did not initiate accounting for sustainability or create any significant change in its practices; but it did provide strong legitimacy as to the validity of current practices and a focus to promote future accounting for sustainability system developments. In all interviews conducted it was stated that there was no shortcut for effective connected accounting for sustainability systems. These systems had to be built upon effective financial, environmental and social management and accounting systems, integrated with programmes designed to reduce the organization's social and environmental impacts. Within the Environment Agency the purpose of accounting for sustainability was to bring about change in organizations and not just to improve reporting practices.

The sustainability reporting framework developed by the FRAB sustainability working group was seen to contribute to the Environment Agency's accounting for sustainability initiatives in ways aligned with the initiatives under way. Even though the Environment Agency did not consider the CRF to be a perfect framework, it found it useful in helping to reinvigorate the debate on sustainability reporting within the public sector. It was deemed as useful to 'sell' the notion of sustainability reporting to the rest of the organization, as well as having the potential to work in both the public and 'for-profit' sector. There was a feeling in the organization that it was time for action in sustainability reporting, rather than seeking the 'perfect' accounting for sustainability standards.

One useful principle within the CRF is the importance of focusing on the most material sustainability impacts, within the organization as well as their downstream and upstream impacts. The Environment Agency has developed processes within its existing environmental accounting practices for identifying and prioritizing impacts based on environmental impact and spend. Paul Leinster, chief executive, stated that he was not convinced that the Environment Agency's sustainability accounting and reporting appendix currently accounts for all of its most material impacts – for example, in relation to civil engineering contracting works or reporting on their sustainable outcomes.

Another important point involved the Environment Agency not reporting on the contribution that is made to society by its actions, but rather reporting on the negative environmental impacts of its operations. The Environment Agency and other public-sector organizations generally consume energy and resources to deal with the negative externalities of for-profit organizations. Much of the public-sector environmental footprint is about remediating, mitigating or improving the social, economic and environmental state of the nation and cannot always be regarded as 'bad'.

Simply measuring this footprint without linking it to the consequences of the resource consumption is only providing a partial account of the sustainability of an organization. For example, the Environment Agency measures the mileage used by staff in carrying out regulatory visits, but not the improved environmental impact of the regulations that it is enforcing. As mentioned previously, the Environment Agency uses a considerable amount of concrete and steel, not to make profits for shareholders, but for building flood defences to reduce the social and environmental risks and costs of flooding. Reporting the environmental impacts of its activities without linking it to the purpose and impact of its activities arguably creates a partial and misleading account of the organization. Further development is therefore required if the Environment Agency is able to provide an account that helps with the stated goal of wanting to maximize the environmental outcomes per pound of funding.

There is a clear recognition of the lack of system completeness; but the Environment Agency has a strong vision of the next set of challenges to be addressed within its sustainability accounts. This includes further developing full costing methods, carbon accounting, better waste metrics and accounting for the impact of its contractors. However, it has in place a number of systems/metrics that could be further evolved and integrated with the current environmental accounting systems.[7]

An important factor in the Environment Agency's piloting of the CRF was the potential inclusion of a version of this framework as part of the public-sector accounting standards, backed by the Treasury and subject to audit by the National Audit Office. An adapted version of the CRF was seen as an ideal starting point for developing a public-sector sustainability reporting standard. The CRF has a holistic dimension and incorporates a range of accounting techniques intended to deliver more sustainable outcomes, while recognizing the essential changes in the way that businesses and organizations work. The CRF contains a set of principles that link strategic planning, decision-making, actions and performance with the need for clear, concise external reporting. However, the Environment Agency identified a need for those principles to be translated into standards and guidance to help achieve this change in the short to medium term.

Within the FRAB, the Treasury and public-sector organizations, it was felt that a principles-based approach (looking at policy and other material aspects of performance) was too difficult to achieve. A standards-based approach, with a core set of metrics calculated, defined, normalized and measured in a consistent format that all public-sector organizations could apply, was a necessary first step. The Environment Agency staff believed that a clearly defined standards approach needed to be in place so that organizations could not simply 'pick and use' or arbitrarily define issues to be reported. There was consensus within the FRAB for a strategy of starting with the CRF, establishing a core set of indicators, reflecting on the outcome, modifying their practices, engaging with the standard to develop it further, and then standardizing its use across the public sector.

There was a strong and consistent view that without some form of regulatory backup or assurance process the CRF could be abused or captured by organizations not fully committed to meaningful sustainable change. While financial accounts were not considered to be the most effective method of communicating, there was support for the power of the technology in providing accounts of organizational behaviour (at all levels, internal and external), as the discipline of being held to account was felt to make a difference to behaviour. However, reporting without reliable data or meaningful programmes of action was regarded as problematic since it runs the risk of covering up and/or misleading external and internal stakeholders.

Conclusions

The Environment Agency is a special case. It is an unusual organization in relation to social and environmental sustainability, as its core mission is to minimize the environmental damage done by others in England and Wales. Environment Agency staff have a very high commitment to environmental issues and very high levels of environmental expertise. The Environment Agency has expressed an objective to be an exemplar sustainable organization where good environmental management is an 'act of faith'. It seeks to demonstrate practical sustainable changes by doing the things that it expects others to do, showing, where possible, that this does not involve excessive expenditure and, in many cases, will reduce costs. Bob Branson, head of financial management, stated that the Environment Agency's strategy is to 'show ourselves to be a good example of what anybody could do and it not to be something you've got to pump loads of money into'.

The Environment Agency also sees a need for the public sector to improve its environmental impact and wishes to lead change in this field. Part of this change process includes reforming internal and external accounting systems, an area that has been sidelined in the past and acted as an obstacle to change.

The Environment Agency believes that external reporting could have a direct role in changing organizations' behaviour and performance, and for this reason it calls for meaningful and mandatory sustainability reporting, building on the CRF. It believes that the consistent reporting of a narrow, yet clearly defined, core set of indicators and costs could contribute to a transformation of UK public-sector organizations. Basic comparative data need to be in place, with organizations incorporating environmental performance indicators and costs within their annual reports before they can reflect on how they can become less unsustainable and how to embed sustainability in their DNA.

If one were trying to sum up the key lessons from this short investigation of the Environment Agency, one would conclude that it is important to do the simple things well. Organizations should not wait until they have a perfect environmental or sustainability accounting system in place before they attempt to report on their sustainability, simply because it is not possible at this point in time to design such a system. However, organizations must think carefully about how to reduce their impacts, what specific purpose they want to achieve, design an appropriate accounting system, and then just do it. It is critical that organizations continually reflect upon and review the performance of this system in order for it to evolve based on experience with its operation.

The Environment Agency feels that too many organizations are using this quest for perfection prior to action as an excuse to keep doing what they have always done with potentially disastrous consequences for people and the planet. It believes that in order to create a better place, organizations should do the small, seemingly trivial, things correctly.

In summary, the key lessons are:

- establishing environmental accountability methods and measures throughout the organization;

- the importance of solid, reliable, consistent data management systems and integrating non-financial information within accounting systems;
- clear environmental decision protocols built into organizational routines;
- ensuring that the most sustainable options are properly rewarded and the easiest to adopt;
- making visible the potential cost savings associated with certain sustainable options;
- integrating environmental improvement targets with performance measures and peer benchmarking;
- an evolutionary approach, building on organizational successes from the bottom, but inspired from the top;
- persistence, attention to detail and the continual need to educate staff and suppliers;
- awareness of limitations of current systems, clear vision of necessary changes and not resting on laurels;
- the importance of conventional 'old-fashioned' accounting values in accounting for sustainability – consistency, reliability, verifiability, relevance;
- awareness of how effective systems can emerge from the intentional assemblage of small, apparently simple, reforms; and
- a need for external standards and regulatory underpinning for meaningful sustainability reporting.

'Inspire from the top and build from the bottom' seems to be the best description of accounting for sustainability and environmental management in the Environment Agency and a pragmatic implementation of the well-worn but important environmental mantra 'think global, act local'.

Acknowledgements

The authors thank all those who participated in this case study and especially the officers and staff of the Environment Agency. We would also like to thank Professor Anthony Hopwood, Professor Jeffrey Unerman, Jessica Fries and Karen McCulloch for their comments and support. This work was funded, in part, by the Consultative Committee of Accountancy Bodies (CCAB) and the Environment Agency and their financial support is greatly appreciated.

Notes

1   The Environment Agency was created by the Environment Act 1995 and assumed the functions of the National Rivers Authority (NRA), Her Majesty's Inspectorate of Pollution (HMIP) and the waste regulation authorities in England and Wales
2   See www.environment-agency.gov.uk/aboutus/default.aspx

3   See www.environment-agency.gov.uk/aboutus/work/35696.aspx
4   Full details of these publications can be found at www.environment-agency.gov.uk/
    business/topics/performance/32348.aspx
5   See www.environment-agency.gov.uk/business/topics/performance/36974.aspx and
    www.environment-agency.gov.uk/business/topics/performance/36979.aspx
6   This information was sourced from www.environment-agency.gov.uk/business/
    topics/performance/36979.aspx
7   Examples of these can be found in 'Appendix B: Performance measurement review'
    in the Environment Agency's 2008/2009 *Annual Report* (Environment Agency,
    2009b)

References

Environment Agency (2009a) *Creating a Better Place: Environment Agency Corporate Strategy 2010–2015*, Environment Agency, Bristol, UK
Environment Agency (2009b) *Annual Report and Accounts 2008–2009*, Environment Agency, Bristol, UK

seven

Evolution of Risk, Opportunity and the Business Case in Embedding Connected Reporting at BT

Jeffrey Unerman and Brendan O'Dwyer

Introduction

BT Group plc is a global telecommunications company, supplying a range of markets with services and equipment in over 170 countries, and is the UK's largest telecommunications supplier. In 2009 it had 15 million customers (including many large multinationals), 107,000 employees and more than 1 million shareholders; sales revenue was UK£21.4 billion and it invested UK£1.1 billion in research and development. BT's worldwide emissions of CO_2 equivalents (CO_2e) in 2009 were 906,000 tonnes, representing a reduction of 44 per cent (per unit of BT's contribution to gross domestic product, or GDP) compared to their level in 1997, and a reduction from 920,000 tonnes in 2008.

As part of its long-standing commitment to effective policy and action on its social, environmental and ethical impacts, BT published its first *Environment Report* in 1992. Over the ensuing years, as social and environmental reporting practices have evolved at BT, the company has been at the forefront of innovative developments in sustainability reporting. Many of these have subsequently been adopted by a number of other organizations.

This chapter explores some of the key processes underlying current sustainability reporting practices at BT. It looks at how issues of business risks, commercial opportunities and associated materiality have driven the evolution of connected thinking at BT that underlies its connected reporting practices. These connected thinking processes seek to embed sustainability considerations within decision-making processes at all levels in the organization by linking economic, social and environmental considerations through the articulation of a business case for corporate responsibility. The chapter also examines how the business case has to be nuanced to make it an effective sustainability embedding mechanism at different levels within the organization. It also looks at how materiality issues central to the business case are used to help determine the sustainability issues that are reported within BT's annual sustainability and financial reports. To provide a focused illustration of how business case thinking has been applied to foster connected thinking and connected reporting, the final part of the chapter investigates aspects of BT's approach to managing one of its key corporate responsibility risks – supply-chain labour practices – through its Sourcing with Human Dignity Initiative.

Changes in directions of causality: Reporting driving action, action driving reporting

A key issue that needs to be addressed by any organization when engaging in sustainability reporting, and an issue at the core of the Connected Reporting Framework (CRF) developed by The Prince's Accounting for Sustainability Project (A4S), is the degree to which reporting is an activity largely integrated with, or an activity isolated from, underlying organizational change processes. It is common for many organizations that are just starting to engage with issues of sustainability to initially focus on sustainability reporting, often using reporting to foster sustainability awareness amongst managers throughout the organization and thereby seeking to influence managerial decision-making.

Over the many years that BT has been engaged in sustainability reporting, the role and impact of reporting within BT have evolved considerably. As there are currently many processes in place within the company that embed sustainability considerations within decision-making at all levels, thinking in a connected way about the social, environmental and economic impact of policies and practices is the norm and does not need to flow from reporting practices. This means that the social, environmental and economic impacts, in terms of opportunities and risks associated with strategic and operational decisions, are currently identified and linked at the time that decisions are made – and this will often be some time before the reporting stage is reached. Therefore, for BT, the content of sustainability reporting now primarily reflects sustainability-related strategies and actions during the reporting period, rather than the reporting being a predominant driver of these strategies and actions. One key exception to this prevailing direction of causality is target-setting (e.g. through key performance indicators reported within the annual and sustainability reports), which is an overarching process integral both to the reporting process itself and to driving changes and improvements in sustainability practices.

Evolution of risk and opportunity considerations in sustainability decisions: Making the business case

An important element that facilitated evolution of a connected understanding of environmental, social and economic impacts, and embedding of this understanding within strategic and operational decision-making processes at BT, was the refining of the business case for corporate responsibility. Initially, the business case was explicitly developed from about 2003 at the strategic level among senior executives. This involved articulating and partially quantifying the direct and indirect economic impacts (e.g. related to risk, reputation, customer satisfaction, employee motivation and so on) potentially flowing from a variety of major social and environmental issues.

The business case for CR

Good management of CR issues supports our business performance in five ways:

1. Risk management and mitigation
Reducing significant social, environmental and ethical risks to BT, including those relating to breach of integrity, climate change, diversity, health and safety, privacy and supply chain working conditions.

2. Our reputation
Our consumer customers who believe that BT takes its responsibility to society seriously are 49% more likely to be very or extremely satisfied with BT.

3. Reducing costs
Our programmes to reduce the environmental impacts of energy use, waste and business travel have saved us over £400m since 2005.

4. Motivating our people
Our annual employee survey showed that this year 69% of employees felt proud to work for BT as a result of our CR activities.

5. Marketplace opportunities
Our CR credentials supported bids worth a potential £1.9bn to BT in 2009. Climate change is creating new commercial opportunities. We are developing new products and services that help our customers live and work more sustainably.

Figure 7.1 The BT business case for corporate responsibility

Source: BT Group plc (2009a, p12)

At present, the elements of the business case for corporate responsibility at this strategic level within BT are explained in the 2009 *Sustainability Review* as comprising risk management and mitigation, reputation, cost reduction, employee motivation and marketplace opportunities (see Figure 7.1).

The above factors indicate that both risks and commercial market opportunities are important elements of BT's business case for sustainability at the broad strategic level. From this perspective, commercial opportunities arise primarily from BT's good record on sustainability (in many areas) being seen as a key reputational factor in distinguishing BT from its competitors, thereby giving BT competitive advantage. They also arise from identification through sustainability of completely new products, services and markets. While the reputational impact helps to distinguish BT from its competitors, identification of new markets contributes *directly* to revenue generation.

Once the business case had been embedded at the strategic level, the broader sustainability considerations identified at this level were divided into a series of component issues that could be embedded and enacted at a more operational level. Embedding sustainability via the business case at this operational level helped to highlight for individual managers that social and environmental issues, when managed more sustainably, could contribute to achieving that manager's economic objectives. It also highlighted issues where there was a weaker economic case for improving environmental or social sustainability, such as situations where it could not be demonstrated that customers or employees were really demanding action on the particular issue.

As an example of the more detailed operational-level sustainability tensions highlighted by the business case, BT's stringent carbon reduction targets require a highly energy efficient network and meeting these environmental targets with new equipment has a clear financial benefit in reduced energy bills. However, in a complex environment such as an individual telephone exchange, where new equipment has been added and integrated with existing equipment regularly over many years, the impact on service delivery of switching off some of the very old equipment will not always be known. Managers need to decide whether to invest finite resources in investigating the potentially complex engineering impact on individual customers of switching off old, possibly energy-hungry, equipment within an exchange, or to focus on commissioning new equipment to meet new customer demands. As the latter will often generate additional revenue with a reasonable degree of certainty, whereas the former will probably contribute no direct revenue generation but may lead to disgruntled customers (and, thus, a risk of lost revenue) if their telecommunications service is disrupted through an unforeseen problem from switching off an old piece of equipment, business case reasoning in the context of finite resources will almost inevitably lead to some old equipment being left running and continuing to consume energy. However, through a combination of increased costs of energy, the need to address climate change becoming a higher priority and tightened government regulation, the business case for investing resources in turning off old equipment has become even more compelling, thus driving more effective action.

Nuancing the business case:
Degrees of uncertainty and appealing to the interests of managers at different levels

BT's experience in seeking to successfully embed sustainability considerations within strategic and operational decisions by appealing to the business case has shown that different approaches are needed at different levels of the organization.

At the senior executive and board levels, sustainability is seen primarily in the strategic terms of its potential impact on, and risks to, BT's social licence to operate (its social contract). Damage to the social licence to operate from failing to address BT's corporate sustainability values could negatively affect BT's brand and reputation. Conversely, enhancing the social licence to operate through meeting BT's social values more effectively can increase the economic value of BT's brand and reputation. As a demonstration of the strength of board-level buy-in to sustainability issues at BT, during 2009/2010 15 per cent of board-level bonuses will be awarded for 'each individual [director's] contribution to the company's environmental, social and governance (ESG) objectives' (BT Group plc, 2009b, p58), with this performance being assessed largely qualitatively.

This predominantly qualitative assessment of the sustainability performance of board members and senior executives is consistent with the partially qualitative nature of information used to help make sustainability decisions at this strategic level. The use of qualitative sustainability information in conjunction with quantitative sustainability information in decision-making at board level is necessary to help set forward-looking strategic direction. By their nature, many innovative future sustainability-related opportunities considered at board level will not currently lend themselves to quantification that can 'prove' the business case. This contrasts with the situation further down the organization, where there is a perceived need for greater quantification in order to help embed sustainability considerations within decision-making processes at operational levels.

At these middle management operational levels, it has been necessary to recognize differences between the personal, social and environmental priorities of different individuals in seeking to embed the business case. Where individual managers have been personally deeply committed to principles underlying social and environmental sustainability, it has been relatively straightforward to embed sustainability considerations connecting social, environmental and economic outcomes. However, as in any organization, some individual managers will not be so deeply personally aware or committed to social and/or environmental issues. To successfully embed sustainability considerations into the decisions taken by these managers, it is even more important to demonstrate to them

effective business case benefits from taking sustainability issues seriously in
terms of how this will help them to achieve their targets:

> Don't go in as tree huggers saying: 'If we don't do this the world's going
> to be a worse place.' Ask them what business problems they have and try
> and find a link to sustainability. If their scorecard is about driving up
> revenue or reducing costs, then link these to sustainability. If you can't
> help them meet their objectives, then it's tough to convince them. (Chris
> Tuppen, BT Chief Sustainability Officer)

A key problem that needed to be overcome in achieving embedding through
the business case at this middle management level was linked to many managerial targets being set in quantified terms. To clearly demonstrate how addressing
sustainability issues could contribute to achieving these quantified managerial
targets, it was necessary to articulate sustainability business case impacts
through metrics. However, in many areas of sustainability for BT, several aspects
cannot be readily or reliably captured in metrics. For other issues, quantification involves an evolutionary process where the issue starts off being evaluated
in qualitative terms and then metrics evolve over a period. Even where metrics
can be derived for an individual sustainability issue, these metrics are often
incompatible with those for other sustainability issues, so it is not possible to
simply add the different sustainability metrics together for an individual
manager to derive a single metric to put on their scorecard. The example drawn
from BT's operationalization of their Sourcing with Human Dignity Initiative,
examined later in this chapter, provides an illustration of how some of these
tensions have been addressed within BT.

Aside from developing the business case, there can also be more subtle
barriers that need to be overcome in taking middle-level managers across large
organizations such as BT forward on the journey of embedding sustainability
within their decision-making processes. For example, people tend to feel more
committed to solutions that they, or their close colleagues, have developed,
whereas embedding sustainability in the most effective manner will often
involve innovative solutions and thinking developed in one department being
disseminated to other departments. So it is necessary to take account of, and
seek to overcome, the 'not invented here' syndrome in most large organizations such as BT. Similarly, an overall sustainability gain to the organization as a
whole can generate revenues or reduce costs in one department, while requiring resource/investments in another department, and in decentralized
organizations this can hinder cross-organization connected thinking on sustainability matters.

Another difficulty is the time horizon. Where managers have financial
targets to meet, behaviour or actions that can contribute to short-term achievement of this quarter's or year's target can have a damaging longer-term
sustainability impact – including longer-term economic damage. For example, it

may be possible for a manager to drive up sales and/or drive down costs this month by engaging in highly aggressive bullying behaviour with more junior employees if there were not procedures, policies and evaluations in place to prevent this. While such bullying behaviour may help to achieve this month's targets, it not only has a negative social impact (on the people being bullied), 'but over the longer period actually that's not going to create the right kind of working environment to drive innovation and [get] people going the extra mile' (Chris Tuppen, BT Chief Sustainability Officer).

At non-managerial levels within BT, where individual employees are not making strategic or tactical decisions, a 'softer' approach to embedding sustainability has often found success. For example, seeking to persuade employees to change their behaviour to a more sustainable basis by providing messages around the negative impacts of issues such as climate change and other social and environmental matters tends to elicit a positive reaction.

Therefore, there is not a 'one size fits all' approach to embedding sustainability, or to the articulation of the business case, at BT. Rather, a wide variety of different approaches have been found to be necessary to change the culture in order to embed sustainability considerations connecting social, environmental and economic outcomes within strategic and day-to-day decisions and behaviour.

Materiality helping to determine the content of connected sustainability reporting

Having advanced the embedding of sustainability considerations in decision-making at all levels, there is a considerable range of sustainability actions and practices within BT. Information about each of these issues could potentially be of interest to a number of stakeholders and could therefore form part of BT's external connected sustainability reporting. Although information on a wide range of sustainability issues exists internally within BT, choices have to be made regarding which of the many issues should be reflected in BT's sustainability reporting. The materiality, or significance, of individual corporate responsibility risks and opportunities is a key factor in deciding which of these many sustainability strategies and actions are taken forward to BT's external reports.

The relative materiality of each type of sustainability issue is determined systematically on an annual basis through plotting on a graph the internal BT view on its significance against an external stakeholder perspective of its importance (see Figure 7.2, which, in the version actually used by BT, would show each sustainability issue as a data point). The internal perspective is primarily a combination of the views of the managers within BT whose area of responsibility encompasses the issue, along with quantified risk assessments undertaken in relation to the issue. The external stakeholder perspective of an issue's signifi-

Identifying our material issues

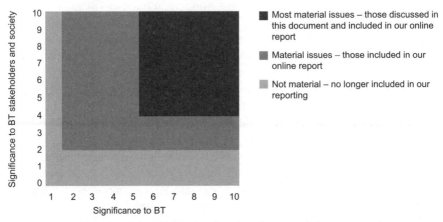

Figure 7.2 Materiality identification graph

Source: BT Group plc (2009a, 'Introduction', p7)

cance is determined by reviewing an array of external information, including sources such as the media coverage devoted to the issue (not just regarding BT, but more broadly), investor questionnaires, employee focus groups, questions in parliament about the type of issue and so on.

Once the significance of all the identified sustainability issues has been plotted, a senior-level committee within BT then reviews the positioning of each issue in terms of its internal significance and can take a more holistic overview and adjust the relative *internal* materiality of individual issues. BT's external Corporate Responsibility Leadership Panel examines the relative *external* significance assigned to each issue, and has the ability to adjust this for each issue if it believes that external stakeholders would consider an issue more or less significant than BT's initial evaluation suggested.

Through this process, in addition to quantification, factors that may be held to reflect BT's values as a business can be brought to bear in determining the materiality of an issue. This is partially necessitated because the potential impacts of many issues are not of the nature that can be quantified precisely in monetary terms, so judgements of probability have to come into the decision-making process. For example, in energy saving initiatives, BT's total energy costs in 2009 amounted to UK£227 million. While this figure would be above the financial materiality threshold for BT's *Annual Report*, a percentage saving of this UK£227 million direct cost through energy-efficiency initiatives may well be below the threshold. However, in addition to using the direct cost saving from reduced energy bills in determining the materiality of energy saving as a corporate responsibility issue, BT will also take into account an evaluation of other possible (and often more subjective) economic impacts indirectly flowing from strong energy saving performance – such as the positive impact on BT's reputation from leading on environmental initiatives, the extent to which major customers (such as large government contracts) may take account of sustainability performance in their procurement processes, and so on.

As can be seen from Figure 7.2, the materiality attributed to each issue as a result of the above processes is then used to determine whether and where each issue will be reported upon. Many of the actions taken by BT that contribute towards greater social and environmental sustainability may not be reflected anywhere in BT's reports if they are not judged to be sufficiently significant. Where issues are judged material or significant enough to BT to be reported in BT's detailed online sustainability report, the person responsible for managing the issue will be asked to write some relevant content for the website. This content will then be copy-edited by an external agency to ensure consistency of expression. The sustainability report website (www.btplc.com/Responsiblebusiness/Ourstory/Sustainabilityreport/index.aspx) has considerable detail on many aspects of BT's sustainability policies and practices, clearly connecting economic, social and environmental considerations over many areas, and using a mix of narrative and quantitative reporting.

The more material issues within the most strategically important sustainability themes will be taken forward and reported in the summary *Sustainability Review*. The core sustainability issues will then be reported in summary form in the *Annual Report* in a way that provides a high level understanding of these issues. For several years, these issues have been reported throughout the *Annual Report*, seeking to connect a reader's understanding and appreciation of each issue with the aspect of BT's business that the issue most closely affects – thereby reporting the key sustainability information alongside the economic information for each issue.

In 2009, BT included in its *Annual Report* for the first time a summary table of the 'Non-financial corporate responsibility KPIs' as a high-level connected reporting summary of the most material strategic sustainability issues (this table also appears in the summary *Sustainability Review*).

Although this key performance indicator (KPI) table was published in the corporate responsibility subsection within the 'Business review' section of the *Annual Report*, discussion and explanation of the issues covered in the KPI table are still located throughout the *Annual Report*. This is because, consistent with the principles embodied in the CRF, BT believes that placing all sustainability content in a separate section of the *Annual Report* would not reflect the company's embedding of considerations of these matters throughout its business operations.

The 2009 'Non-financial corporate responsibility KPIs' table is reproduced in full in Table 7.1 to illustrate the issues that it covers and, therefore, the sustainability issues that BT considered the most material and strategic in 2009, along with the non-financial and financial metrics (or indicators) used to evaluate these issues.

Table 7.1 Non-financial corporate responsibility key performance indicators (KPIs) table

	Key performance indicators	Direct company impacts: Non-financial indicators Target 2010	2009	2008	2007
Customers	**Customer service** A measure of success across BT's entire customer base	To improve customer service based on getting things right first time (RFT) in line with our corporate scorecard	**17%** improve-ment in RFT service from 2008	**9%** improve-ment in RFT service from 2007	**3%** increase in customer satisfaction (our previous measure)
Employees	**Employee engagement index** A measure of the success of BT's relationship with employees, through its annual employee attitude survey	Maintain or improve the 2009 level of employee engagement. We moved to a five point scale this year, and have restated previous scores	**3.61**	**3.60**	**3.62**
	Diversity A measure of the diversity of the BT workforce	BT will maintain a top 10 placement in four of five major diversity benchmarks. Includes four UK benchmarks and the Schneider-Ross Global Diversity benchmark (from 2008)	BT is in the top 10 placement in four out of the five major diversity benchmarks	BT is in the top 10 placement in four out of the five major diversity benchmarks	BT is in the top 10 placement in three out of four main UK diversity benchmarks
	H&S: lost time injury rate Lost time injury cases expressed as a rate per 100,000 hours worked on a 12 month rolling average	Reduce to 0.157 cases	**0.160** cases	**0.188** cases	**0.238** cases
	H&S: sickness absence rate Percentage of calendar days lost to sickness absence expressed as a 12 month rolling average	Reduce to 1.9% calendar days lost due to sickness	**2.17%**	**2.43%**	**2.43%**
Suppliers	**Supplier relationships** A measure of the overall success of BT's relationship with suppliers, based on our annual supplier survey	To achieve a rating of 80% or more, based on the question: 'How would you describe the quality of your company's relationship with BT?'	**85%**	**78%**	New measure in 2008
	Ethical trading A measure of the application of BT's supply chain human rights standard	To achieve 100% follow up within three months for all suppliers identified as high or medium risk, through our ethical standard questionnaires	**78** risk assess-ments with 100% follow up	**234** risk assess-ments with 100% follow up	**413** risk assess-ments with 100% follow up

Direct company impacts: Financial indicators				*Indirect company impacts*
	2009	*2008*	*2007*	
Total revenue	£21,390m	£20,704m	£20,223m	
Average annual revenue per (UK) consumer household	£287	£274	£262	
Employee costs	£5,506m	£5,358m	£5,223m	Employee engagement is a driver of customer satisfaction
Number of employees	107,021	111,858	106,200	
BT will develop a relevant financial indicator for diversity next year				Establishing a diverse workforce promotes social cohesion
Cost to the business arising from injuries resulting in time off work	£7m	New measure in 2009		Lowering lost days from injuries and sickness reduces societal health care costs and improves productivity
BT sick pay costs	£85.2m	£89.8m	£84.7m	
Total spend with suppliers	£8.9bn	£8.6bn	£6.8bn	Economic multiplier effect (e.g. employment) arising from BT's supply chain procurement
Value of procurement contracts where our suppliers agree that we work with them to improve sustainability impacts (extrapolated from a representative supplier survey)	£7.4bn (83% of supplier spend)	£5.7bn (66% of supplier spend)	First measured in 2008	Quality of life – especially working conditions in emerging economies

Table 7.1 *continued*

	Key performance indicators	Direct company impacts: Non-financial indicators Target 2010	2009	2008	2007
Improving society	**Community effectiveness measure** An independent evaluation of our community programme	Maintain evaluation score at over 90%	**91%**	**79%**	**70%**
	Investment to improve society	Maintain a minimum investment of 1% of underlying pre-tax profits	**1.01%**	**1.02%**	**1.05%**
Environment	**CO_2 equivalent emissions** A measure of BT's climate change impact	By December 2020, BT group will reduce its CO_2e emission intensity by 80% against 1997 levels. New target set in 2008	CO_2e 906,000 tonnes **44% reduction 43%** intensity reduction	CO_2e 920,000 tonnes **43% reduction 52%** intensity reduction	CO_2e 896,000 tonnes **45% reduction 52%** intensity reduction
	Waste to landfill and recycling A measure of BT's use of resources	BT group will reduce the tonnage of waste sent to landfill by 8% from 2009	**17%** reduction in waste to landfill from 2008 (UK only)	**22%** reduction in waste to landfill from 2007 (UK only)	**8%** reduction in waste to landfill from 2006 (UK only)
Integrity	**Business practices measure** How our Statement of Business Practice is implemented. Measured through a regular employee survey	We plan to make this indicator more broad-ranging to include all relevant policies including our new anti-corruption and bribery, and gifts and hospitality policies	**77%**	**83%**	**87%**

Source: BT Group plc (2009b, pp24–25)

The main added dimension for BT's sustainability reporting derived from adopting the CRF was drawing together into the overview KPI table this key summary of sustainability information that is reported throughout the *Annual Report*. It is felt that this helped to provide a more embedded sustainability picture, demonstrating the associations between different elements of BT's sustainability practices and clearly drawing together the key financial and non-financial impacts. As the information in the connected reporting KPI table is also published in separate sections of the report, there was very little additional resource required to bring the information together on a more systematic basis within the KPI table.

Direct company impacts: Financial indicators				Indirect company impacts
	2009	2008	2007	
Community investment (time, cash and in-kind support)	£25.0m	£22.3m	£21.8m	BT's community programme focuses on improving communication and ICT skills. This helps improve people's employment prospects and increase social inclusion
Total energy costs (fleet fuel + gas + oil + diesel for back up generators etc; UK and Ireland only)	£227m	£194m	£185m	Indirect negative impacts occur in the manufacture of equipment and through energy consumption in customer premises. Positive impacts arise from application of ICT to support low carbon economy
Income from recycling	£7.42m	£6.70m	£4.48m	Dealing with end of life products sold into the market place. Acting to reduce obsolescence
Landfill tax savings	£1.15m	£0.89m	£0.84m	
Waste costs	£(7.90)m	£(7.27)m	£(5.15)m	
Net waste savings	£0.67m	£0.32m	£0.17m	
Revenue Support (customer bids with a sustainability component)	£1.9bn	£2.2bn	£1.8bn	A responsible business culture, banning corrupt practices including facilitation payments, supports better international governance

The manner in which BT undertakes this reporting demonstrates the potential power of the CRF in seeking to integrate throughout a company's *Annual Report* a clear demonstration (via a combination of both quantified and narrative reporting) of the connection between sustainability performance and corporate strategic objectives, rather than relegating all of the sustainability information to a separate section in the report. It also demonstrates the helpfulness of drawing together a summary of the sustainability information (in BT's case, in the overview KPI table) to provide clear overall signals to stakeholders connecting the different aspects of sustainability strategy and performance.

Box 7.1 BT's corporate responsibility risks

During 2009, we continued to develop our knowledge and understanding of our corporate responsibility [CR] risks. Our most significant CR risks continue to be:
- *breach of our code of business ethics;*
- *climate change;*
- *diversity;*
- *health and safety;*
- *privacy;*
- *supply-chain working conditions.*

Each of these risks has an owner and a mitigation strategy in place.

Source: BT Group plc (2009b, p23)

In addition to the 'Non-financial corporate responsibility KPIs' table in BT's 2009 *Annual Report*, the corporate responsibility sub-section contained a brief narrative summary of the following key issues (BT Group plc, 2009b, p23): BT's community support programmes and actions, both in the UK and worldwide; BT's policies and actions to protect the environment; and a list of the six 'most significant corporate responsibility risks' (see Box 7.1).

The last of these risks, supply-chain working conditions, is explored in more depth in the case example below in order to provide a more focused illustration of how many of the issues discussed above are embedded, in practice, in connected thinking and connected reporting about sustainability within BT.

Case example: Supply-chain initiatives – Sourcing with Human Dignity

The 'significant' corporate responsibility risk of 'supply-chain working conditions' is managed primarily through BT's Sourcing with Human Dignity Initiative. This initiative was launched as an internal BT standard in 2001, having been developed over the previous few years, drawing on insights from International Labour Organization Standards and the United Nations Global Compact. As such, it does not seek to impose UK standards in other countries, but to use internationally recognized standards.

A key impetus for development of this standard within BT was media coverage during the late 1990s of child labour in the clothing industry. Although these stories did not involve BT, they led BT's senior procurement managers to question whether there was a risk of such human rights issues arising within BT's supply chain. The early motivation for this initiative being developed and rolled out across BT's suppliers was therefore an ethical concern that BT should take action to ensure that its suppliers were treating their workforces with dignity, not employing child labour and so on:

> I think it was, at that stage, less a risk assessment and more a human reaction in terms of that story that hit the headlines and [it] has quite an impact on you as an individual in terms of BT tending to have quite strong ethics running through it. (Liz Cross, Head of Corporate Social Responsibility Strategy and Policy for Procurement)

The standard was initially applied to suppliers of clothing for BT employees and to suppliers of telephones. This was because it was felt that, given their location of manufacture, these areas of the supply chain had the highest risk of poor employment practices, with the use of relatively unskilled workers in the manufacturing process. However, these areas were not highly strategic supply areas for BT at the time – partially because there were many alternative suppliers that could have been used if a problem had been found in one supplier. The initiative was then rolled out relatively quickly across other parts of the supply chain that, by their nature, were considered to be a lower risk in terms of poor employment practices but of much more strategic importance to BT, such as sourcing of network equipment, which requires long-term commitments to a small number of suppliers.

In common with other corporate social and environmental responsibility issues at BT, it was only relatively recently that formal business case justifications for the initiative, in terms of risk, brand reputation and, possibly, additional sales, have been connected with the social issues underlying the Sourcing with Human Dignity Initiative.

Reporting the Sourcing with Human Dignity Initiative

Using the 'Non-financial corporate responsibility KPIs' table from the 2009 *Annual Report* (see Table 7.1) as a starting point, this section drills down to demonstrate how the KPI table is supported by more detailed information published both elsewhere in the *Annual Report* and within BT's sustainability reports.

As can be seen from the second row of the *supplier* section of the KPI table, ethical trading is one of BT's non-financial corporate responsibility KPIs. The table states that the non-financial KPI used is 'a measure of the application of BT's supply-chain human rights standard' with the target for 2010 of achieving '100 per cent follow-up within three months for all suppliers identified as high or medium risk, through our ethical standard questionnaires'. The fourth column of the table shows that in 2009, 78 such risk assessments were conducted with 100 per cent follow-up. The financial KPI used in the right-hand side of the table for this area is 'value of procurement contracts where our suppliers agree that we work with them to improve sustainability impacts (extrapolated from a representative supplier survey)', with a procurement value amounting to UK£7.4 billion in 2009 (representing 83 per cent of supplier spend). The table also notes that this financial KPI was first measured in 2008, demonstrating the evolutionary nature of metrics in areas of sustainability. The indirect company impacts for this area (in the right-hand column of the table) are 'quality of life – especially working conditions in emerging economies'.

Drilling down within the *Annual Report* itself, the Sourcing with Human Dignity Initiative is discussed almost 50 pages after the KPI table, on page 71, in the responsible business subsection of the 'Business policies' section within the *Report of the Directors*. Here, it is explained that:

> We have had in place for nearly ten years a written statement of business practice (The Way We Work). This covers all our operations and applies worldwide to all employees, and to all agents and contractors when representing BT, and is available in nine languages. During 2009, we have refreshed and reissued The Way We Work and our policy on Anti-corruption and Bribery to all our people worldwide...
>
> Through our Sourcing with Human Dignity initiative, we seek to ensure that working conditions throughout our supply chain meet internationally recognized human rights standards. We investigate potential social and environmental shortcomings and are committed to achieving 100% follow-up within three months for all suppliers identified as high- or medium-risk. During the 2009 financial year, we completed 27 on-site assessments (2008, p25). The majority of assessments were conducted in China, although we also conducted assessments in the Philippines, South Korea, Thailand, France and the UK. We now employ our own assessor based in Shanghai, which has enabled us to focus our efforts on suppliers in China. We work with our suppliers to help them improve their performance. In 2009, 83% of our suppliers agreed that we work with them to ensure our purchases are made, delivered, used and disposed of in a socially and environmentally responsible manner.

Within the 2009 summary *Sustainability Review*, supply-chain ethics are described as one of the key corporate responsibility risks for BT. Along with the other such key risks, a graph of the risk frontier is provided (see Figure 7.3). This shows the likelihood of an impact occurring (on the vertical axis) plotted against financial cost of the impact on the horizontal axis. In the *Sustainability Review*, a section entitled 'Working with our suppliers' explains (BT Group plc, 2009a, p8):

> BT buys from thousands of suppliers, many in emerging economies. We aim for all our suppliers to meet high standards on human rights, employment and environmental practices. We have a long-established supply-chain management programme to assess potential suppliers,

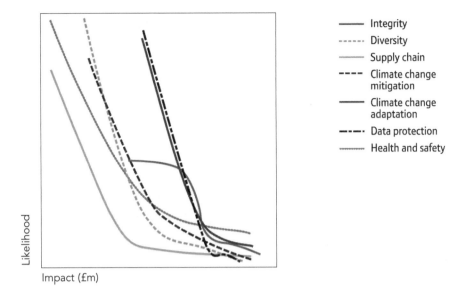

Figure 7.3 BT's key corporate responsibility risks frontiers

Source: BT Group plc (2009a, p5)

> monitor their performance and work with them to improve standards.
>   In 2009, we conducted 27 onsite assessments of our high- or medium-risk suppliers. The most common, significant issues found during assessments of medium- and high-CR risk suppliers related to health and safety, the welfare of employees and working hours. We discussed assessment findings with suppliers and are monitoring their progress through follow-up reports, review meetings, and, in some cases, return visits.

Within the 'Running a responsible business' section of the main *Sustainability Report* the Sourcing with Human Dignity Initiative is discussed under the subsections dealing with BT's procurement standards, on–site assessments and implementing human rights.

The remainder of this case study example will explain the connected thinking on sustainability issues that underlies the above information about the Sourcing with Human Dignity Initiative that was reported in the various BT 2009 reports.

Evolution of embedding the Sourcing with Human Dignity Initiative

Although initial development of BT's Sourcing with Human Dignity Initiative was motivated largely by the ethical standards of BT and of the individuals within procurement who developed the initiative, latterly it has been embedded by articulating the social and economic (business case) impacts in a more connected manner:

> *As discussions around this area, and particularly the Sourcing with Human Dignity standards, have extended further into the company, the risk side of it is probably a message that is more upfront. Because, in a business context, it is more straightforward to discuss the risk than the ethics side, which tends to be more personal, and sometimes people get a little uncomfortable talking about that side of things. And, certainly, in terms of making the business case for why we use this standard with suppliers and should continue to do so, and that resources are required to support its use, clearly the risk and the brand reputation piece is a very strong message to remind people of.* (Liz Cross, Head of Corporate Social Responsibility Strategy and Policy for Procurement)

Two important factors combined to facilitate the embedding of the Sourcing with Human Dignity Initiative. The first of these was that the initiative, by its nature, could largely be owned and operationalized within BT's procurement operations, and there was therefore no need initially to take time selling the ideas underlying the initiative to other areas within BT. The second important factor was strong support and leadership from successive chief procurement officers helping to signal to all those within procurement the importance of the initiative.

The manner in which the initiative was applied to procurement decisions was also important in winning the support both of those working within BT procurement and of suppliers. Initially, the initiative was applied to individual suppliers post-contract, so it was not used pre-contract to differentiate between suppliers. In entering a supply contract, suppliers would be asked to sign up to the standard and then, post-contract, BT would require the suppliers to complete a *Sourcing with Human Dignity Questionnaire* (an updated version of which is still in use today). This helps BT to understand the risks attached to each supplier in terms of supply-chain labour practices, and then work with each supplier to help the supplier both understand the issues and draw up a plan to improve their policies and practices where necessary. BT then undertakes periodic reviews of suppliers (both direct, tier one, suppliers and the indirect suppliers to BT's suppliers: tier two and higher) to ensure that they are abiding by commitments in their agreed improvements plan:

> *We expect an improvement plan to be agreed and delivered against. It's not a question of 'You're either in our supply chain or you're out of our supply chain'; it's about: 'We expect you to engage and work on delivering improvements.'* (Liz Cross, Head of Corporate Social Responsibility Strategy and Policy for Procurement)

Issues that commonly arise with suppliers that have an identified need to improve their practices have tended to be predominantly in the area of health and safety – for example, handling of chemicals and exposure to lead, worker protection and protective equipment. Other issues also arise, such as excessive working hours and low pay. Addressing these issues in a proactive manner has delivered positive risk management returns to BT. For example, when BT started to use some call centres in other countries, the procurement team applied the Sourcing with Human Dignity Standard (among assessments of suppliers against BT's other requirements). When questions were subsequently raised publicly about working conditions in overseas call centres, BT had the evidence to show how the call centres they were using had addressed potential problems in this area in an effective way. This included an independent report commissioned earlier to substantiate BT's activities in this area.

An additional benefit for BT is felt to be the development of a strong reputation for its commitment to, and effectiveness in, supply-chain labour standards – having been one of the early innovators in this area. It is felt that, among its actions in many other areas of corporate responsibility, this has helped to significantly reduce the risk of BT becoming the focus of the types of social and environmental protest campaigns that have been held against many other corporates.

Developments of metrics around the Sourcing with Human Dignity Initiative

As in other areas of sustainability within BT, metrics are used, where possible, to help connect economic to social impacts arising from the Sourcing with Human Dignity Initiative in making an effective business case. The primary metrics used involve evaluation of risks to the value of the BT brand from a negative incident leading to a potential loss of trust in the brand, and the commercial opportunities for enhancing the BT brand value and sales through such corporate responsibility initiatives being a positive differentiator for customers, employees and investors in choosing to support BT:

> In commercial bids from both government organizations and large corporates, we are now asked questions around sustainability and included in our response to that is the message around what we do in terms of our suppliers and our supply chain. So that's one element of value around these activities. (Liz Cross, Head of Corporate Social Responsibility Strategy and Policy for Procurement)

In evaluating and quantifying the economic risk around supply-chain labour as part of evaluating a connected business case, in common with other aspects of BT's corporate responsibility risks, a regular review is undertaken that graphs the likely financial impact to BT from a particular type of incident against the probability of that incident occurring (see Figure 7.3). For each identified potential supply-chain labour risk, these evaluations take into account, for example, the costs of lost sales to customers who may stop buying from BT if a particular type of incident occurred; the fines that may be incurred; breaks in the supply of critical products at critical times; delays in supplies of critical network equipment and so on. Combining all the identified potential risks from supply-chain labour incidents produces a 'risk frontier'. Given the size of BT, this risk frontier for supply-chain labour issues (in common with the risk frontiers for other key areas) shows a higher probability of incidents with relatively low potential financial impacts occurring and a much lower probability of an incident that carries much greater financial implications occurring. Having quantified the economic risk arising from the social risks around supply-chain labour issues in this graphical manner, the economic paybacks from lowering the risk frontier on both the likelihood and financial impacts axes become much more readily apparent. This is a very helpful outcome of this form of connected reporting.

However, there was a sense, while conducting the case study, that issues around supply-chain labour practices are perhaps not as significant or material in economic risk terms to BT as several other corporate responsibility issues. Nevertheless, they are reported in the top level KPIs table and elsewhere in the narrative in the *Annual Report* because senior executives decided that this was an intrinsically important issue for the company. This demonstrates how management discretion is used, informed by the metrics, in deciding the significance of issues to report.

For external reporting, the number of Sourcing with Human Dignity risk assessments that have been undertaken with 100 per cent follow-up within three months has been chosen as the key non-financial metric because it has been found that reporting this particular KPI externally helps to bring issues of supply-chain labour standards very effectively to the fore internally in procurement decisions and actions:

> When buyers are very busy, when they're asked to do more and more things, this could easily be pushed to another day, and perhaps just not happen. So the fact that it is reported in this way, and it's very visibly reported as a KPI, does help us to ensure that the required engagement and follow-up does happen. (Liz Cross, Head of Corporate Social Responsibility Strategy and Policy for Procurement)

Supplier and BT buyer reaction to the initiative

Initially, there was a range of reactions to implementing the initiative. Some people immediately saw the positive aspects of the initiative and were keen to implement it. But for others, particularly those working in areas of procurement where there was very little perceived risk related to the issues covered by the initiative, there was questioning of the relevance of them using scarce time and resources to implement the initiative – for example, for buyers procuring from small-scale suppliers in low-risk areas. This initial resistance from some was largely overcome when they had experienced applying the standard and the questionnaire. They realized that the process from BT's perspective was relatively straightforward and could readily become part of routine discussions with a range of suppliers. The embedding was made even more effective when business case financial risk and reputation issues were connected more systematically to the social issues around sourcing with human dignity.

Embedding this initiative within procurement decision-making has made managers more aware of the criticality of these issues:

> The kind of thing that hits my desk would be an email from a product manager saying 'We're just about to launch a new product and have discovered a potential supplier down the supply chain of this product in a country that is on the extreme of acceptability ... what do we do about it?'... The fact that the product manager is asking the question at all and understands the reputational impact that might flow out of that demonstrates [that] ethical procurement is embedded in the organization.
> (Chris Tuppen, BT Chief Sustainability Officer)

Good management of supply-chain labour standards has also become increasingly embedded within the strategic decision-making of several of BT's suppliers during the period since BT launched their initiative in this area. Some suppliers have developed systems where they will make the outcome of supply-chain labour assessments available to other customers, recognizing that there are benefits to them of doing so that are broader than just their relationship with BT. These systems help to make the processes involved in assessing supply-chain labour standards less onerous and more cost-effective, as a single assessment can be used with multiple customers. Each customer can then use its resources devoted to this initiative to take the baseline of information in a previously conducted assessment and probe in more depth and develop a more focused dialogue with a supplier.

Many of BT's customers, as suppliers to other organizations or consumers, have also become increasingly aware and demanding of BT in this area:

> This is not diminishing as a business issue, and the risk side is being more clearly understood. The fact that there are now significant customers out there who are engaged in this agenda and taking actions themselves, I think that has focused minds. (Liz Cross, Head of Corporate Social Responsibility Strategy and Policy for Procurement)

Challenges in the process

There have, however, been several challenges in embedding the Sourcing with Human Dignity Initiative. One such difficulty has been that many of the issues are not clear-cut 'right or wrong' issues. Rather, they involve perhaps 'softer' qualitative decisions across a range of possible issues. This has posed challenges to some procurement managers for whom problems portrayed in more definitive terms resonate better than softer issues:

> When managers who are used to clear-cut business issues start to come on board with the Sourcing with Human Dignity Initiative, it can be quite difficult to start with because they see it in shades of black and white. A supplier is in or out, they fix it or they don't fix it. Our ethos is about driving lasting improvements in working conditions, which can take longer and more effort. So if you want to stay with that supplier and drive improvement, you've got to get the management on board to allow the time for some of that to work its way through. (Liz Cross, Head of Corporate Social Responsibility Strategy and Policy for Procurement)

This also demonstrates that for the initiative to work effectively involves a long-term engagement process with suppliers to systematically embed, within their management, proactive thinking and action consistent with the ethos of ethical labour standards.

Coupled with this, some managers feel uncomfortable bringing ethical issues to the fore in decision processes. However, when the business case connection was made between the economic and the social dimensions, through bringing the real nature of business risks addressed by the initiative to the fore, there was much less reluctance from managers to engage with the issues. In all these aspects, it has been necessary to appreciate that different individuals will take different lengths of time to appreciate the real economic and social benefits delivered by the initiative, and each person needs to be given the space and encouragement to develop their understanding of these benefits.

Conclusions

This case study of BT reveals a number of issues that can inform the integration of sustainability practices and connected reporting within other companies. First, the business case needs to be clearly articulated at a strategic level and afforded top-level support if it is to be embraced substantively at an operational level. This articulation does not necessarily wholly require quantitative indicators, which in many cases are not available, but a clear link to brand and reputational risk factors is needed. Second, embedding practices throughout the organization requires tailoring articulation of the business case to suit the specific needs of different internal constituencies. For example, operational managers need to be given a sense of ownership of proposed practices with the benefits arising from their adoption framed in the context of the risks and opportunities for them. They also need to be allowed the space to establish their commitment to, and understanding of, the benefits from adopting new practices. Third, the development of annual reports should clearly reflect the embeddedness of sustainability practices, with sustainability as an issue being addressed *throughout* annual reports and not in an isolated fashion, seemingly separate from core business concerns. This can facilitate clearer communication of the embeddedness and interconnected nature of sustainability in organizations. Fourth, metrics in many areas of sustainability take time to evolve and their absence should not deter companies from addressing, in a connected manner, potential risks and opportunities that may need addressing in the context of the companies' strategic direction, or from reporting these issues in their annual reports and in standalone sustainability reports.

Acknowledgements

We are very grateful for the time and help that staff at BT provided in assisting us to collect information for this case study – in particular, Chris Tuppen (Chief Sustainability Officer) and Liz Cross (Head of Corporate Social Responsibility Strategy and Policy for Procurement). We are also grateful for input and comments from Jessica Fries, Karen McCulloch and Thomas Ahrens. However, analysis of the information and opinions expressed in this chapter are those of the authors, and do not necessarily represent the views of BT.

References

BT Group plc (2009a) *Sustainability Review*, BT Group plc, London
BT Group plc (2009b) *Annual Report*, BT Group plc, London

eight

Sustainability and Organizational Connectivity at HSBC

Alnoor Bhimani and Kazbi Soonawalla

Introduction

HSBC is one of the largest banking and financial services organizations in the world. Headquartered in London, its international network comprises some 8500 offices in 86 countries and territories in Europe, Hong Kong, the rest of Asia-Pacific, the Middle East (including Africa), North America and Latin America. HSBC provides a comprehensive range of financial services to more than 100 million customers and shares in HSBC Holdings plc are held by about 220,000 shareholders in 119 countries and territories.

HSBC considers long-term thinking to be central to its success. Established in 1865, HSBC has weathered change and believes that it has adapted to survive by building on its foundations of capital strength, strict cost control and development of long-term relationships with customers. For HSBC, this long-term thinking is central to its sustainability strategy and it regards the management of environmental and social risks and opportunities as a critical part of business sustainability. The HSBC *Sustainability Report 2008* offers a broad definition of sustainability: 'At HSBC, a sustainable business means achieving profits for our shareholders, underpinned by good governance, long-lasting customer relationships, and highly committed staff delivering the corporate strategy and managing the social and environmental impact of our business' (2008b, p4).

In line with the external context and changing stakeholder expectations, HSBC has sought to formalize its management of corporate sustainability over the last 20 years by establishing and embedding policies, a reporting structure and a culture in which all employees have a role to play in protecting the environment and contributing to wider society. This chapter aims to highlight the role of the broader principles of The Prince's Accounting for Sustainability Project (A4S) – in particular, those underlying the Connected Reporting Framework (CRF) – in HSBC's journey of embedding sustainability into the business. For the purposes of this chapter, these principles include:

• a focus on the needs of long-term investors and executive management;
• the connection between the organization's strategic objectives and context within which the business operates and the associated risks and opportunities that it faces; and
• the connection between financial and non-financial performance.

This chapter looks at the approach taken by HSBC to embed sustainability by examining three broad themes. 'Implementation of the Equator Principles and sector policies' highlights how HSBC has sought to embed sustainability within one of its core businesses through the Equator Principles and HSBC's own sector policies as a means of managing the environmental and social risks of lending to corporate clients. The chapter then goes on to review the ways in which sustainability, particularly the impacts of climate change, have been integrated into the organization and culture of the bank. 'The role of sustainability reporting' looks at the evolution of, and influences on, HSBC's external sustainability reporting and the role that it has played in communicating sustainability issues to stakeholders. Finally, concluding thoughts are provided.

Linking financial and non-financial performance and risk

Sustainability risk is covered in HSBC's *Annual Report and Accounts* (HSBC, 2008a, p254), alongside reputational risk, credit risk and operational risk, demonstrating the connectedness between all of these different elements. In an investor seminar in 2009, sustainability risk was included in the analysis provided. Both of these examples are an indication of the integration of sustainability within HSBC's financial management and reporting.

In the case of sustainability risk, the link to core business success is clear. Lenders have a commercial rationale for assessing the social and environmental consequences of their borrowers' actions. Extensive risk-taking or actual damage by borrowers will influence their ability to repay loans or manage their reputation and credit effectively. As regulatory stipulations concerning environmental and social impacts of corporate actions become more significant, due process by a lender in monitoring client adherence becomes more relevant. From a purely commercial perspective, then, lenders may be inclined to establish lending precepts on client sustainability practices and to institutionalize controls for monitoring compliance and good practice.

Beyond this, and of increasing significance, are the strategic reputational and branding objectives of financial institutions in their pursuit of sustainability. HSBC's Group Reputational Risk Committee oversees existing and potential reputational issues and provides guidance on aspects of the business where reputational risk is perceived to be a particular challenge. Reputational risks – including environmental, social and governance issues – are considered by the HSBC Holdings Board and its committees, subsidiary company boards and senior management during the formulation of policies and the establishment of HSBC standards. The group head of corporate sustainability sits on the Group Reputational Risk Committee and raises issues of investments in sensitive sectors in that forum, where relevant.

These reputational aims require that external stakeholders' demands for transparency are met, and providing a full public report on progress is often deemed at least as important as being able to demonstrate excellent performance. Following the issue of the Forest Land and Forest Products Sector Policy in June 2004, 98 per cent of HSBC's customers in this sector met, or were on a credible path to meet, the requirements of the policy in 2008. HSBC recognizes the value of transparency to stakeholders, as the head of sustainability risk states: 'That is why we openly engage with our own teams internally, other businesses, investors and NGOs when developing our sector policies.'

Implementation of the Equator Principles and sector policies

Financial institutions have become increasingly aware of the significant impacts that their strategies and decisions can have, not only on the business community and economy, but also on individuals and society as a whole. Sustainable finance has become a critical means through which financial institutions can influence and promote sustainability. In determining the creditworthiness of clients, a number of financial institutions now look beyond economic return criteria to identify other types of risk that may affect the long-term success of the investment. This assessment may culminate in additional lending stipulations or a refusal to lend. In order to consistently analyse the social and environmental risks, standards and policies are required to guide decision-making. In response to this need, international guidance such as the Equator Principles and internal organization-specific policies have been developed.

Application of the Equator Principles at HSBC

The Equator Principles were developed in 2003 by a group of leading international banks, with input and guidance from the World Bank and the International Finance Corporation (IFC), to enable categorization of project finance applications according to social and environmental risk. The guidelines are voluntary and are being adopted by an increasing number of banks over time, once their internal policies and systems are sufficiently sophisticated. The principles are intended to help financial institutions assess and monitor the impacts of project finance loans specifically, as an environmental and social risk assessment requires that the bank has some knowledge of what the loan will be used for. A fundamental precept of the Equator Principles is that organizations that have signed up to them will not provide loans to projects where the borrower will not, or is unable to, comply with the underlying social and environmental policies and procedures that organizations have established in implementing the principles.

The Equator Principles provide a process framework that is underpinned by the standards of the IFC. There are ten principles – the first nine refer to the process of determining and managing environmental and social risk, while the final one requires institutions to report publicly on their application of the principles. They require processes to be in place to:

- categorize finance projects based on the magnitude of potential impacts and risks in accordance with the environmental and social screening criteria of the IFC;
- conduct an assessment of the relevant social and environmental impacts and risks of the proposed project and propose mitigation and management measures relevant and appropriate to the nature and scale of the proposed project;
- establish the project's overall compliance with, or justified deviation from, the applicable IFC Performance Standards and relevant industry-specific guidelines;
- prepare an action plan that addresses the relevant findings and draws on the conclusions of the assessment;
- consult with project-affected communities in a structured and culturally appropriate manner;
- ensure that consultation, disclosure and community engagement continues throughout construction and operation of the project, and that a grievance mechanism is established as part of the management system;

- ensure that review of the assessment, action plan and consultation process documentation is conducted by an independent social or environmental expert not directly associated with the borrower;
- ensure specific elements are covenanted in financing documentation; and
- ensure ongoing monitoring and reporting over the life of the loan.

The IFC's Performance Standards define clients' roles and responsibilities for managing their projects and cover such areas as social and environmental assessment, labour and working conditions, pollution prevention and community health.

HSBC adopted the Equator Principles shortly after their launch in 2003 and extends their use to export finance loans and other facilities where the use of proceeds is known to be directly related to a project. The principles apply to all new project financings globally with total project capital costs of US$10 million or more, and across all industry sectors. In addition, HSBC goes beyond the requirements of the principles by applying them to all project finance transactions covering expansion or upgrade of an existing facility where changes in scale or scope may create significant environmental and/or social impacts, or significantly change the nature or degree of an existing impact. The principles also extend to project finance advisory activities. In these cases, HSBC commits to making the client aware of the content, application and benefits of applying the principles to the anticipated project, and requests that the client communicates to HSBC its intention to adhere to the requirements of the principles when subsequently seeking financing.

HSBC's sector policies

In addition to the Equator Principles, HSBC has developed its own policies for dealing with 'sensitive' sectors – namely, forestry, mining and metals, freshwater infrastructure, energy and chemicals. These are based on the international standards of good practice set out by the IFC, as well as other inputs, such as HSBC's own experience, research and engagement with shareholders. The sector policies set out HSBC's global standards to be followed for all lending or investing in companies or projects operating in the sector concerned, and specify areas where an involvement is prohibited or restricted.

In the development and review of sector policies, HSBC actively seeks and receives input from clients, industry associations, shareholders and non-governmental organizations (NGOs). The policies are issued by the Group Corporate Sustainability Department in collaboration with the appropriate sector team within global banking and markets and with commercial banking. The policies are signed off following review by the Corporate Sustainability Committee of the board and final approval by an internal risk management meeting.

Implementation and reporting

A network of specialist risk managers in 22 countries around the world ensures that the policies are implemented, and the wider risk management community is trained on sustainability risk. HSBC's deputy head of group corporate sustainability also highlights the importance of implementing controls that help employees to act sustainably in an effective manner. Controls such as the standard operating procedures within the credit and risk function and the controls that are built into the internal systems, as well as relevant training, are seen as key to ensuring proper implementation of the Equator Principles and sector policies. These include automated system controls, where flags or triggers prompt certain checks or actions and final approval cannot physically be given unless all necessary steps and sign-offs have been completed. Outside the system controls, further checks and reviews are performed by the compliance and group audit functions and, ultimately, by independent assurance with regard to the information reported under the Equator Principles.

The risk team in group corporate sustainability works with all parts of the business to develop sustainability initiatives and provides specialist guidance on specific transactions. To ensure consistent analysis and clearance procedures, HSBC introduced the Sustainability Risk Rating System, which allows tracking and rating of every corporate customer globally who operates in 'sensitive' sectors and to provide improved data on the group's exposure to sustainability risk. Assessing the environmental and social impacts of providing finance to HSBC's customers and monitoring the implementation of the Equator Principles and sector policies in this way helps to embed them into the overall risk management processes of the group.

HSBC's approach to these sensitive sector transactions is to engage with the client to help them meet its policy standards, with the aim of making a bigger contribution to sustainable development. There is a clear business rationale for this: HSBC's head of sustainability risk says: 'It is in our own interests to work with our customers in this way as the global economic emphasis is shifting increasingly towards long-term sustainable business values.' The bank has a public commitment to exit relationships as a last resort if satisfactory progress is not being achieved and HSBC's specifications outlined in its policies are not met by the client.

The tenth and final Equator Principle requires institutions to report publicly on their application, and in its reporting HSBC seeks to demonstrate the emphasis it places on the transparent implementation of its policies. Detailed reports are provided with year-on-year comparisons, outlining the number of transactions approved in each of the three levels of risk. The value of the loan is provided in each case, providing a financial context to the reporting.

HSBC's *Sustainability Report 2008* also provides data on the implementation of the Forest Land and Forest Products Sector Policy, including the

Table 8.1 The Equator Principles: Transactions vetted by HSBC

Equator Principles: transactions vetted by HSBC	2008		2007		2006	
	No.	Value (US$m)	No.	Value (US$m)	No.	Value (US$m)
Transactions approved	148	6,842	129	8,705	76	5,171
By mandate						
- Lending	100	6,842	103	8,705	76	5,171
- Advisory	48	n/a	26	n/a	n/a	n/a
Loans by category						
- Category A	3	178	7	1,407	1	80
- Category B	59	4,348	57	5,184	41	2,708
- Category C	38	2,316	39	2,114	34	2,383
Loans by type of facility						
- Project finance loans	47	3,508	63	4,516	42	2,921
- Export finance loans	44	2,403	32	2,878	29	1,350
- Mix of project/export finance	9	931	8	1,311	5	900
Transactions declined	1	n/a	4	n/a	4	n/a

Category A: Projects with potentially significant adverse social or environmental impacts that are diverse, irreversible or unprecedented.

Category B: Projects with potentially limited adverse social or environmental impacts that are few in number, generally site-specific, largely reversible and readily addressed through mitigation measures.

Category C: Projects with minimal or no social or environmental impacts.

Source: HSBC (2008b, p17)

percentage of clients who are compliant, non-compliant and near-compliant, both by value of loans and by number of clients. The group states that it plans to report more widely on other sectors in the future.

The impact of adopting the Equator Principles is viewed positively by the organizations involved. The Equator Principles' website (www.equator-principles.com) states that the Equator Principles Financial Institutions (EPFIs):

> ... have not seen any decline in business because of adoption, application or implementation of the Equator Principles over the past three years. Indeed, the Equator Principles have been championed by the project finance business heads of participating EPFIs. They continue to believe that having a framework for the industry will lead to greater learning among project finance institutions on environmental and social issues, and that having greater expertise in these areas will better enable them to advise clients and control risks. In other words, they continue to believe it is good for business.

Integration of responses to environmental impacts of HSBC's business and culture

The Equator Principles and sector policies are one way in which HSBC has responded to the social, environmental and economic concerns that specifically affect financial institutions in terms of their core business (Chen and Macve, 2010). This part of the chapter looks at some of the ways in which HSBC has embedded management of environmental impacts, risks and opportunities into its day-to-day operations – in particular, those relating to the issues of climate change. It also looks at the potential benefits that involvement in climate change initiatives can have for both the workforce and the business as a whole.

Operational environmental management

Energy use is HSBC's most significant direct environmental impact. The remainder of the group's environmental footprint arises from water and paper use, carbon dioxide emissions from business travel, and production of waste. From 2008, new four-year targets were set for reducing consumption of energy and water, and production of waste and carbon dioxide from energy. These apply to HSBC's offices and branches in 23 countries and territories where 91 per cent of employees are located, and to its global service and technology centres. The targets and progress towards them are reported externally in the group's *Sustainability Report* (HSBC, 2008b, p21). The overall achievement of the group targets are supported by the existence of environmental targets within the scorecards that form part of the appraisal and reward system, although these are only applicable to certain individuals within the organization and as such may therefore have a limited impact in driving changes in underlying behaviours.

Prior to 2004, when HSBC invested in a group-wide online system, relevant sustainability data was collected via a series of spreadsheets. The online system, which was tailored for HSBC's specific requirements, collates energy, water, waste and carbon dioxide emissions data on a half-yearly or quarterly basis from 37 countries, representing 95 per cent of HSBC employees. Some 200 named individuals have responsibility for ensuring that the appropriate data is accurately gathered, calculated and entered, including responsibility for measurement and estimation where 'actual' data is not available (e.g. due to the nature of some environmental parameters such as carbon dioxide emissions). HSBC sees several benefits from the implementation of the online system:

- The use of a common format of data collection helps to prevent errors and facilitates the identification of variances.
- Triggers are built into the system at set intervals that prompt the input of data on a timely basis.

- Controls, such as a hierarchy of approvals, are automated within the system, helping to ensure that the data goes through all the necessary levels of review and sign-off.
- Training and additional information and explanations are incorporated within the system, which can help to educate users and should consequently improve levels of data consistency and accuracy.

Operationally, HSBC has contracted out certain activities to service companies specializing in the sustainable management of business services and the provision of facilities management and other support services, which provides the flexibility to adapt to changing needs and circumstances – for example, the outsourcing of a variety of support services centred on integrated property management and site management at HSBC retail branches.

This approach indicates at least three possible consequences of out sourcing:

1 It creates a market that specializes in and provides scope for knowledge transfer, which in turn provides efficiency gains for a wider range of companies.
2 It provides the client with the flexibility to adapt to changing needs and circumstances.
3 It potentially decreases the pressure to internally educate and monitor staff.

The environment and sustainability manager for corporate real estate notes a significant dependence on external companies for monitoring, recording and advising on sustainability issues. This is logical given the expertise, resources and technology available to the external contractor. Overall, there is a clear distinction between branch management (where the manager deals with banking issues) and facility management (where the bricks and mortar are expressly dealt with). Usually a range of environmental issues would be covered in the monitoring, including usage of lights and personal computers, air conditioning and heating, and weekend energy consumption.

This dependence on external suppliers means that branch staff do not, themselves, need to manage and monitor sustainability issues. In some cases this could be more cost-effective than trying to change ingrained underlying behaviours of employees. Conversely, the outsourcing approach could potentially lead to a situation where employees feel less committed to sustainability issues than if they were given responsibility for such matters. This is not to say that HSBC considers employee commitment to be unimportant. The environment and sustainability manager noted that the out-sourcing approach would not preclude more sustainability-oriented objectives being included in an individual's specific job or role. HSBC also runs a number of initiatives to encourage employee participation in, and commitment to, sustainability matters, such as a training programme for Climate Champions, some of which are explored later in this chapter.

The chain of partnerships to monitor and facilitate buildings and branch maintenance and sustainability creates a web of connection and possible scope for efficiency gains in knowledge and technology transfer. For each building or property, the actual consumption is compared to the benchmarks and circulated to the relevant facilities managers for the particular buildings. A typical report broadly monitors electricity and gas usage and tracks the sum of these two. Information about the type of office is provided (i.e. in this case whether it is a branch office (and subcategories within) or a call centre, the size of the premises, a code to capture specifics as to the type of air conditioning, level of refurbishment, running hours, quality of computer and communications rooms, and whether the sites include catering kitchens). The gas and energy consumption is then benchmarked against 'good' and 'typical' consumption for each property. Any learning observed through a particular site (provided it was not confidential) would be conveyed to the rest of the contractor's organization and the benefits would be passed on to other clients.

The use of facility management suppliers also provides further scope for enhancing the information and experience web. For instance, Glovers Constructing Partnerships, a Lancashire-based company, was engaged in a series of external inspections and building surveying for over 400 properties of HSBC through Carillion Facilities Management. In their description of this project, Glovers stated: 'The expertise gained by Glovers on this project is easily transferrable to any large-scale stock condition or asset management survey programme.' This is just one example of how the web of knowledge and information on facilities management and support services can become highly specialized and result in higher efficiency gains through contracting.

Cultural and behavioural change

As Stephen Green, HSBC's group chairman, recently noted:

> We should remember that no amount of rules will be sufficient if an organization's culture does not encourage people to do the right thing. It is the responsibility of boards to supervise, and management to embed, a sustainable culture into the very fibre of the organization. For HSBC, this is fundamental. (HSBC, 2009)

One way in which HSBC is trying to engage employees across the bank in sustainability issues is by transferring responsibility for delivering environmental management programmes away from the Corporate Sustainability Department. The aim is to embed responsibility for environmental impacts within relevant departments of the business where it can become part of 'business as usual'. As part of this, in 2008, HSBC introduced environmental criteria into personal performance objectives for the Group Management Board and regional heads. In 2008, the bank established a new working group comprising the heads of sustainability for corporate real estate, information technology (IT) and purchasing, with the aim of embedding the management of its direct impacts within operational business units.

Several of the initiatives that HSBC is involved in provide further opportunity for employee engagement, while also potentially helping to enhance the bank's reputation. For example, HSBC's Global Environmental Efficiency Programme is investing US$90 million over five years (2007 to 2011) to promote innovative and technology-driven environmental initiatives. The projects support HSBC's environmental reduction targets as well as the roll-out of low carbon and environmental technology into its property portfolio and other infrastructure. The programme is viewed by HSBC as a sort of research and development (R&D) project, seen as above and beyond the bank's 'business as usual' investment decision-making. Many of the initiatives that are proposed under the programme are higher risk in nature, and management recognizes that a different business case (e.g. longer pay back periods) may need to be applied. In some cases, the financial benefits may not be quantifiable; but HSBC's willingness to invest in such projects indicates that importance is also attached to less tangible non-financial outcomes that they are seen to generate, such as changes in culture and behaviour. There is also an acceptance that some projects may not work, while others may deliver higher benefits than expected. So, for example, a small-scale wind-turbine project had to be abandoned, while a solar photovoltaic project is exceeding expectations. HSBC has an international network of employees with specific responsibilities for measuring and managing performance against targets in these areas. Performance against the initiatives is captured as part of the reporting within the CRF, discussed further below.

Climate change initiatives

In response to the need to shift the organizational culture, HSBC established a major partnership programme. Launched in 2007, the HSBC Climate Partnership is a five-year US$100 million commitment to work with The Climate Group, Earthwatch, the Smithsonian Tropical Research Institute and the World Wide Fund for Nature (WWF) to combat climate change by inspiring individuals, businesses and governments worldwide. One of the aims of the partnership is to engage HSBC employees through the Climate Champions Programme. Five regional climate centres have been opened in partnership with Earthwatch in the US, Brazil, India, the UK and China. Climate Champions from HSBC complete an intensive Earthwatch-designed residential training programme on climate change and sustainability to equip them to initiate change within their business area.

HSBC is creating a network of champions with the knowledge and remit to incorporate considerations for climate change within their roles all across the group. Over 800 HSBC employees have trained as Climate Champions at the half-way points of the five-year programme. The objective is that the Climate Champions will themselves create a project incorporating sustainability elements that is related to their day job and therefore has direct relevance to them.

In line with the strategic themes that the bank sees as vital to future lending and investment activity, the HSBC Climate Partnership organizations are also involved to help develop understanding, identify future trends, and prepare the business for the risks and opportunities associated with the water industry, the forestry sector and emerging markets – specifically, China and India. The growing employee task force of Climate Champions, created as part of the HSBC Climate Partnership, also has a role to play in identifying and developing new sustainable business opportunities.

Programmes and initiatives may also combine commercial opportunities with reputational benefits. Examples of this are HSBC's involvement in the Climate Principles and its achievement of carbon neutral status. HSBC attained carbon neutrality in 2005. For HSBC, the business rationale for carbon neutrality involves using carbon neutrality as a tool to encourage further efficiency, as the cost of the offsets is charged to the HSBC entity concerned. It also saw reputational benefit to be gained from being the first bank to become carbon neutral.

In 2008, HSBC chaired the development, by the Climate Group, of the Climate Principles. The Climate Principles are a voluntary code to guide best practice across the financial sector to deal with the risks and opportunities of climate change. Guidance is tailored to suit each part of the finance sector. For example, retail banks address the level of customer enthusiasm for tackling climate change and the barriers currently preventing them from taking action; corporate and investment banks work on financing solutions to facilitate investment in low carbon technologies and greenhouse gas (GHG) reduction projects, as well as measuring the climate impacts of their investments. In addition, investment banks will build expertise to support development of trading in emissions, weather derivatives, renewable energy credits and other climate-related commodities. Project financiers will also request that clients assess project GHG emissions and seek reduction and offset solutions.

During the same year, an HSBC Climate Team was established, including representatives from each of HSBC's customer groups, global businesses and key product areas, to ensure adherence to the Climate Principles and to formalize the sharing of best practice across the group on climate change. The information and data collected to support HSBC's adherence to the Climate Principles is subject to similar processes and controls to embed in day-to-day decision-making by relevant individuals across different functions as those described earlier in this chapter for the Equator Principles and sector policies.

The companies that have adopted the Equator Principles are required to report on their progress. Following the first year of implementation, the Climate Group, which has facilitated the principles, commissioned Pricewaterhouse-Coopers to conduct a review summarizing progress overall. In time, financial institutions may be expected to produce updates on their implementation of the Climate Principles, which will be integrated within existing sustainability or wider corporate reporting.

The HSBC Climate Team enables learning to be shared between parts of the group where climate-related products and services are being developed. One example is the HSBC Climate Change Benchmark Index, launched in 2007. The breadth of the companies listed in the index goes beyond clean energy and the basis for stock inclusion focuses on revenues generated from climate-related services and products. The index gives clients the opportunity to invest in specific elements of global climate change on a selective and focused basis, and enables investors and asset allocators to track and monitor climate-related investments and the transition from a high to low carbon economy for listed companies on a global, regional and country basis. In practice, this means that clients can build a climate change portfolio with targeted exposure to one country or region, which may better fit their overall investment strategy and objectives.

The role of sustainability reporting

An analysis of HSBC's sustainability reporting from 2000 to 2008 reveals a continuing evolution of style, content and presentation. The early years (i.e. 2001 to 2004) illustrate an emphasis on community investment, with grassroots contributions in terms of education, community activities, etc., with a smattering of environmental issues. These were reported on in a rather ad hoc and unconnected basis. This changed from 2005 with an increasing focus on environmental issues, especially those that could be quantified and presented in charts and tables. By 2008, the report covered a range of sustainability issues, as well as the risks and opportunities, and incorporated the principles of the CRF, which HSBC first adopted in 2007. This section looks at the evolution of what is now the *Sustainability Report* and the influences upon it in more detail.

Much of the material in the 2000 to 2002 reports focuses descriptively on each geographic region in turn, with case studies of local success stories or efforts interspersed throughout the report. In 2002, the shift towards environmental reporting becomes more evident. The section on the environment discusses how environmental reporting systems are being implemented and target reductions set in place. For the first time, more detailed data on direct environmental impacts is provided: energy, travel, greenhouse gas emissions, freshwater estimated capture, and waste disposed estimated capture are given in disaggregate form for the main geographic regions.

In 2003, HSBC published the first report where an attempt is made to present a business case for corporate social responsibility. The 2003 report also emphasizes the robustness of internal systems and responsible financing issues, and continues to expand the detail of environmental impact data.

In 2004 the importance of climate change is acknowledged with more detailed tables and graphs, using the Global Reporting Initiative (GRI) guidelines for the first time. At the same time there were developments in International Financial Reporting Standards that would require greater reporting on emission rights and allowances, which themselves arose from the implementation of the European Union Emissions Trading Scheme. Against this background, the 2004 report contains a number of climate change related information: HSBC became a founding member of the Climate Group; the offsetting of CO_2 emissions is discussed; and HSBC made a commitment to be the first major bank in the world to become carbon neutral across all of its operations. The external events of 2004 highlight the potential impact that regulation in areas such as financial reporting can have on sustainability reporting, as well as on an organization's strategy and policy decisions. Frequently, however, organizations do not make the link between financial reporting requirements and sustainability reporting.

The HSBC *Corporate Social Responsibility Report 2005* continues the documentation of internal processes and strategy, sustainable growth, anticorruption and microfinance, as well as implementation of the Equator Principles. The reporting, in 2005, presents a shift towards reporting on banking- and finance-related issues that could affect sustainable growth rather than general community-based projects. To further validate HSBC's commitments to these topics, the report also incorporates HSBC's inclusion in external benchmarks such as the Business in the Community Environment Index ranking, the Dow Jones Sustainability Index, FTSE4Good, the AccountAbility Rating of the Fortune Global 100, and Interbrand top 100 brands. A sizeable section of the report is entitled 'Managing for sustainable growth', and this provides considerable documentation of HSBC's processes in this area. The report shows environmental management and reporting as being integrated within the organization.

The 2006 *Corporate Responsibility Report* starts with upfront reporting of financial accounting data, such as profitability and assets across geographic regions and lines of business. The report also emphasizes themes of responsible lending and financing, with details on lending based on the Equator Principles. As in the previous year, the report makes an effort to integrate sustainability issues with management and internal processes. There is extensive discussion on climate change and offsetting carbon emissions. Key economic, social and environmental amounts are all tabulated together in a key facts table.

In 2007 the report differs from previous ones most strikingly in appearance and provides minimal discussion of HSBC's community involvement. The terminology has now changed from 'corporate responsibility' to 'sustainability' – an indication of the centrality of social and environmental issues to the long-term prosperity of the bank. This also reflected an internal shift as responsibility for direct environmental footprint, sustainability risk and business opportunities, and community investment activities were brought together into a department called corporate sustainability. The changes also reflected HSBC's adoption of the CRF. As well as presenting a specific summary of greenhouse gas emissions, waste, resource usage and energy intensity that link financial and non-financial impacts, the report includes broad discussion of a wide range of sustainability risks and impacts, including discussion of many of the initiatives mentioned earlier in this chapter.

Strategic sustainability pursuits do not necessarily find ready translation into economic cost savings, but can positively affect the company's valuation via institutional and individual investor perceptions of the value of such engagements. As sustainability becomes increasingly embedded within the core business of an organization, financial implications are clearer to see, as in the example of sustainability risk reporting at HSBC. Similarly, the wider the definition of corporate sustainability, the closer is the link to long-term financial health of a business.

HSBC has found that the CRF itself can be applied most readily to direct environmental impacts: energy, water, waste and carbon dioxide. The principles of the CRF, however, have much wider application. The way in which the implementation of the Equator Principles is reported is one clear example of how this sustainability commitment is set in a financial context. Importantly, the figures that are communicated are those that are used to monitor application of the Equator Principles internally.

In presentation and emphasis, the 2008 *Sustainability Report* is similar to that of the previous year. HSBC also continues to convey the importance that it attaches to external initiatives. This is further accentuated in the choice of a major audit firm to provide independent assurance on selected information in the report. Mainstream financial information is interwoven with supplementary sustainability information throughout the report.

In studying the development of HSBC reports from 2000 to 2008, a few features are striking. Primarily noticeable is HSBC's drive to adopt a number of external initiatives that offer a useful benchmark, and often include additional voluntary reporting – for example, that relating to the United Nations Global Compact.

HSBC's most recent sustainability reports are designed to complement the group's *Annual Report and Accounts* and *Annual Review*. While the majority of sustainability-related information is contained in the separate *Sustainability Report*, in line with changes to reporting legislation in the Companies Act 2006, the *Annual Report and Accounts* also contains details of the group's sustainability activities that are considered to have the greatest relevance to the success of the company's strategy.

Following the experience of producing sustainability reports for a number of years, HSBC now has a clear reporting strategy. The intended readership for the reports is a global audience of stakeholders with a professional interest in the issues. In line with the broad definition of corporate sustainability outlined earlier, the scope of the reports includes a range of non-financial issues that are considered material to the business. It is worth noting that a tension can be seen here in the use and understanding of the term 'corporate sustainability'. HSBC's Corporate Sustainability Department is responsible for overseeing, developing strategy and representing the group solely on sustainability risk and business development, community investment and management of direct environmental footprint. However, reporting on corporate sustainability also includes employee and customer issues, and details of engagement with other stakeholder groups managed elsewhere in the business. In this regard, sustainability touches on all areas of the business and over time the role of the Corporate Sustainability Department may become less closely involved in operational delivery as responsibility is devolved and sustainability considerations embedded across the organization. This may be regarded as an indication of the continuous change in stakeholder expectations of what corporate sustainability involves and HSBC's response to this.

One final point of note with regard to sustainability reporting is HSBC's decision to have both its carbon neutrality and application of the Equator Principles formally assured by an independent third party. These areas have been selected as suitable for assurance as they are both of interest to stakeholders, particularly the sustainable and responsible investment (SRI) community and NGOs, they both utilize a set of quantifiable data and are required to follow a clear process, and both have significant financial implications for the group. The decision to obtain external assurance would seem to indicate that stakeholders are increasingly interested in sustainability reporting. Feedback from SRI contacts suggests that the involvement of a formal assurance organization in the reporting process does provide some comfort that proper rigour is being applied.

Conclusions

The impact of information conveyed in HSBC's publication of a sustainability report based on the CRF is reflective of an increasingly standardized and uniform approach to what is seen to matter in sustainability reporting. The CRF does not alter the diversity of approaches that are used by organizations to report on sustainability related matters, whether they are financial, social, environmental or other. However, it does bring together in a coherent comparability-enhancing manner those dimensions of sustainability that are regarded, in the current context, to matter to stakeholders. HSBC's sustainability report evidences this strongly.

HSBC recognizes that what it does as an organization, and what and how this is reported, affects stakeholder perceptions. Given the diversity of HSBC's shareholder base, measures of short-term economic impact are perceived to hold value for certain stakeholders; but longer-term considerations and investments, the current impact of which often enhance the organization's image (as well as having potential non-financial or indirect financial benefits in the future) are also seen to be valuable. So HSBC engages in both types of sustainability resource allocations and reports the results. Strategic sustainability pursuits may not find ready translation into economic cost savings, but can positively impact upon the company's valuation via institutional and individual investor perceptions of the value of such engagements. An economic effect thus does tie in to strategic reputational and branding motivations, though not necessarily with the preciseness of quantifiable savings or cost effects.

Successful embedding of sustainability often requires a different and more open mindset, and a space where innovation is allowed and encouraged facilitates such new ways of thinking. An organization must not only to be prepared to take a longer-term perspective in terms of the timing of any potential financial benefits, but there also needs to be an acceptance that not all initiatives will be successful and, for those that are, the benefits may not be financially quantifiable. In other words, the parameters for the business case for some sustainability decisions will differ from those used in 'traditional' decision-making, as is the case with HSBC's Global Environmental Efficiency Programme. The external reporting of such initiatives can also help to encourage and facilitate the embedding of sustainability internally.

A clear governance framework to support the management of sustainability initiatives needs to be in place, including appropriate targets and commitments and clear policies. However, embedding cannot be achieved without a supportive organizational structure and, importantly, the buy-in of senior management to allow such an environment to be created. The implementation of standard procedures and controls, such as those automated within information systems, is viewed by HSBC as an important facilitator in embedding sustainability in terms of day-to-day operations; but embedding goes beyond simply following rules and processes – it is also about the underlying culture of the organization, its management, employees and other stakeholders along the value chain.

One also observes the wider impact of HSBC's sustainability reporting via supply-chain linkages. Sustainability practices become propagated across organizations because of both the adoption of the CRF, as well as the nature of operational activity linkages. HSBC's use of Carillion's integrated property management services makes it a possible conduit for advancing particular sustainability practices through to Carillion's wider customer base, whose sustainability practices it monitors and possibly reshapes, allowing good practice to be more quickly shared between different organizations. This is characteristic of firms that act as nodes within wider value chain industrial contexts. An organization can influence and affect its customers, and if it itself has operational practices which are, in turn, influenced by providers of services on which it relies, then the potential exists for transmitting sustainability practices within and across industrial value chains. This is so particularly for a lender such as HSBC, which has a wide customer base spanning many industries and geographic borders.

Ultimately, reporting under the CRF brings together all of these different strands, which are driven by two main forces: one operational and more quantifiable in financial terms, and a set of strategic pursuits, which are less easily measured via traditional accounting measurement mechanisms. The adoption of relevant voluntary guidance, such as the Equator Principles, can help to bring these together in terms of external reporting. For example, in HSBC's reporting of the Equator Principles, quantitative financial and non-financial information is brought together side-by-side to clearly communicate outcomes from applying the Equator Principles, putting these outcomes in the context of the number and value of project finance loans.

What ultimately emerges through the adoption of CRF is a more standard approach to the communication of an organization's sustainability activities – both operational and strategic. The application of the CRF by different organizations enables the unique reporting focus of individual companies to be maintained, while also allowing for some level of uniformity of approach. This potentially enhances comparability across organizations and demonstrates the impact of these activities along financial conventions to a certain extent, through the linkage of financial and non-financial information. Sustainability reporting that aligns to the principles of the CRF thus becomes more accounting convention orientated and is a significant step on the way to achieving reporting that supports the information needs of long-term investors and reflects the interconnected nature of environmental, social and governance factors – the ultimate goal of The Prince's Accounting for Sustainability Project.

Acknowledgements

We wish to thank HSBC executives for their time and resources. We also thank Carillion plc for allowing interview access and internal documents.

References

Chen, X. and Macve, R. (LSE Working Paper, 2010) 'The "Equator Principles": A success for voluntary codes?', *Journal of Accounting, Auditing and Accountability*
HSBC (2008a) *Annual Report and Accounts*, HSBC Holdings plc, London
HSBC (2008b) *Sustainability Report 2008*, HSBC Holdings plc, London
HSBC (2009) *Annual Report, May*, HSBC Holdings plc, London

nine

'One Aviva, Twice the Value': Connecting Sustainability at Aviva plc

Martin Brigham, Paraskevi Vicky Kiosse
and David Otley

Box 9.1 Prologue: Helping the war effort

The urgent need for economy in the use of fuel and restriction of the use of power was well recognised, and the formation of the Ministry of Fuel and Power only served to emphasize the necessity. No doubt a helpful response has been made at all Offices of the Allied Companies, but figures are not available at the moment. The result at 24 Cornhill may be of interest.

Two stewards were appointed from the staff of each floor to the building to supervise the saving of light wherever possible, and in the main, the delicate task was carried out with consideration and tact, resulting in the following savings: 266,766 units used in 1942, 196,196 units in 1943, a saving of 26 per cent.

Naturally, this diminution of light, causing in some cases eye-strain and headaches, was not welcomed, but it was tolerated as part of our contribution to the War Effort and in the hope the necessity will pass soon.

Box 9.1 CONTINUED

All short journeys by lift were stopped, and everybody was expected to walk two floors – a regulation that might well be enforced in the post-war years, as we were getting lazy in this respect and all the better for the exercise. Of course, this rule does not apply to any suffering from physical disability.

The period of artificial heating was limited and heat was reduced. At times we felt cold, but temperatures rose as we reflected that our enemies were the primary cause of our discomfort and anathematized them accordingly.

The result in power and heating ... may be explained to the uniniti-ated that the total saving was equivalent to $116\frac{1}{2}$ tons of coal.

Table 9.1

	Power Units used	Heating Units used
1942	52,960	519,230
1943	43,274	366,300
Saving	9,686 = 18%	152,930 = 29%

Source: Extract from The Cuao Link (Commercial Union 1943, pp76–77), courtesy of the Aviva Group plc archive, Surrey House, Norwich

---

'One Aviva, one world'

'Helping the war effort': so reported the staff magazine of the Commercial Union in the last period of a large-scale mobilization for resource conservation and financial restraint. Today's preoccupation with climate change has resonances with previous concerns about finite natural resources and financial stability. However, in contrast to previous eras, the sustainability of the natural environment can no longer be taken for granted, nor are ecological impacts considered as external to the operations of companies. As we look to the future, after the financial crisis, individual, organizational and societal responses to ecological changes in a connected and complex world have become one of the leitmotifs of our century.

'One Aviva, twice the value': this is the vision for the future announced in October 2007 by Andrew Moss, Aviva's group chief executive. Transforming Aviva into a company able to compete on a global scale arose out of a series of mergers within the insurance sector that led to its formation – between Commercial Union and General Accident in 1998, and with Norwich Union in 2000. Aviva is now a global provider of life and general insurance, long-term savings, pension products and fund management, with operations in 28 countries, 54,000 employees and around 50 million customers. Aviva, the group's worldwide name, was introduced in 2002, replacing the UK brand name Norwich Union in June 2009.

Taking Aviva's global strategy and vision as our cue, in this chapter we cast the spotlight on Aviva's global sustainability initiatives and steps taken to embed these into business processes. We first introduce Aviva Group plc and outline its corporate responsibility, environmental and sustainability practices. We then present four important themes in Aviva's approach to embedding sustainability: implementing connected reporting for environmental performance; embedding carbon-neutral operations; managing stakeholders and the value chain; and the integration of sustainability within core business products through sustainable and responsible investment. The penultimate section outlines Aviva's reporting systems for corporate responsibility and sustainability. We conclude the chapter with lessons and implications for those thinking about how to manage corporate change in the direction of sustainability.

Linking responsibility and sustainability

Aviva has embedded a wide range of corporate responsibility (CR) and sustainability policies and practices over the last decade. The company currently reports CR under five integrated themes: customers, environment, people, suppliers and communities. Aviva produced its first annual corporate social responsibility (CSR) report in 2002, extending a report focused on environmental issues that had been initiated in 1999. Before this, environmental concerns were less developed – Commercial Union began, for example, an internal environmental programme in 1997 after the appointment of its first environmental manager.

In addition to producing a standalone CR report, Aviva's sustainability activities are also reported in the *Annual Report and Accounts* using the Connected Reporting Framework (CRF). This integration is consistent with Aviva's overall approach to responsibility and sustainability, which covers operations worldwide and is based on interlocking levels of governance and activity across the company. There is significant board level support: the Board Corporate Responsibility Committee, established by the current chairman in 2006, comprises the chairman, three non-executive directors and the group chief executive, and meets quarterly. Specialist CR professionals report to this committee and are responsible for implementing the CR strategy and integrating sustainability within operations and other functions across Aviva, in addition to monitoring and reporting performance. The Global Corporate Responsibility Advisory Group meets twice a year and provides additional group-wide input. An internal Corporate Responsibility Summit also brings together corporate responsibility representatives from across the Aviva Group once a year.

Taking part in citizenship activities is an integral part of Aviva's approach to demonstrating leadership in responsible and sustainable practice. Engagement with forums and networks builds consensus on issues and facilitates inter-organizational learning. Michelle Wolfe, a senior CR manager remarks: 'Aviva

**Greenhouse
gas emissions**

Benchmark information
Carbon Disclosure Project
Score 83 out of 100

BREEAM minimum ranking
'Good' for new build and
refurbishment

Non-financial indicators

Aviva's CO₂ emissions

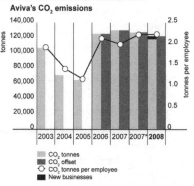

▨ CO₂ tonnes
■ CO₂ offset
○ CO₂ tonnes per employee
■ New businesses

* The 2007 CO₂ emissions have been restated. Each
year the conversion factor for electricity generation
varies. Aviva restates these figures every four years
including 2007 figures.

Direct company impacts

**Cash flow performance: CO₂
emissions**
Total cost of offsetting 105% of
our global CO₂ emissions –
128,931 tonnes in 2008 – was in
the region of £750,000. We incur
up to a 2% premium for zero
emission/renewable electricity
compared to fossil fuels.
Following the publication of the
2008 UK DEFRA carbon reporting
guidelines, at the end of our
current electricity contract we will
no longer pay a premium for zero
emission electricity in the UK.

2008 has been a benign year for
weather-related claims, although
we do see a trend in the
increased incidents of such events
and believe the occurrence of
these will rise with climate
change.

**Cash flow performance:
Other significant emissions**
Our operations do not generate
material quantities of any other
significant greenhouse gases.

Waste

Benchmark information
200 kgs of waste per employee
per year

Recycling rate of 60–70%
(BRE Office toolkit)

Non-financial indicators

Aviva's waste

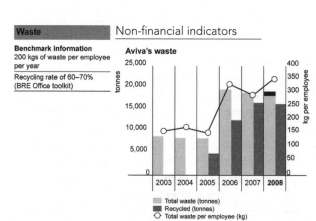

▨ Total waste (tonnes)
■ Recycled (tonnes)
○ Total waste per employee (kg)
■ New businesses

Direct company impacts

**Cash flow performance:
Hazardous and non-hazardous
waste**
Total disposal cost for hazardous
and non-hazardous waste in the
UK was £629,000 (2007: £464,000),
which includes UK landfill tax.

**Cash flow performance:
Conservation investment**
Total capital expenditure for
storage and recycling in the UK
was minimal (2007: £200,000).

Figure 9.1 Environmental performance

Source: Aviva Group plc (2009, pp18–19)

Commentary

Our performance, strategy and targets

In 2008, our total CO_2 emissions decreased with all businesses reporting consistently on their footprint and applying practices to reduce their emissions. They have achieved this by using technologies, changing behaviours, and by purchasing zero emission and renewable electricity. We anticipate our carbon footprint reducing to 108,000 tonnes in 2009 through our divestment of AutoWindscreens and AGS – 10,000 tonnes – and by reducing business travel. There will be an increase from our new data centre reaching full capacity but expect that this will reduce over time through a programme of virtualisation and consolidation of data.

Our RAC business has fitted speed limiters on its breakdown vehicles providing an anticipated saving on fuel and associated carbon emissions of 7.4% over the year to October 2009. We are trialling retrofitted hybrid drive systems on two of the breakdown vehicles which could save up to another 25% in associated emissions in 2008/09. We will continue to purchase zero emission/ renewable electricity where it is practical to do so. Currently 65% (2007: 61%) of our electricity worldwide is purchased from zero emission sources. Our remaining emissions will continue to be offset on a retrospective basis compensating for the carbon output of our consumption of non-renewable sourced electricity, gas and oil from buildings and business travel.

Indirect impacts

Products/Suppliers/Investments

We anticipate having a complete UK carbon footprint of the properties we own through our Property Fund managed by Aviva Investors. Under the new UK Government Carbon Reduction Commitment scheme, electricity, gas and oil used in the properties will be subject to an additional cost of £12 per tonne.

We regularly review the viability of new products and services that can encourage customers to reduce their own CO_2 emissions. Our Prestige Property Owners Policy includes a free energy assessment, advice and guidance on energy saving technologies and reassessment to demonstrate improvements.

This year the UK general insurance business worked with public bodies to create a best practice template in flood planning, involving local authorities, emergency services and utilities companies. The planning should help improve response times, raise awareness and reduce damage. See www.floodplanuk.org. This development complements the work completed earlier in the year. See www.floodsim.com

Aviva Investors' new European Renewable Energy Fund specialises in developing and financing renewable energy infrastructure projects in the European Union. The Environmental Technology Fund and New Energy Fund managed by Delta Lloyd asset management business and the Renewable Energy and Clean Technologies fund in Aviva Spain focuses on climate change mitigation.

Commentary

Our performance, strategy and targets

In 2008, the total volume of waste generated has increased globally by 2% and the proportion of waste recycled has decreased by 4% on 2007 data to 84%. Our waste figures will reduce by some 6,000 tonnes due to the divestment of AutoWindscreens.

The learning from our bin-less office system is being applied to the Canadian business in 2009 and complements their efforts in 2008 around the composting of organic waste.

The rebranding of our businesses in the UK, Ireland and Poland to Aviva in 2009 and 2010 will inevitably generate increased volumes of waste. This, however, is being closely monitored to ensure this waste is kept to a minimum.

Indirect impacts

Products/Suppliers/Investments

We are working with our upstream partners to eliminate waste from the business through take back of packaging and switching to biodegradable wrapping etc. Environmental clauses are included in contracts with suppliers. Each new supplier has to sign up to Aviva's CR Supplier Code of Conduct – focusing on environmental impact as well as human rights and social issues.

We adhere to all building regulations (insulation, proper disposal of waste material including building waste and white goods) and we are members of a responsible motor repair network which disposes of waste and spare parts in accordance with sustainable environmental practices.

Continued

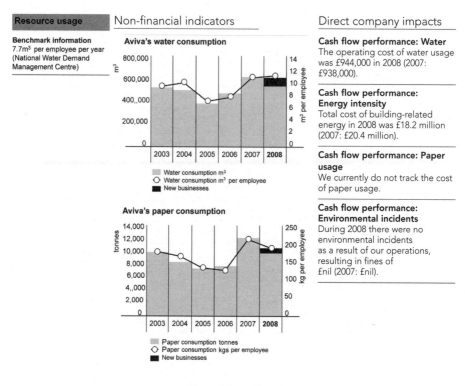

Resource usage	Non-financial indicators	Direct company impacts

Benchmark information
7.7m³ per employee per year
(National Water Demand
Management Centre)

Cash flow performance: Water
The operating cost of water usage
was £944,000 in 2008 (2007:
£938,000).

**Cash flow performance:
Energy intensity**
Total cost of building-related
energy in 2008 was £18.2 million
(2007: £20.4 million).

**Cash flow performance: Paper
usage**
We currently do not track the cost
of paper usage.

**Cash flow performance:
Environmental incidents**
During 2008 there were no
environmental incidents
as a result of our operations,
resulting in fines of
£nil (2007: £nil).

Figure 9.1 *continued*

participates in numerous external forums to contribute to developing the external agenda on important CR issues.'

This proactive involvement in corporate citizenship includes external associations for policy development and advocacy forums. Since 1998, Aviva has chaired the Forge Group, a sector-led initiative comprised of insurers and banks with government industry associations as partners. Aviva oversaw the development of guidance on *Environmental Management and Reporting 2000*, the business case for CSR best practice in 2002 and the *Managing Climate Change in Financial Services* guidance in 2007. It signed the United Nations Global Compact in 2001, was a founder member of the UK network of the Global Compact in 2003, and is the co-author and founding signatory of the ClimateWise principles. Aviva joined The Prince's Accounting for Sustainability Project (A4S) in 2007 and its current group corporate responsibility director, Marie Sigsworth, sits on the Executive Board, having taken over from her predecessor, Louella Eastman. It was one of the first companies to fully integrate the CRF into its *Annual Report and Accounts* – an approach to reporting we outline in detail in the next section.

Aviva is one of three UK listed insurers included in the Dow Jones Sustainability World and Stoxx Indexes and is a member of the FTSE4Good

Commentary

Our performance, strategy and targets

Our focus on water reduction increased in 2008; Aviva's businesses in the UK set a target of 10% reduction. Trials of flow straighteners for taps, reduced water consumption urinals, and water saving devices on toilet cisterns have been successful, resulting in a combined reduction to 5.5m³ per employee per year at the test locations. A group target of 4% has been set for 2009, through the sharing of these good practices around the world.

Our energy strategy is to invest in new energy-saving technology and to reduce our energy dependency on fossil fuels. We are prepared to pay up to 2% premium for purchasing electricity from renewable/zero emission sources.

We have trialled the use of boiler optimisation valves fitted to all our boilers. The trial suggested a reduction in gas use of 15% and our investment of £154,000 should see a positive return in just 38 weeks.

Capital expenditure work on energy conservation is proceeding with a payback period of less than three years.

Our strategy is to increase the use of recycled content paper, while reducing overall paper use. Cost and quality of recycled papers are now comparable with virgin content paper.

We have introduced self-selection options, which enable policyholders to receive and save policy documentation online, thus reducing paper usage, printing and postage cost.

Indirect impacts

Products/Suppliers/Investments

Work is continuing with our marketing departments and suppliers to provide marketing materials with recycled content and remanufactured stationery products.

Shareholders have been asked to make the switch to receive company information electronically including the electronic transfer of dividends.

Index Series. The company has received various awards, including the Global Diversity and Innovation Award at the World Diversity Leaders Summit in 2007, hosted by the United Nations Global Compact. Aviva was awarded the Best in Class recognition by the Carbon Disclosure Project in 2007 and in the Carbon Disclosure Leadership Index for FTSE350 and Global 500 in 2009.

Connected reporting

Interest in accounting for environmental and social impacts began to emerge during the 1990s in recognition that such issues are likely to be significant features of the future corporate landscape.

Aviva is an exemplar within the financial services sector in being able to provide figures for carbon dioxide (CO_2) emissions, resources and waste dating back to the early 2000s on a comparable basis. Aviva was the first insurer in the UK to report on environmental performance indicators – greenhouse gas emissions, energy, resource use and waste. Aviva's legacy company, CGU, had established an environmental management reporting system, compiling figures for paper usage (including recycled materials), energy consumption in buildings (i.e. electricity and gas) and for transport (including car, rail and air travel), and waste (print cartridges, neon tubes, office furniture and so forth) from 2000 onwards, with waste reported from 2001.

While Aviva is unusual in having an archive of environmental information dating back a decade, it does suggest that there are established ways of measuring direct environmental impacts – energy and water use measured through metering and so on – which can be readily drawn upon. From 2007, Aviva reported its environmental impacts using the CRF. Aviva currently uses the framework to report on what it sees as its key environmental impacts – greenhouse gas emissions, energy usage, water use and waste. The CRF provides a format for reporting on sustainability that integrates economic, financial and sustainability information in a connected way, showing the link between a company's strategy, and the financial costs and benefits of sustainability impacts and performance. Information on sustainability is presented alongside financial information to provide a more complete picture of the organization's performance – to demonstrate that sustainability and financial performance cannot be viewed in isolation.

The latest CRF figures and commentary from Aviva are shown here together with comparatives over the last five years. Figure 9.1 is extracted from the 2009 *Corporate Responsibility Report* (Aviva Group plc, 2009). This information is also reported in the 2008 *Annual Report and Accounts* (Aviva Group plc, 2008a, pp78–79) in the 'People and responsibility' section of the report.

The CRF provides clear summaries of environmental performance. Zelda Bentham, group senior environment manager, suggests that one of the valuable lessons of this form of reporting is the way in which data can be collated to provide reliable evidence of how sustainability performance is interdependent with financial performance:

> The data was getting too unwieldy and we were collecting too much information ... audiences just wanted to know the headlines, they didn't really want to know how many plastic cups we recycled in a year ... [it's about] pulling out the important things to the company.

Since 2008 Aviva has begun to publish metrics in the form of key performance measures across all dimensions of corporate responsibility, including environmental metrics for greenhouse gas emissions, water and waste. The following is from the 2008 CSR report:

> Now for the first time, we are publishing CSR key performance indicators (KPIs) across more areas of our business. Some of these KPIs were monitored in 2007, and will be strengthened in 2008, while others are being introduced. We have also established targets for many KPIs in 2008. (Aviva Group plc, 2008b, p8)

Integrating sustainability reporting and targets within the *Annual Report and Accounts* has meant that sustainability has become a part of Aviva's mainstream reporting activity. Reporting across Aviva has also become a platform for managing change, demonstrating the 'business case' for sustainability through figures that can be compared across Aviva's regions and businesses, and over time. While Aviva has reported on environmental impacts for a decade, the deployment of the CRF has fostered a greater dynamism between environmental considerations and organizational strategy and practice. Louella Eastman, former group corporate responsibility director, states that there is a 'double cost saving from decreasing energy use – that of payment for the energy and payment for the carbon offsetting ... water costs were highlighted for the first time, resulting in action to reduce usage with financial benefit'.

Aviva's experience of the CRF also suggests that collaboration across internal organizational boundaries is a significant effect of this form of connected reporting – bringing together people from finance, estates management, human resources and CR. Sharing best practice with other organizations and communicating with a wide range of stakeholders such as shareholders and investors is a further important dimension of the impact of the CRF.

Climate change and carbon-neutral Aviva

In recognition of the importance of addressing climate change, Aviva announced in December 2006 that it would be the first insurer to carbon neutralize its operations worldwide on a retrospective basis from 2006. As a provider of financial and insurance services, Aviva's direct carbon footprint is comprised of emissions from business travel and energy use in office buildings and data centres. Aviva continues to reduce carbon emissions through monitoring resource usage and purchasing renewable electricity, but also by offsetting residual emissions, a mechanism seen as an important element of the transition to a low carbon economy by providing private-sector funding for green investment. The impact of the CRF is evident on Aviva's approach to managing carbon emissions as it provides the basis for reporting CO_2, but also facilitates reductions in emissions by identifying areas for improvement and internalizing environmental impacts.

Aviva's strategic decision to become carbon neutral was driven by a range of factors. These included its continuing emphasis on minimizing its contribution to environmental impacts; proactively identifying future risks, particularly climate change; maintaining the position as a 'thought leader' in its sector; fostering the development of new forms of competitive advantage (such as sustainable and responsible investment and general insurance products with an environmental dimension, such as digital flood mapping and the 'Pay As You Drive' motor insurance); and encouraging employee engagement at work and home.

Aviva's decision to push for carbon-neutral operations worldwide has board-level support. Aviva's chairman announced the move to becoming a carbon-neutral company, giving a clear insight into the strategic importance attached to this issue:

> Aviva's purpose is to provide prosperity and peace of mind to our customers. Sustainability, an issue of global significance to our stakeholders and to our business internationally, is central to achieving that purpose... I'm very pleased that we have managed to find projects that not only offset our carbon output, but also promote local community benefits. (Lord Sharman of Redlynch OBE, Aviva Group plc, 2008b, p2)

The remaining carbon is offset through projects sourced by carbon brokers and directly with project owners. The total cost of offsetting 105 per cent of global CO_2 emissions – 128,931 tonnes in 2008 – was around UK£750,000. Offsetting emphasizes the win–win between Aviva and offsetting projects, mostly in developing countries. Projects include 'green' cement production in The Netherlands and Ireland, a biogas project in Sri Lanka, the provision of efficient wood-burning stoves in Africa, treadle pumps for irrigation in India and wind turbines in India and China.

Over the last nine years Aviva's emissions have reduced by 14 per cent 'in the context of strong company growth' (Aviva Group plc, 2009, p3). In 2007 the then newly formed Energy Steering Group developed a UK energy policy – the 5, 4, 3 Strategy – with a target of a 5 per cent reduction for electricity, 4 per cent for gas and CO_2, and 3 per cent for water, targets which Aviva were able to meet. Furthermore, Andrew Moss, reporting on 2008, states that 'Our performance in battling climate change saw our CO_2 emissions from energy consumption down by 6.6 per cent this year' (Aviva Group plc, 2009, p3).

Examples of the kinds of practical changes to organizational routines that Aviva has made in reducing its carbon footprint include reducing business travel by hosting meetings through high-definition videoconferencing (telepresence) facilities (available from London, York, Norwich, Pune in India, and regional offices in North America and Asia Pacific). Between April and November 2008 videoconferencing was used for 1700 hours of meetings with a 25 per cent reduction of air travel for those using the facilities (Aviva Group plc, 2009, p3). Progress has also been made from simple changes that often have a significant impact. More than 50 energy-saving initiatives have been introduced, ranging from backlights in vending machines, power-saving modes on PCs and low-flushing toilets, plus the construction of new buildings with high environmental credentials.

To demonstrate ongoing leadership commitment, from 2008 carbon emission targets are included in the personal objectives of Aviva's senior executives – an example of how the company is linking individuals' remuneration with environmental performance measures at a global and regional level. This has support from Chief Executive Andrew Moss, who wanted carbon reduction targets in the personal objectives of Executive Committee members. Martyn Fisher, the director of group reward, describes how a personal target for carbon is currently operated: 'Thirty per cent of the bonus comes from personal objectives... One aspect of those personal objectives for the Executive Team including the regional CEOs is a carbon emission target.'

Engaging and educating employees about the importance of reducing CO_2 emissions is another important feature of Aviva's carbon-neutral strategy. Through Aviva's annual global employee survey, staff rate managers – around 1200 worldwide. Marie Sigsworth, the new group corporate responsibility director, remarked that working for a progressive and sustainable company has become an important issue for staff:

> My immediate experience on the ground [in the Asia Pacific region] is managers becoming much more engaged in community and social activities in response to building actions off the back of the survey. And also the increasing pressure; staff are saying they want to work for a company they can be proud of.

Stakeholders and the value chain

Sustainability is 'not just environmental, it covers customers, suppliers, people and a lot of legal standards', says Tom Oxley, corporate responsibility manager for Aviva UK. Aviva seeks to exert influence over its suppliers and customers, extending consideration of sustainability issues beyond the boundaries of the company to indirect impacts.

Aviva's annual procurement is around UK£6 billion. Each of Aviva's businesses is expected to establish CR performance improvement plans with its five most important suppliers. Supplier policies are further integrated through a comprehensive purchasing and supply management policy, with all new suppliers signing the company's code of conduct.

Aviva introduced a range of new performance metrics in 2008 for suppliers, customers and community relations, which are reported alongside environmental performance. These include reporting the number of suppliers signing Aviva's Supplier Code of Conduct – 983 in 2008 and a target of 2500 for 2009. Aviva has also begun to undertake detailed corporate responsibility assessments of suppliers and measure progress on this front. The target for 2009 is 100 assessments, trebling the 2008 figure of 30. Aviva contributes to best practice approaches for the financial services sector through the CSR forum of the Chartered Institute of Purchasing and Supply.

Connecting purchasing to core products and services is an important feature of Aviva's approach to sustainability and one that is likely to have an increasing impact. Zelda Bentham, group senior environment manager, remarks that:

If the Sustainable and Responsible Investment Team decided that a company shouldn't be invested in, to be excluded from investment because of their business practices, then why should we purchase from them? So we wanted to make sure that we had a coherent message across the two areas of the business.

Aviva attempts to influence customer behaviour by seeking to design sustainability into financial and insurance products and services and by educating consumers. When it comes to its customer base, sustainability is manifested in two forms. First, institutionalizing the company's commitment to sustainable business practices externally and internally conveys to customers and potential customers the values of the company. It is taken as a predictor of the long-term sustainability of the company, which is important for customers entrusting their savings to Aviva on a long-term basis. Trustworthiness is, similarly, an important feature of Aviva's general insurance, as Martyn Fisher, director of group reward, explains: 'When your house gets flooded you know you're not going to get a guy who says well, actually, on clause 23, subsection b, it says, well, if your house gets flooded we're not going to help you. You want to know you're going to be looked after.'

Second, Aviva is experimenting with new forms of general insurance. An example of this is the 'Pay As You Drive' motor insurance policy launched in 2003 and designed to reduce carbon emissions by providing incentives for customers to change their driving habits. The 'Pay As You Drive' policy offers motorists an informed choice about when, where and how often a car is used, with lower premiums for lower mileage. Pricing per mile is calculated to reflect higher accident times – during the early morning commuter period and between 11.00 pm and 6.00 am for younger drivers – with the aim of increasing road safety.

This initiative is also an example of the difficulties of establishing more sustainable products – of connecting sustainability issues to mainstream company strategy in order to change consumers' attitudes and behaviour. While the 'Pay As You Drive' scheme remains available in Canada, France and Turkey, it was removed from the UK market in June 2008, a decision Aviva took after carefully reviewing the viability of the product. Such initiatives serve to demonstrate the uncertain boundaries between company, individual and government responsibility in terms of providing incentives to consumers to change, in this instance, driving habits.

Aviva is also involved in enhancing financial literacy and designing new financial products in response to consumers' concerns. For the last six years Aviva has undertaken a global survey of attitudes to saving, which covered over 28,000 people in 25 countries in 2008. Factors that have been found to influence such attitudes include pressures for short-term returns, financial vulnerability and risk aversion, and anxiety about adequate provision for retirement. Another of Aviva's companies, the RAC, distributes information about more economical, and greener, driving methods and includes this on its website.

Aviva's people management strategy is another dimension of the company's approach to sustainability – emphasizing employee engagement and ethical behaviour in the conduct of business, rewarding staff through the Talking Talent programme, and fostering workplace well-being and diversity through corporate responsibility initiatives. Staff in the UK can volunteer to be Environmental Champions as part of an internal Think Global, Act Local Network that fosters learning, innovation and commitment in the workplace. Linking staff engagement and participation with company sustainability initiatives aligns these issues with human resource development, focusing on win–win outcomes for the company and staff. The 'business case' for diversity in terms of staff, customers and reputation is significant, says Louella Eastman, former group corporate responsibility director:

> Aviva has worked to embed diversity into Aviva as our competitive advantage depends on having a motivated and valued workforce that reflects the diversity of our customers... As we aim to become the world's most trusted financial services provider, it is essential we achieve unprecedented diversity of people across the globe.

As part of wider community engagement, staff can apply for three days' paid volunteering per year with 67,700 hours reported in 2008. Levels of engagement, progress on sustainability issues and line managers' leadership are monitored annually through Aviva's global *employee climate survey* – with responses linked directly to directors' remuneration. Aviva has a corporate Business Ethics Code that reflects the company's values of 'progressiveness, integrity, performance and teamwork'. As in other aspects of Aviva's activities, external benchmarking is an important feature of the people management strategy – Aviva is, for example, in the top 100 for its diversity policies according to Stonewall, recently sponsored the first Global Empowerment Award for Women of the Future Summit and was ranked ninth in the *Observer Good Companies Guide* in 2008, being singled out for its work in seeking to shape policy and promoting consistency in climate change matters.

Embedding sustainable and responsible investment practices

We now turn our attention to the integration of sustainability and responsibility within a significant part of Aviva's core business – fund management:

> Increasing numbers of investors now see the sense of investing in situations where the major long-term environmental and social trends are in their favour. They understand it's best to avoid companies with poor governance and environmental performance; they also want to use their

influence as shareholders to improve the corporate responsibility of the companies they own. (Dr Peter Michaelis, Head of Sustainable and Responsible Investments, Aviva Investors, 2009)

As an insurance company, a core part of Aviva's business involves the investment of funds received from policy-holders. This part of the business, Aviva Investors, manages global assets of around UK£236 billion in 15 countries. Aviva is therefore able to exert influence on sustainability outcomes through the way in which it invests the monies entrusted to it. Sustainable investment practices are thus a prime example of how sustainability criteria are embedded in core business areas at Aviva. Aviva Investors seeks to integrate material environmental, social and governance (ESG) issues within all assets under management. This is achieved by embedding the corporate governance and sustainable and responsible investment (SRI) teams within Aviva Investors' overall investment process and also by voting at the annual general meetings (AGMs) of the companies in which it invests. The former indicates that responsible investing does not sit on top of the overall investment process, but is integrated within it. One example supporting this is that mainstream (i.e. non-SRI fund) desks have dedicated SRI champions, with ESG ratings from the SRI team also being made available to all research desks. Furthermore, AGM voting is seen as an important way of encouraging improvements in corporate disclosure and narrative reporting on ESG issues. Aviva Investors votes against the reports and accounts at the AGM if the company has not met the required standards of reporting.[1] In 2008, Aviva voted on corporate responsibility disclosure at 558 AGMs for FTSE350 and FTSE EuroFirst 300 Index companies, indicating how the company is actively involved in shaping ESG policies in other companies.

Aviva Investors has taken a number of other initiatives aiming to improve the ESG-related standards of the companies in which they invest. For example, Aviva Investors encourages stock market authorities to consider updating their corporate governance codes and requires companies to 'consider how responsible and sustainable their business model is and to put a forward-looking sustainability strategy to the vote at their AGM' (Alain Dromer, CEO, Aviva Investors, Keynote Speech, TBLI Conference, 13 November 2008).

Aviva Investors currently has approximately UK£2 billion of funds under management invested in SRI funds. Sustainable and responsible investment strategies aim to invest in companies that are regarded to be socially and environmentally responsible. Sustainable and responsible investments at Aviva Investors are considered to be:

> ... *those that have a positive impact on society or the environment. This might include companies which develop technologies to reduce carbon emissions, or those that improve the lives of people through medical innovation. Our team actively avoids investing in companies that cause*

unsustainable environmental damage or operate in an unethical manner,
often engaging with companies to improve the way they operate. (Aviva
Investors, 2009, p3)

Even though Aviva Investors attempts to incorporate sustainability within the
entire investment process, it is important to note that the SRI criteria apply
only to the SRI funds[2] and that these might be appropriate in different ways
for different clients. Dr Steve Waygood, head of sustainability research and
engagement at Aviva Investors, comments that:

We manage money for a range of very different institutions, including the
French government, the Fairtrade Foundation, Friends of the Earth and
the Church of Finland. There is a range of issues that these organizations
have; but all of these issues come together in a concept of sustainable devel-
opment which underpins our SRI funds' investment philosophy.

Prior to investing in a company, Aviva Investors identifies and evaluates ESG
issues that are likely to affect a company's earnings and valuation. For example,
the carbon factor is used to distinguish between clean and dirtier (carbon
dioxide) companies. Aviva Investors uses a sustainability matrix that evaluates
companies using two criteria: a product sustainability rating (rated from A to E)
and a management quality rating (rated from 1 to 5) (see Figure 9.2).

The first dimension evaluates the impact of a company's core business on
society and the environment. An 'A' rating signifies a company's commitment to
sustainable business practices (e.g. renewable energy), whereas an 'E' rating
signifies that not only does the company not adopt sustainable development,
but that there is a conflict with such practices (e.g. tobacco business). The
second dimension assesses whether a company can successfully manage its
environmental, social and governance risks: this is accomplished by evaluating
structures, policies and practices of the company in question. More specifically,

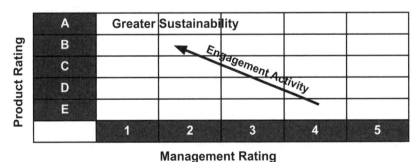

Figure 9.2 Aviva Investors' sustainability matrix

Source: Aviva Investors (2008)

Aviva Investors seeks to better understand the company's strategy and competitive position and engages in discussions with the company regarding corporate governance and corporate responsibility issues; it also assists companies in improving ESG-related areas.

However, evaluating the quality of management requires an amount of effort and time: considering that there is a cost–benefit trade-off involved, Aviva Investors carefully chooses the companies with which it will further engage. Even if a company is not deemed to be an appropriate investment opportunity (based on the evaluation criteria discussed above), Aviva Investors still uses its influence and works closely with some of these companies in order to help them improve. This is hoped to be a win–win situation because, on the one hand, Aviva Investors ultimately has a bigger selection of companies to consider as potential investment candidates and, on the other, it helps companies to adopt more sustainable practices (Aviva Investors, 2009).

Aviva Investors has a coherent set of four SRI strategies. These strategies, which are described in more detail below, are on offer in the market. However the Aviva Investors' Sustainable Future funds combine all the four strategies in an approach that they consider to be optimal:

1   integration;
2   engagement;
3   positive screening;
4   negative screening.

Each one of these strategies can be deployed independently of the rest or, alternatively, some of the above strategies can be combined.

The first strategy, integration, considers explicitly the impact of ESG issues on corporate earnings and valuations. The underlying assumption is that there is market inefficiency and that investors might not value accurately sustainable and responsible business. If this is the case, adoption of this strategy should reduce risk and enhance returns. This strategy has the potential to foster responsible long-term business behaviour, especially if a market inefficiency is identified when analysing ESG issues. This is a prime example of how sustainability considerations actually reinforce rather than conflict with investment performance-related objectives.

The second strategy, engagement, involves working with companies aiming to improve corporate performance on ESG-related issues; as a result, adoption of this strategy is expected to reduce risks and enhance long-term wealth creation. Even though this strategy can be adopted to justify investing in a company with poor ESG performance, when used as intended, it can result in significant ESG-related improvements, especially when it is used in both investment decision-making and proxy voting actions at company AGMs. The adoption of the engagement strategy suggests that sustainability is embedded not only within Aviva, but also across the value chain by encouraging the companies that they would like to invest in and which do not meet the ESG requirements to proceed in improvements.

The third strategy, preference or positive screening, involves investing in companies with responsible business practices or which offer beneficial goods or services. This strategy may therefore involve investing in the exemplars of a sector or sustainability-thematic investment (e.g. environmental technologies). Depending on the approach adopted when picking stocks, this strategy may result in substantial volatility, particularly when there is a bias towards smaller companies. However, it can also lead to improvements in performance, especially when using ESG thematic analysis. Overall, this strategy can result in a reduction in the cost of capital for more sustainable businesses, which can be used to raise capital for smaller companies.

The fourth strategy, avoidance or negative screening, involves the exclusion of companies that do not satisfy the ethical standards of the fund. For example, Aviva Investors' UK Ethical Fund cannot consider investing in tobacco or defence companies.[3] Although it might be expected that such funds are likely to underperform the overall market because of their restricted set of opportunities, there is research evidence suggesting that risk-adjusted returns can be equally good.

Aviva Investors' deployment of SRI criteria indicates how the company has chosen to mobilize its considerable position in the investment business to encourage sustainability in the companies in which it chooses to invest. This is an extension of the issues of exerting influence upstream and downstream in the conventional linear value chain. Aviva mobilizes the specific power available to an institutional investor, although always within the constraints of the capital markets. No doubt, many of its customers would be unwilling to see such strategies implemented if they were to yield significantly poorer returns on investment. However, this is a further example of how Aviva has chosen to embed positive sustainability policies within its mainstream corporate strategy. Given that recent history has indicated such investment choices have had good profitability, a win–win situation has developed. Indeed, it might be seen that the reaction against excessive short-termism can be helpfully progressed by taking a long-term position both financially and in terms of sustainability.

Reporting practices

Regional and national managers report quarterly to the Group Corporate Responsibility Team in London. In 2008, Aviva introduced a group-wide computerized reporting system to facilitate greater comparability of reporting. This replaced a largely paper-based system that involved a CR representative writing a report and completing an Excel spreadsheet. Data from the new computerized reporting system is analysed by the CR team at the London Group Centre and this information feeds into the *Annual Report and Accounts, Corporate Responsibility Report* and briefings to the Corporate Responsibility Board. As Emma Medd-Sygrove, a senior CR manager, remarks:

> *The paper-based system performed a useful function, but it was laborious and made it more difficult to collate aggregate information for the group on key topics. Part of the rationale for a web-based system was to create an environment where it was easy to input information as it became available, lessening the burden of having to do a detailed report at the end of the year.*

Information collected via the computer-based system spans qualitative data from all aspects of the CR programme and quantitative data from the environmental, community investment and diversity areas. One or more nominated CR representatives are responsible for submitting data in a timely manner. The CR representative also has to input their own details – this is designed to enhance accountability through the audit trail. The purported advantages of the computer-based system are that it enables Aviva to assess the extent to which its businesses around the world adhere to the required standards and, if not, to take corrective action. Local initiatives can also be documented on the system. Emma Medd-Sygrove continues:

> *The system is invaluable as the information can be easily retrieved when auditors ask for evidence of our programmes and performance. Longer term, we aspire to extend the use of it, so that we can map our current performance against targets in real time and use this with a wide range of internal stakeholders.*

The main challenge of maintaining such a system rests on choosing the information to be collected and reported. Considering that Aviva is engaged in a varied spectrum of activities, the company cannot collect and maintain information for each activity in which it is involved. Aviva therefore assesses 'materiality' in numerous ways when deciding what information to collect and report. Staff actively involved in corporate responsibility related issues are well positioned to assess the materiality of alternative activities, coupled with advice from consultants. One good example is the number of plastic cups used – a piece of information which might be useful for internal decision-making, but which is nevertheless not of much interest to other stakeholders:

> *So it was all about the materiality and pulling out the important things to the company and then we still do collect [information on the number of] plastic cups because that is of interest to some employees, but we report on the main figures publicly.* (Zelda Bentham, Group Senior Environment Manager)

Aviva also plans to use more proactive approaches when deciding which information to collect and report – for example, to seek the views of various stakeholders. This includes engaging directly with stakeholders, including 'ones that love us and ones that don't', to ask them what they think are Aviva's material issues and then to classify their responses to understand what different stakeholders think are Aviva's material issues.

Aviva subsidiaries around the world have to report on key metrics on a regular basis; in addition, there are also plans to introduce a CR scorecard and the different operations around the world will have to report against key metrics twice a year. This will eventually become part of the company's overall performance management and monitoring process. Actual performance indicators will be benchmarked against the targets; incentives are attached to the achievement of the targets set and senior staff remuneration is partly linked to this.

Conclusions and lessons from Aviva

We began this chapter with an image of wartime mobilization necessitating cutbacks in energy use. Over half a century later we have returned to questions of resource use at a global scale. What lessons might be learned from Aviva's experience of sustainability? In this concluding section we attempt to identify some lessons and principles from the experiences that Aviva has had with the CRF and embedding sustainability, carbon management, stakeholders, and responsible and sustainable investment. We should emphasize that these are our conclusions; but we believe that they can provide some useful guidelines for other organizations attempting to integrate and embed sustainability policies into their strategies, practices and behaviours.

Quick wins

There is much to be said for harvesting the 'low-hanging fruit' first. Focus on things that can be done quickly and which are based on existing organizational practices. Aviva had a long track record of monitoring its environmental impact in a variety of ways that made the implementation of the CRF relatively straightforward. A wider range of issues or an increased level of detail can be added later and built upon some early successes. Actions with relatively small impacts can be useful in generating an organizational culture that fosters sustainability and improves efficiency. Aviva chooses not to provide waste paper baskets in offices, thus requiring all employees to take their waste to recycling points. Printers are set so that the default position is that printing is produced double-sided. Such small mechanisms make the commitment to sustainability visible to a large number of staff on a frequent basis. Once some quick wins have been achieved, more formal information and reporting systems can be used to monitor progress, followed by an increased emphasis on targets.

Small wins

Be prepared for small wins, particularly at first. There may not be large instant successes and setbacks are likely to occur. Sustainability will not become embedded in any company overnight. Some things may work well in one context, but not transfer easily to other contexts. For example, the 'Pay As You Drive' initiative did not prove successful in the UK market although it is still offered in non-UK markets. If one approach does not work, try a different tack. A variety of small initiatives may be better than concentrating on a single major policy in that the successful ideas can be expanded and replicated. Less successful approaches can be revised and tried in a different form without embarrassment. Remember, the objective is steady progress towards some overarching aims and objectives, despite inevitable setbacks.

Big wins

Big wins will probably be built upon the foundation of smaller wins. For example, Aviva has a long history of environmental monitoring and reporting since the early 2000s, but only recently was able to consolidate this into being the world's first insurer to be fully carbon neutral (including offset payments). The policy of voting at AGMs by Aviva Investors has been under way since 2001 with Morley, Aviva Investors' legacy company, but is developing in scope with the announcement in 2008 that its AGM voting strategy will apply to global assets held on the MSCI World Index. This development appears to have the potential to exert significant influence over the longer term. In both cases, the company is promoting its initiatives in the hope of enhancing corporate reputation in a variety of arenas and using its influence to change other companies' practices.

Tone at the top

Executive commitment and support is absolutely vital. The signals that senior executives can provide through speeches, policy statements and personal support cannot be underestimated. However, it is probably not sufficient in itself. Not everything starts at the top and trickles down. Much useful innovation occurs at lower levels in the organization, with successful ideas being picked up and transplanted to different areas of the business. We suggest that there is no need to wait for a fully integrated strategy from day one. Rather, allow things to happen – notice and support what seems to work by engaging staff, then replicate what works in different places. Bottom-up approaches are as important as top-down initiatives. Frontline employees often have important insights into actions which can have a significant impact on the overall operations of the business, particularly with regard to their own work context. Senior managers can learn from local practices and ensure that they are disseminated more widely – something which we suggest is going to remain important for Aviva as it operates in 28 countries worldwide.

Working with others

Support is necessary both internally and externally. Aviva has a central team at the group headquarters with responsibility for sustainability issues. This is both a powerful internal message, and also a vital focus and resource for making progress on a variety of initiatives; but it needs to be managed in such a way for it to be seen as a support service without taking away responsibility from operating unit managers and staff.

External support is also vital particularly at sector level. Companies can learn a lot from what is being done elsewhere, both in terms of good practices and also from mistakes which others may have made. This will also help in preparing for any future regulation and, potentially, help to shape policy. Attendance at meetings of organizations and associations that are committed to various aspects of sustainability seems to be very helpful, even though it is less immediately quantifiable in impact. Becoming an active member of forums and associations can provide motivation and stimulus for your company, as well as fostering inter-organizational learning.

Stakeholders

Sustainable practices are not confined to a company's employees, important though it is to ensure that these are implemented internally. Organizations can influence other participants in their value chains. Suppliers can be required to report on their own sustainability practices as part of the contract negotiation process and some weight given to preferring those who act in sustainable ways. Customers can be encouraged to purchase products or services that have desirable characteristics from a sustainability perspective, and there is the potential for a cost advantage to be gained from such an approach. Aviva invests a considerable amount of capital on behalf of its clients and has used its position in this respect to influence the policies of companies in which it invests. Capital investments can be initiated and evaluated on the basis of criteria that include environmental impacts. For example, buildings can be designed to have energy-efficient characteristics, which may involve greater initial costs, but which will also have lower operating costs.

Business cases

Sustainability should be built into the 'business case' for all innovations and changes, including new products and services. However, it needs to be recognized that there are different types of business cases as companies attempt to progress a variety of goals at the same time. Some will have cost or risk reduction benefits. For example, energy saving both reduces carbon footprint and operating costs. Some may focus on reducing risk and enhancing returns for investors, as is the case with sustainable and responsible investment strategies. Other innovations may help to give the organization a competitive advantage relative to competitors. Each of these may combine to help improve the reputation and legitimacy of the organization, and may also prevent the intervention of regulatory authorities. Finally, value may be created in multiple contexts, with a variety of stakeholders benefiting from a particular course of action. All of these aspects need to be taken into account in developing a wide-ranging 'business case', which may need to have multiple criteria for evaluation. Successful companies are often those that work on multiple fronts at the same time.

Experimentation

Given the long-term nature and complexity of sustainability, innovation to foster sustainability should not be confined to the few. Ideas and initiatives can be widely scattered within an organization, and good ideas need to be recognized and exploited wherever they occur. It is often difficult to predict what might work or not be feasible. A sensible way forward seems to be to allow small-scale experimentation across a wide range of areas. The 'suck it and see' approach has much to commend it. Some initiatives may be immediately successful and can be disseminated. Others may take time to develop and require further refinement; yet others will almost certainly prove to be failures. But small-scale failures are not disasters and can lead to alternative approaches being tried. Experimentation is often the best route to organizational learning and success. At Aviva this has taken the form of a shift in focus in relation to climate change away from reporting on environmental impact as a form of risk management to connecting environmental performance with financial performance and experimenting with new products and services against the backdrop of climate change.

Formalized reporting

Formal reporting systems are a powerful mechanism for embedding organizational practices. Managers know that 'what gets measured, gets done'. The development of formal information systems for capturing important non-financial data such as carbon footprint, waste and other resource usage are a vital part of managing for sustainability. Indeed, it can be seen that developing formal monitoring and reporting procedures is an important stage in the maturity of sustainability reporting. The performance management of sustainability is, in many respects, similar to managing any other aspect of performance. It needs to start from a strategy, to develop appropriate performance measures and targets, and to report on these on a regular basis. The incorporation of the CRF as part of both Aviva's *Corporate Responsibility Report* and, even more importantly, as part of the *Annual Report and Accounts* is a major sign of progress. However, it also needs to be recognized that such reporting systems take time to develop and can be costly to operate, and should therefore be focused on a few key factors.

Key performance indicators

Companies adopt targets for a range of internal and external reasons – to manage costs, to enhance sustainability and for stakeholder recognition. The introduction of key performance indicators (KPIs) at Aviva is a relatively recent feature of its approach to sustainability despite its long record in this arena. Care should be taken in selecting major performance indicators to ensure that they capture the key factors required. Before targets can sensibly be set, some history of actual performance is needed. Non-financial data may not have the same reliability as long-established financial information, and trade-offs may need to be made between relevance and reliability. But measurement is a vital tool that can be mobilized to implement sustainable strategies.

Our suggestion is that all of the above can be seen as a consistent approach to embedding sustainability into organizational activities. Both top-down commitment and bottom-up mobilization of innovation are required. Experimentation is an important tool in developing innovative approaches. All stakeholders and actors in the value chain need to be considered. Business cases need to be recognized as having multiple dimensions of evaluation. Connectivity outside the organization is important, both as a motivator and as a source of ideas, as well as a public service. By such a combination of small and loosely coupled activities, a sustainable approach can emerge, grow and become embedded within a company's ongoing activities.

Acknowledgements

We would like to acknowledge Aviva plc for generous research access and to thank all interviewed at Aviva – in particular, Marie Sigsworth, Louella Eastman, Tom Oxley and Zelda Bentham. Anna Stone, Aviva Group archivist, kindly sourced the quote from *The Cucao Link*. Gunther Haberkamm provided invaluable assistance in undertaking data collection for this project. We would also like to thank Professor Anthony Hopwood, Professor Jeffrey Unerman and Jessica Fries for their editorial support, and Karen McCulloch and Gordon Wilson at A4S.

Notes

1   Aviva Investors helped to initiate the Carbon Disclosure Project (CDP), which encourages disclosures related to the risks and opportunities associated with climate change from over 2000 companies. Since 2007, 39 companies that did not disclose any information related to climate change emissions were informed that Aviva Investors would vote against their report and accounts if they do not provide these disclosures. As of 2009, 82 per cent of the companies including impact extractive companies, such as Vedanta Resources (mining, UK) and SOCO International (oil and gas, UK) and Porsche (automobile, Germany), have responded positively.
2   Sustainable investments are required, as a fiduciary responsibility, to make financial sense; supporting sustainable development is not necessarily in conflict with profitability. It often proved to be the case that these two objectives were mutually reinforcing. For example, adopting sustainable development practices may lead to cost reductions.
3   Aviva Investors excludes ExxonMobil from its Sustainable Future Funds since the company does not meet Aviva Investors' selection criteria. In addition, Aviva Investors also exerts its influence in other ways. For example, it supported a shareholder resolution at ExxonMobil regarding the separation of the roles of chairman and chief executive on the grounds that decision-making authority, such as that related to ExxonMobil's climate change policy, should not reside with the same person (Aviva Investors, 2009).

References

Aviva Group plc (2008a) *Annual Report and Accounts 2008*, Aviva, London
Aviva Group plc (2008b) *Corporate Social Responsibility Report 2008*, Aviva, London
Aviva Investors (2008) *Sustainable and Responsible Investing (SRI)*, Aviva Investors, London
Aviva Group plc (2009) *Corporate Responsibility Report 2009*, Aviva, London
Aviva Investors (2009) *Sustainable Future funds*, Aviva Investors, London
Commercial Union (1943) *The Cucao Link*, Staff Magazine of the Commercial Union, Commercial Union, London, autumn, pp76–77

ten

Integrated Reporting at Novo Nordisk

Colin Dey and John Burns

Introduction

In 1994, the Danish pharmaceutical company Novo Nordisk became one of the first companies in the world to produce an environmental report. Since then, the company has continued to expand and develop its voluntary disclosures and has gained a reputation as a leader in the area of sustainability reporting. Although Novo Nordisk has not yet adopted the Connected Reporting Framework (CRF), it has spent the last five years developing its own approach, which it calls 'integrated reporting' and which seeks to measure social, environmental and financial performance within a single comprehensive document. Underpinning this approach, and aligned closely with the recommendations of the CRF, is Novo Nordisk's bold aim to 'fully integrate' sustainability within business strategy. The pursuit of what the company calls full integration is not limited to the development of new disclosure practices: instead, Novo Nordisk has developed a 'way of management' that encompasses corporate governance, employee culture, specific management tools and rigorous performance measurement methods. In this way, sustainability reporting may be viewed as just one element of a broader approach that may offer the potential to further strengthen and 'embed' a sustainability mindset within the organization. The purpose of this chapter is to examine the background and development of integrated reporting at Novo Nordisk and to explore the extent to which the company's goal of full integration and its use of reporting and other control systems have succeeded in making sustainability an embedded feature of the organization.

Context and background

Novo Nordisk is widely regarded as a leader in diabetes care, employing over 27,000 people across 81 countries. A controlling share in Novo Nordisk is owned by the non-profit-making Novo Nordisk Foundation, which means that the company has a degree of operational freedom by comparison with the rest of the pharmaceutical industry and is protected from the threat of possible takeovers. In 2000, Novo Nordisk was de-merged from its enzymes business, Novozymes, and the two companies have remained separately listed since then. Novo Nordisk Foundation effectively owns a controlling interest in both companies and acts as a stable platform for the two operating companies. A holding company, Novo A/S, creates a link between the foundation and the two operating companies: importantly, Novo A/S has the voting majority at the annual general meeting of Novo Nordisk. This structure has given the company relative freedom to choose its strategic direction, not least in relation to the integration of sustainability within business strategy. Novo Nordisk was founded in the 1920s with a specific mandate to help people, and this mandate continues to influence the company's strategic direction. In 2004, Novo Nordisk amended its Articles of Association to explicitly commit itself to 'strive to be economically viable, socially responsible and environmentally sound'. This decision was endorsed by the company's investors, who regard the company's strategic direction as being particularly compatible with the company's business model:

> For the majority of our investors, financials are still the most important – R&D [research and development] spend, sales prospects, etc. But we do benefit from investors taking a long-term perspective. It's not just our unusual capital structure – it's the fact that a lot of what we do, our business model, has a ten-year development lead time. So a lot of our institutional investors understand our concern with sustainability. They see the sustainability issues as a fundamental perspective on Novo Nordisk. In other words, we are less risky. (Corporate Vice-President, Head of Investor Relations)

The origin of the company's modern interest in sustainability may be traced to specific incidents over the last three decades, where the company suffered criticism from external stakeholders and associated negative media coverage. The first of these incidents occurred during the early 1970s when the company faced allegations from the then consumer advocate Ralph Nader, who claimed that new detergent enzymes were affecting the health of the American employees involved in the production process. The reputational damage caused by this episode caused sales in the company's US market to fall by half; as a consequence, management attention became focused on the vulnerability of the business to public opinion.

In response, the company sought to better recognize the broad set of stakeholders to whom the organization owed a responsibility and to explore the impact of that learning curve on the company's strategic direction. In 1990, when the company faced the prospect of further negative media attention in relation to its use of genetically modified organisms, Novo Nordisk was this time ready to initiate a more proactive form of stakeholder engagement, designed to identify and address issues of concern. The company successfully persuaded those involved in making the allegations to revise and correct them and, in so doing, to limit the extent of negative media coverage. More importantly, however, the engagement also led to the recruitment of one of the principal authors of the allegations, John Elkington, to undertake a review of the company's business practices in relation to the environment. A year later, the company launched its first sustainability strategy, focused primarily on the environmental issues of concern at the time.

Since then, stakeholder engagement and trend analysis have become essential tools to enable the company to identify new issues that are (or could become) material. The company uses what it calls a 'learning curve' – a tool that aligns the process of defining materiality with integration into business practices (see Figure 10.1). Emerging issues that are identified as relevant and potentially material are included at the beginning of the learning curve. The company then reviews the implications for Novo Nordisk's long-term business: often, an independent expert will be commissioned to undertake this review. The review is considered by the Executive Management Team, comprising the vice-presidents of seven corporate divisions. Strategies are then developed for those issues that are deemed material. To manage the strategy going forward, data, indicators and targets are identified. Over time, as management of the issue gradually develops, the strategy may be revisited and reappraised.

One of the most visible early outcomes of the new strategy was the company's publication of environmental reports. Novo Nordisk produced its first environmental report in 1994, a year ahead of Danish legislation requiring that certain companies disclose information about their environmental impacts. In 1997, Novo Nordisk commissioned an independent expert to undertake a review of the company's human rights; by 1998, the first social report was published. In 1999, both social and environmental reports were merged into one document, and in 2001, Novo Nordisk explicitly adopted the triple bottom line (TBL) approach to sustainability reporting, in which social and environmental impacts were measured alongside economic performance. In 2003, for the first time, the *Sustainability Report* was published at the same time as the

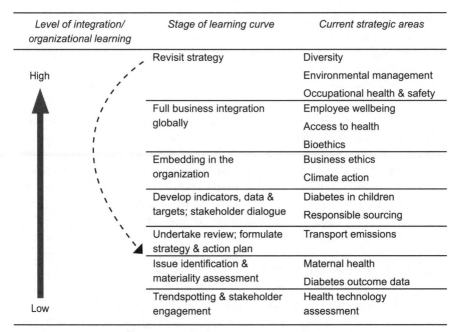

Level of integration/ organizational learning	Stage of learning curve	Current strategic areas
High	Revisit strategy	Diversity
		Environmental management
		Occupational health & safety
	Full business integration globally	Employee wellbeing
		Access to health
		Bioethics
	Embedding in the organization	Business ethics
		Climate action
	Develop indicators, data & targets; stakeholder dialogue	Diabetes in children
		Responsible sourcing
	Undertake review; formulate strategy & action plan	Transport emissions
	Issue identification & materiality assessment	Maternal health
		Diabetes outcome data
Low	Trendspotting & stakeholder engagement	Health technology assessment

Figure 10.1 Novo Nordisk's current sustainability agenda

Source: Novo Nordisk (2009)

Annual Financial Report and distributed to shareholders. Novo Nordisk believed that this move was well received by shareholders and other stakeholders because the two documents together provided a more comprehensive overview of the company's performance, progress, positions and strategic initiatives. As a result, Novo Nordisk took the decision to fully merge its financial report and its sustainability report into one inclusive, integrated report. According to the company's official documentation:

> ... the aim is to drive business performance and enhance shareholder value by exploring the interactions between financial and non-financial objectives. This entails alignment of key priorities, target setting and definition of key performance indicators, in consultations that involve internal and external stakeholders. (Novo Nordisk, 2008)

The 2004 *Annual Report* was the first such integrated report and was compliant with International Financial Reporting Standards (IFRS), the AccountAbility AA1000 Framework, the Global Reporting Initiative (GRI) Sustainability Reporting Guidelines, and the United Nations Global Compact. Novo Nordisk does not use the CRF; but there are numerous similarities between the CRF and the company's published reports. However, Novo Nordisk's non-financial indicators are not currently financialized or connected to financial outcomes.

It is important to emphasize that sustainability reporting at Novo Nordisk is one element of a wider strategic approach that has gradually evolved since the early 1990s, which is intended to integrate sustainability into business practices. Of key importance here are the economic, social and environmental 'commitments' underpinning the integrated reporting approach. While the use of integrated reporting serves as an accountability mechanism for the organization as a whole, attempts to further embed the company's stated commitments within the organization have been driven by a number of other innovative developments. For example, at the corporate governance level, the explicit adoption in 2004 of these commitments in the company's Articles of Association was especially significant. In addition, however, and of particular concern within this chapter, are internal control and feedback systems that together comprise a larger formal framework of management guidelines and systems within the organization. The next section introduces some of these elements in more detail.

The Novo Nordisk 'Way of Management'

In 1997, Novo Nordisk introduced a comprehensive formal management framework known as the Novo Nordisk 'Way of Management' (the 'Novo Nordisk Way'). It comprises a set of principles and guidelines designed to help embed and operationalize its vision. The Novo Nordisk Way was originally set up as a framework for managers in the company's foreign subsidiaries to better understand and align to 'the way we do things', yet allow a degree of flexibility at local/divisional management level. It was intended to provide sufficient control over global company operations and to ensure common direction (including sustainability), yet at the same time allow enough malleability to absorb challenges arising from diversities in national and cultural aspirations, as well as multiple stakeholder expectations.

The Novo Nordisk Way consists of three main components: vision, charter and policies. The vision establishes broad direction and sketches out a general theme of striking a balance between commercial endeavours and behaving in a responsible manner. Of particular interest here is the second component, which is the charter (see Figure 10.2). The charter describes an overall framework of guidelines for all corporate activity based on three main elements: values, commitments and fundamentals. Values are intended to further define the general ethos outlined in the vision, while the fundamentals set out in more detail a number of management principles. The commitments mirror the three dimensions of the TBL approach described earlier, and the commitments reflect those defined in the company's Articles of Association. Finally, the third element of the Novo Nordisk Way is a set of 13 policies on specific operational issues, covering bioethics; business ethics; communications; environment; finance; global health; information technology; legal; people; health and safety;

Values
• Accountable, ambitious, responsible, engaged with stakeholders, open & honest, ready for change

Fundamentals
• Business units share and use better practices
• Units are clear with regard to their respective accountabilities and decision-making powers
• Units have an action plan to ensure improvements in both business performance and the working climate
• Teams and individuals have up to date business and competency targets, against which they receive timely feedback on performance
• Units have action plans to ensure team and employee development, as required
• Managers establish and maintain procedures in their units to align and adhere to relevant laws, regulations and corporate commitments
• Units and individuals know how to create customer value
• Managers explain to others the actual use and added value of any reports they require
• Managers enable employees to easily and speedily turn attention to any customer related issues
• Managers and units actively support inter-unit projects and other relevant working relationships
• Individuals continuously seek to improve their work

Commitments
• Financial responsibility: growth, value creation, compliance with standards
• Environmental responsibility: improve performance, integrate into strategy, maintain open dialogue and reporting transparency, support ICC Charter for Sustainable Development & UN Convention on Biological Diversity
• Social responsibility: improve performance, integrate into business, dialogue, reporting transparency, support UN Universal Declaration of Human Rights

Figure 10.2 The Novo Nordisk Charter

Source: Novo Nordisk (2007)

purchasing; quality; and risk management. To link the operational policies with the overall TBL approach, a governance structure known as the TBL Leadership Forum has been established. This body has a cross-functional remit, spanning the work of a number of high-level committees, with specific responsibility for overseeing the operational policies identified previously and with an aim of securing implementation and development of Novo Nordisk's TBL strategy.

The charter forms the central mechanism in the Novo Nordisk Way since it defines both a framework for corporate activity, as well as the feedback and control mechanisms needed to measure and manage such activity. Three key dimensions of action (values, fundamentals and commitments) are supported by a number of 'follow-up methodologies'. Those relevant to the management of sustainability are shown in Figure 10.3.

TBL management typically operates at an aggregated level across all business units, enabling the company as a whole to measure its performance against the economic, social and environmental commitments enshrined in the corporate charter and Articles of Association. In addition, the headline non-financial

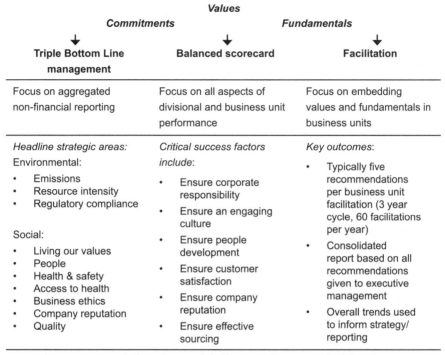

Values		
Commitments		*Fundamentals*
↓	↓	↓
Triple Bottom Line management	**Balanced scorecard**	**Facilitation**
Focus on aggregated non-financial reporting	Focus on all aspects of divisional and business unit performance	Focus on embedding values and fundamentals in business units
Headline strategic areas: Environmental: • Emissions • Resource intensity • Regulatory compliance Social: • Living our values • People • Health & safety • Access to health • Business ethics • Company reputation • Quality	*Critical success factors include:* • Ensure corporate responsibility • Ensure an engaging culture • Ensure people development • Ensure customer satisfaction • Ensure company reputation • Ensure effective sourcing	*Key outcomes:* • Typically five recommendations per business unit facilitation (3 year cycle, 60 facilitations per year) • Consolidated report based on all recommendations given to executive management • Overall trends used to inform strategy/ reporting

Figure 10.3 The Novo Nordisk Charter: Follow-up methodologies relevant to sustainability strategy

Source: adapted from Novo Nordisk (2007)

indicators relevant to sustainability are used to inform the development of a corporate balanced scorecard, which is designed to assess overall performance of each corporate division and cascades down to both business unit level as well as to individual senior managers' targets. Hence, a mechanism exists to link individual managers and business units to the social and environmental dimensions of the company's overall strategy. The facilitation methodology, in contrast to TBL reporting and the balanced scorecard, is designed to focus on the underlying principles guiding corporate behaviour: the values and fundamentals in the corporate charter. Rather than performance indicators, the facilitation methodology is based on more qualitative data-gathering, especially interviews.

While each feedback methodology focuses on a specific dimension of the company's management charter, taken together, the different elements in the Novo Nordisk Way act to reinforce each other: 'There's no way that we'd be where we are solely based on our reporting system. It's got a lot to do with the corporate governance structure' (Director, Global TBL Management).

We will now examine each of these three feedback mechanisms in more detail.

Triple bottom line (TBL) management

TBL reporting was formally adopted by Novo Nordisk in 2001. TBL reporting measures the extent to which the company is progressing in relation to its stated economic, social and environmental commitments. Table 10.1, extracted from the 2008 *Annual Report*, highlights the main strategic areas, or 'non-financial accounting policies', for which it currently sets indicators and targets.

The TBL approach has been steadily developed and refined since its introduction. For example, one of the most visible recent examples of this has been the decision to present its headline non-financial results directly alongside its financial results. In addition, in order to manage the gradual inclusion of social as well as environmental strategic objectives, the company has gradually increased the number of non-financial indicators that it uses. Having initially focused mainly on the environmental concerns of the 1990s, it has sought to develop more indicators in the area of social responsibility, with a focus on areas such as access to health and business ethics.

Just as in the 1990s, the emergence of these issues as strategic areas of importance may be attributed to the influence of external stakeholders and the proactive management of stakeholder concerns using the corporate learning curve approach described earlier. In 2001, Novo Nordisk jointly undertook legal action with 38 other pharmaceutical companies against the South African government for violating intellectual property agreements, particularly in relation to AIDS medications. Although Novo Nordisk does not manufacture such products, it participated in the court case because it believed that the agreement balanced the rights of the pharmaceutical industry against the needs of developing countries. The case caused public concern in Denmark, and as part of its response to the backlash, the company invested in a number of new initiatives designed to improve access to healthcare in developing countries. Currently, the company sets specific TBL targets in relation to this issue in terms of the number of developing countries to which it sells insulin products at or below cost price, as well as the number of healthcare professionals and diabetes sufferers whom it has trained or treated. A further episode of negative public scrutiny in 2005 centred on the role of company sales representatives in negotiating inflated prices of products destined for Iraq as part of the Oil for Food programme. Like the 2001 episode involving South Africa, the incident also influenced the ongoing development of TBL management, and the company now includes a specific target for the number of sales and marketing representatives whom it will train in business ethics.

More fundamentally, however, the company's vision of 'full integration' extends well beyond issues of measurement scope and report presentation: 'Eventually we want to talk in terms of "full integration". We want there to be one of everything – one performance measurement system, one management control system, and one audit system' (Director, Global TBL Management).

Table 10.1 Headline triple bottom line (TBL) indicators and targets

Strategy Area	Indicator	Target
Environment		
Emissions to air	CO_2 emissions	10% Reduction by 2014 compared to 2004
EIR Water	EIR_{Water} Diabetes Care	10% Reduction by 2010 compared to 2005
	EIR_{Water} Biopharmaceuticals	10% Reduction by 2010 compared to 2005
EIR Energy	EIR_{Energy} Diabetes Care	10% Reduction by 2010 compared to 2005
	EIR_{Energy} Biopharmaceuticals	10% Reduction by 2010 compared to 2005
Compliance	Breaches of regulatory limit values	50% Reduction by 2010 compared to 2005
	Accidental releases	50% Reduction by 2010 compared to 2005
Social		
Living our values	Importance of social and environmental issues for the future of the company	Maintain a level of 3.5 or above up to 2014
	Managers' behaviour consistent with Novo Nordisk's values	Maintain a level of 3.5 or above up to 2014
	Fulfilment of action points from facilitations of the NNWoM	Maintain a level of 80% or above up to 2014
People	Engaging culture (employee engagement)	Maintain a level of 4.0 or above up to 2014
	Opportunity to use and develop employee competences/skills	Maintain a level of 3.5 or above up to 2014
	People from diverse backgrounds have equal opportunities	Maintain a level of 3.5 or above up to 2014
Health & Safety	Frequency of occupational injuries	Continuous decrease
	Fatalities	0
Access to health	LDCs where Novo Nordisk operates	Best possible pricing scheme in all LDCs
	LDCs where Novo Nordisk sells insulin at or below the policy price	Best possible pricing scheme in all LDCs
Business ethics	Employees in sales and marketing trained in business ethics	90% by 2008
Company reputation	Improve (or maintain) company reputation with external key stakeholders	Improve (or maintain) brand score
Quality	Number of warning letters and re-inspections	0

Source: Novo Nordisk (2008, p90)

Not withstanding the apparent simplicity of this general ambition to create 'one of everything', as well as strong and collective support towards the corporate strategy, staff recognized the cultural as well as technical implications of the task:

> *I personally think that there are some barriers to full integration, and barriers in our (non-financial data management) department towards the financials. I see challenges ahead in relation to a common under-standing and language between the financial and the non-financial people, a whole cultural thing, a way of thinking. This is about two differ-ent worlds; but, of course, we see the purpose of each other. We're just not always on the same page in terms of what is material.* (Member of Non-Financial Data Management Team)

In its pursuit of full integration, in 2008 Novo Nordisk embarked on a process of structuring the control environment of non-financial reporting. The ambition of this innovative work, to be phased in over a number of accounting cycles, is to gradually achieve full alignment with the control environment of financial reporting. The next section explores the early stages of this work in more detail.

'Sarb-Oxing' the non-financial control environment

The US Sarbanes–Oxley Act lays down requirements for documenting and reporting on the effectiveness of internal controls for financial reporting. Listed on the New York Stock Exchange, Novo Nordisk is obliged to meet these requirements and first did so in 2005, one year ahead of the deadline, and one of the first non-US companies to do so. As part of its objective of full integra-tion, Novo Nordisk has begun the task of applying the principles of the Sarbanes–Oxley Act to *all* of its reporting in order to ensure that are no mater-ial weaknesses in internal controls that could lead to a material misstatement in its non-financial reporting. For the 2008 *Annual Report*, the internal audit committee took the decision to introduce what some staff informally referred to as 'Sarb-Oxing'. The aim was to phase in, over a number of accounting cycles, the same rigour, sophistication and credibility of existing financial systems to non-financial metrics. Over time, the process for gathering data for the headline non-financial indicators would eventually mirror the approach taken for putting together headline financial highlights on the opposite page of the *Annual Report*. The process of emulating best practice even stretched to adopting the same methods for filing, archiving, documentation and using the same reporting templates as employed at operational levels.

Beginning such a task for non-financial reporting was a huge undertaking. The TBL Data Management Team drafted in the Sarbanes-Oxley Consulting Team (previously responsible for applying the act to financial information) to help them begin to apply the same rigorous tests and assurances to non-financial data. Significantly, the general view of those involved in this collaborative work is extremely positive: the difficulty involved in this challenging task was eased considerably by what appeared to be a remarkable willingness to collaborate across different business functions and for the good of the overall business:

> *This is a company that embraces change; but I also think this has high focus within Novo Nordisk. People of Novo Nordisk are proud of what they are doing, proud of the triple bottom line, proud of the Annual Report, and so on. And they are actually interested in making this better. So, generally, the project for integration has been taken positively. There's a general concern that the numbers are correct. People will do what they need to do to achieve this. They don't want to report a wrong number on, say, animal testing or something like that.* (Member of the Sarbanes-Oxley Consulting Team)

The Sarbanes–Oxley team needed to familiarize itself quite quickly with the non-financial metrics of the business, and there was a learning process to go through. Overall, however, team members argued that there was much similarity between the financial and non-financial metrics processes:

> *It was actually the same risks that we needed to cover, and kind of the same controls that we needed in place. The system, the controls and many of the procedures are actually quite similar. So, I don't think the two things are so far apart.* (Member of the Sarbanes–Oxley Consulting Team)

Because of its aggregated long-term basis, the TBL reporting approach is not directly used to assess and monitor the performance of individual business units. This is a task that is, instead, managed through the balanced scorecard. The headline non-financial indicators derived from the company's key strategic aims in relation to sustainability issues are themselves used to inform the development of key performance indicators within the balanced scorecard. The following section explores the relationship between the aggregate measures used to drive TBL reporting and the use of the balanced scorecard to embed strategic priorities within individual business units.

The balanced scorecard

In contrast to external stimuli that originally helped to motivate the company's interest in sustainability issues, the introduction of balanced scorecards was instead rooted in more immediate operational concerns. Balanced scorecards have been used in Novo Nordisk since 1996, and were originally introduced by the Finance Department as part of instilling better local financial management throughout the business units. The Novo Nordisk scorecard begins at the organizational level and is reviewed annually to take account of the key strategic aims and associated non-financial performance indicators used to produce the company's overall TBL reports. The scorecard then cascades down, first to the divisional level of executive vice-presidents, then to the senior vice-presidents at the business unit level. There is no formal requirement to cascade the balanced scorecard below business unit level, although some business units voluntarily choose at least to cascade down particular KPIs to sub-units, such as a plant. In general, long-term objectives and goals used in TBL reporting are broken down into short-term targets in the balanced scorecard. However, while employee performance is generally tied to short-term goals, some managers, particularly those at executive level, are measured directly on achievement of long-term goals, which the company publicly reports against.

As part of their remuneration package, individuals are rewarded for performance that meets or exceeds the non-financial targets in the balanced scorecard. Overall progress is tracked against the targets for headline non-financial indicators in the *Annual Report*. These include socio-economic impacts such as job creation, the ability to manage environmental impacts and optimize resource efficiency, and social impacts related to employees, patients and communities.

The balanced scorecard currently has a total of 24 critical success factors, grouped under the four headings of customers and society; finance; business processes; and people and organization. In broad terms, responsibility for meeting balanced scorecard objectives is cross-functional, meaning that all divisions will to some extent be required to contribute to the overall social and environmental targets set out in the TBL reports. Our investigation included sight of the use of balanced scorecards in the 'responsible sourcing' business unit. A key aim of this business unit is to integrate ethical practice within the company's supply chain. Senior supply-chain managers spend a great deal of their time assessing how ethical Novo Nordisk's suppliers are, which is an enormous task. A more immediate objective is to undertake a mapping of 'risk areas' amongst its supplier base, which, in some instances, has led to Novo Nordisk breaking its ties with a particular supplier. Several staff in the responsible sourcing area highlighted again that this was as much about 'doing things the Novo Nordisk way' than anything else: 'Of course, there is a reputation protection part. But I see this as my responsibility – and I explain to my people – that we have a responsibility to ensuring a sustainable supply of material' (Head of Procurement, Direct Spend).

Senior managers in the procurement area were working hard to articulate and instil amongst suppliers that it made good business sense and promised value creation to go about their work in a sustainable way: 'I think this is an evolution in the whole corporate social responsibility agenda, from being a side function, or an NGO-type function to the company, towards being a more integrated part of value creation' (Director, Responsible Sourcing).

Through their balanced scorecard, the head of procurement for direct spend (i.e. the materials which are used to make the company's finished products) is accountable for two KPIs relating to supplier risk management; these KPIs also influence how his bonus is calculated. Moreover, he pushes such targets to the management level below him, and they too have bonuses that are partly calculated on KPIs, such as those relating to responsible sourcing. There are ten bonus-linked KPIs in total, of which half are non-financial.

The ultimate aim is to link the overall non-financial TBL indicators and associated long-term targets to short-term equivalent KPIs within the balanced scorecard:

> We shouldn't just report on a number just because we can. It should be anchored and there should be a goal. If management [doesn't] have a focus on the number, then we have a risk. We have a risk that it's not the right number being reported or that it's incorrect. So now, if an indicator is in the Annual Report, its equivalent will be in the balanced scorecard, or vice-versa. (Member of the Sarbanes-Oxley Consulting Team)

However, there remained a number of obstacles in the way of this aim with regard to aligning non-financial reporting mechanisms to the quarterly system of financial reporting. First, full alignment between the financial and non-financial reporting mechanisms will require capturing the data for non-financial measures on a quarterly basis – for many such measures this has never been the case. Second, there were issues relating to the consistency of KPI targets:

> We could be more structured in the way we define our KPIs – not just today but three or five years ahead. Long-term targets – stakeholders can follow them and establish proper expectations. In the past we were less consistent. Those issues concern any of our KPIs – it could be CO_2, it could be how we are dealing with culture. (Senior Vice-President, Facilitation and Group Internal Audit)

There is also an issue regarding the quality of information being used to feed not only the balanced scorecard, but other reporting tools. For example, referring again to responsible sourcing, for this Novo Nordisk relies almost entirely on data provided by the (external) supplier. And though it was acknowledged that some key and usually longer-established suppliers were very accommodating with the provision of information relating to their ethical (or not) ways of working, it was proving to be a major challenge to draw the necessary information from some suppliers. In this respect, at least where it is appreciated, Novo Nordisk will usually offer to advise their suppliers on how to make improvements in their practices and now has a handbook for its suppliers on responsible sourcing.

While the balanced scorecard includes success factors relating to employee culture and development, these strategic aims are also reflected in the third key feedback methodology used in the Novo Nordisk Way: facilitation. The next section outlines the significance of this methodology for embedding sustainability within business practices.

Facilitation

Originally introduced in 1996, facilitation is a key mechanism by which Novo Nordisk seeks to ensure that the stated values and fundamentals of the company charter – the underlying principles supposed to guide corporate behaviour – are being practised across the organization:

> We have a set of values, of systems; but I think all companies have those things, that's not unique. What is unique is that Novo Nordisk is actually following up on it in every department, every unit within the company. And then we report back to the units, we give them a rating and also some actions. You don't see that in many companies – normally you have to please your shareholders; but we are saying, we have to please our stakeholders. (Senior Vice-President, Facilitation and Group Internal Audit)

Facilitation is undertaken by a small team of highly experienced staff with broad expertise, usually 'hand-picked' from senior managerial positions within Novo Nordisk. Staff work in pairs on a three-year cycle to review all the business units. The facilitators' tasks include assessing the extent to which a business unit is performing in compliance with the values and fundamentals of the company charter; where necessary, assisting business units to achieve compliance with such requirements and rules by issuing a number of recommendations to unit managers; and identifying and sharing 'best practices' across the whole organization by collating evidence from the 60 or so facilitations undertaken every year and producing a consolidated report that is submitted directly to executive management.

The methodology of the facilitators in all the above tasks is much less quantitative in approach than TBL reporting or balanced scorecards. In particular, evidence is gathered through face-to-face interviewing of business unit managers and other employees:

> Facilitation is not based on data – it's based on interviews. You can go into a unit and select maybe 25 per cent of the people there to speak to. You ask questions, you have a dialogue to try to find out what is working and what isn't. You might find, for example, maybe the unit has a good strategy, the management team know exactly what they would like to do; but they are not communicating this to the rest of the organization, so they're not aware of where you're heading and you end up with a mismatch of expectations. Another example could be that management are not good at staff development, they are too focused on the current task. So based on the interviews we will come up with actions. (Senior Vice-President, Facilitation and Group Internal Audit)

The process is designed to be as constructive as possible in order to result in an agreed plan for business unit improvements. Each facilitation results in around five 'actions' being given to unit managers. The follow-up phase enables facilitation staff to monitor implementation of recommendations issued. Over the course of a year, 50 to 60 facilitations take place, resulting in 250 to 300 actions being given in total to unit managers. In order to assimilate the implications of this for the company as a whole, the facilitations team also produces a consolidated report that is submitted to executive management and the board of directors of the company. The consolidated report considers the areas in which most actions are being recommended, as well as the overall trends from one year to the next.

The consolidated report provides a link between the performance of individual units and the organization as a whole. In some ways this linkage echoes the relationship between the TBL indicators used in the *Annual Report* and the KPIs used in the cascading balanced scorecards. Importantly, however, the operation of the qualitative facilitation process is generally seen as a largely separate, parallel exercise in comparison with the much more quantitative metrics of integrated reporting and balanced scorecards:

> It has no impact on facilitators whether we have integrated reporting. We don't use non-financial data. Of course, we ask the units about their management of environmental and social commitments; but as long as they are aware of their responsibilities, that's all we ask. I don't think our work impacts on the development of non-financial indicators; but we have our consolidated reports that identify trends. For example, let's say we might discover staff engagement levels are going down across the organization. Or we might find we have no focus on training. And then you might set targets using the non-financials. Also, when we set up balanced scorecard targets for the next year, we may use the consolidated facilitation report. We could use KPIs or balanced scorecard targets (e.g. number of days or actual spend on training). It's possible, but it's not a direct link. Our work is still only a small input to TBL management because there are other stakeholders [who] have things that we might like to put into it too. (Senior Vice-President, Facilitation and Group Internal Audit)

The following section concludes the chapter by exploring the extent to which the three main control systems outlined above contribute to the 'embedding' of sustainability within Novo Nordisk.

Full integration at Novo Nordisk: Embedding sustainability

In this chapter, we have examined the company's pursuit of 'full integration' by outlining the development of Novo Nordisk's sustainability strategy, as well as the formal systems and controls that have been developed to measure and manage strategic priorities. At the corporate governance level, Novo Nordisk has explicitly committed itself to being 'socially responsible' and 'environmentally sound', and has sought to deliver on this commitment by means of an unusual combination of formal control systems that emphasize both scope and rigour in quantitative performance measurement, as well as the importance of underlying values and principles of management. By comparison with its peers, Novo Nordisk's achievements in relation to the development of its sustainability strategy are impressive; but the company also recognizes that this is an ongoing incremental task, and the senior managers we spoke to were quite open and honest about the challenges that the company faces.

In response to external pressures, the company has gradually developed a systematic mechanism to integrate stakeholder management within strategic development. However, Novo Nordisk's sustainability strategy is also informed by, and dependent upon, a wider internal assemblage of systems, values, commitments and principles that together comprise 'the way we do things'. This formal internal machinery, known as the Novo Nordisk 'Way of Management', consists of such tools as triple bottom line reporting and the balanced scorecard. In the same way as the emphasis on stakeholder management was triggered by external events, it is interesting to note that the impetus behind the development of some of these systems was rooted in rather conventional concerns, such as expansion into overseas markets (in the case of facilitation) or internal financial control (in the case of the balanced scorecard). Nevertheless, the pursuit of full integration is perhaps most evident at this level, particularly in relation to the evolution of the *Annual Report*. The current focus on 'Sarb-Oxing' and the attention given to the internal control environment for non-financial indicators is especially innovative and ambitious.

In assessing Novo Nordisk's approach to sustainability, an important distinction between integration and embedding may be drawn in the sense that we may consider integration as an assemblage of largely administrative processes, which may, in turn, bring about more substantive institutional change in terms of embedding sustainability within the organization. At the day-to-day operational level, there was recognition on the part of senior management that this dimension of organizational change may be more difficult to assess: 'I can argue that what we do here with TBL management is driving employee motivation. Can I prove it? Probably not. But I can hypothesize, I can make the argument, and then it's up to you to disprove it' (Vice-President, Global TBL Management).

However, while the importance of employee motivation to the company's overall strategy was clearly recognized, the wider challenge facing managers (and the company as a whole) in adopting a sustainability 'mindset' within a patient-focused commercial environment was also acknowledged:

> Sustainability is never the only thing you're thinking about. The biggest
> objective of this company is better medical treatment. And, for example,

for those people who have to inject insulin 15 minutes before they can eat in a restaurant, convenience is a huge part of making sure that they can manage their disease properly. And it's about how you manage that. How do you balance that convenience with the environmental issues of the tools they need to get their treatment? So, it's about the priorities of the company. Can environmental issues really be the most important factor for a company that is really about healthcare? (Director, Global TBL Management)

On a practical level, the difficulties facing Novo Nordisk in embedding sustainability are especially evident in relation to the company's focus on qualitative and cultural dimensions of management in the form of stated values and fundamentals. The facilitation process represents a highly unusual formal control mechanism to measure the extent to which business units, and the organization as a whole, 'comply' with the values and principles set out in the company charter. In defining a benchmark for the underlying managerial 'mindset' within the organization, we may regard this dimension of corporate behaviour as potentially very significant in the context of attempts to embed sustainability.

By comparison with the language used in the company's commitments and values, it is perhaps surprising that the principles defined in the company charter do not explicitly mention or embody sustainability. Indeed, while the formal control systems developed at Novo Nordisk provide a broad and potentially useful approach to establish and manage a sustainability strategy, there nevertheless remain a number of equally important, but less visible, informal dimensions relevant to the embedding of a sustainability 'mindset' within the organization. For example, the operation of the formal control systems, and the success of the wider objective of full integration, remains dependent on the belief and commitment of the staff involved to work together to solve problems. In the case of 'Sarb-Oxing', for example, the application of a strict financial control systems environment to non-financial indicators was not just a technically complex task, but also involved a remarkable level of collaboration and collective action between staff across a number of different departments where one might normally expect to find barriers and obstacles in the way. Likewise, the role of the TBL management forum is crucial in creating a collaborative approach to managing sustainability where different functional areas of the business can share experiences and feed into the development process.

More generally, employees in the company's Danish headquarters appeared to be genuinely comfortable with an emphasis on both quantitative and qualitative aspects of performance measurement and management control. Rather than feeling resentment at being 'policed' by the facilitation process, staff appeared united by such mechanisms and collectively geared towards common organizational aims. It was argued by some Novo Nordisk managers that there was, in general, a deep-rooted and values-based culture in Danish business units that might not be so obvious or prevalent elsewhere in the global company, as well as a widespread assumption that sustainability is simply 'the right thing to do': 'The Scandinavian mindset is very transparent and honest. People come to you with a concern and it's like "Oh! That's a valid concern and we should do something." And there are lots of companies that just wouldn't have such a reaction' (Director, Global TBL Management).

Managing this in the context of global growth presents a particular challenge for Novo Nordisk: 'We are a Danish company and we have a global presence. But there is a difference between being a Danish company with a global presence and being a global company' (Director, Global TBL Management).

Over the last two decades, Novo Nordisk has gradually developed a more proactive form of stakeholder engagement that has shaped its strategic management of sustainability. In addition, it has created a set of control systems to measure the company's performance against its stated social and environmental commitments, and has sought to move closer to full integration. Formal control systems, and the use of quantitative performance indicators, are clearly useful in this context, and Novo Nordisk's ongoing efforts to improve the rigour and sophistication of its internal non-financial control environment are undoubtedly world leading. However, beyond the development of integrated systems based on quantitative non-financial indicators, a particularly welcome dimension of Novo Nordisk's approach is its recognition of the importance of managing values and principles, as well as more tangible commitments and outcomes. In fostering the kind of 'mindset' that many regard as being essential to embedding sustainability within the organization, this is, arguably, a very useful mechanism, with broad appeal, whose potential is, in our view, yet to be fully realized.

Acknowledgements

The authors wish to thank everyone at Novo Nordisk A/S, especially Susan Blesener, Director, Corporate Accountability, who generously offered their time and assistance with this project.

References

Novo Nordisk (2007) *Novo Nordisk Way of Management*, Novo Nordisk, Bagsværd, Denmark

Novo Nordisk (2008) *Annual Report 2008*, Novo Nordisk, Bagsværd, Denmark

Novo Nordisk (2009) *A Focused Healthcare Company: Triple Bottom Line Performance*, Novo Nordisk Presentation, Bagsværd, Denmark

eleven

Summary and Conclusions

Anthony Hopwood, Jeffrey Unerman, Jessica Fries
and Karen McCulloch

Introduction

Adapting organizational strategies and actions to meet the combined needs of a sustainable economy, a sustainable natural environment and a sustainable society is a pragmatic, rational and prudent process that every successful organization needs to undertake. The many interrelated risks from failing to convert an outdated 'business as usual' model that relies on a mirage of economic viability resting on continued production of unaccounted-for social and environmental externalities is simply not economically, socially or environmentally sustainable in the medium or long term. Rather, successful organizations of the future will be those that adapt to effectively embed a connected understanding of environmental, social and economic sustainability into their organizational DNA. Their strategic and operational decision-making will be based on this appreciation of the interconnectedness of different aspects of sustainability.

The cases reported in this book demonstrate ways in which the case study organizations have very usefully employed the principles, tools and guidance developed by The Prince's Accounting for Sustainability Project (A4S) to help embed such sustainability considerations into their DNA. A variety of accounting processes and practices can and do help to embed this connected understanding of sustainability into both internal organizational decision-making and internal and external communications with stakeholders.

The eight case studies reported in this book have, between them, provided a range of in-depth insights and examples of how accounting processes and practices have helped to embed sustainability within day-to-day operations and decision-making in different environments and industries. They have also demonstrated the significant role that accounting, in its very broadest sense, and accountability processes and practices can and do play in helping organizations to meet the urgent challenges of sustainability and to realize the significant opportunities and benefits afforded by adapting to meet the needs of sustainability.

These insights and examples can help other organizations to develop their own accounting for sustainability processes and practices in a way that is sensitive to their own circumstances and context. Given the dynamic nature of the risks, challenges and opportunities flowing from the sustainability agenda, effective sustainability accounting practices will undoubtedly continue to develop, with innovative developments helping organizations to gain and maintain competitive advantage.

While each case study has provided different insights, many of these are complementary across a number of the case studies. Several common key themes have therefore emerged regarding the successful use of accounting for sustainability in helping to embed considerations of sustainability into organizational strategic and operational decision-making in a connected manner. The most common of these themes across the eight case studies are discussed below.

Lessons learned

Sustainability as a strategic objective

A common theme emerging from all the case studies is the importance of embedding sustainability within the strategic objectives of the organization, as demonstrated, for example, by EDF Energy's 'ambitions'. Given that the eight case study organizations that took part in this project were chosen because of their high level of commitment to sustainability and recognition of its importance for the organization's success, it is not surprising that this would be reflected within their strategic objectives. However, the case studies indicate the wider importance of sustainability featuring prominently within an organization's strategic objectives. This is a prerequisite to the organization being able to develop and implement effective processes and practices for sustainability management, including accounting for sustainability. In the case of West Sussex County Council, for example, this was seen to be most effective when there was a recognition of the way in which different aspects of sustainability underpinned all strategic objectives, rather than when presented as a separate objective in isolation.

Governance structures, remuneration and 'tone at the top'

While initiatives to embed sustainability require engagement across the organization, executive commitment is also vital. The importance of the messages, signals and actions of senior executives should not be underestimated. Effective articulation of the business case at board and senior executive levels was found to be crucial in embedding sustainability considerations into strategic and operational decision-making across the case study organizations. Such buy-in from the most senior executives provides clear leadership in terms of signalling how important the sustainability agenda is to help meet the strategic objectives of the organization. It is also important that the vision and commitment of the chief executive or chairman is shared by senior management generally. A common governance structure across the case study organizations was the establishment of a board-level sustainability governance committee, chaired by the chief executive with representation from the leaders of relevant business units and functions, supported by operational committees with equivalent managerial representation at lower levels within the organization. As with the strategic objectives, a clear focus of these committees was the integration of sustainability within normal business activities.

One way of encouraging and publicly demonstrating senior commitment is by the incorporation of sustainability targets within board-level objectives and remuneration. For example, at BT, 15 per cent of board-level bonuses are awarded for each individual director's contribution to the company's environmental, social and governance objectives. At the Environment Agency, selected environmental indicators form part of the directors' 'corporate scorecards', which are discussed at board meetings where each director has to provide an account of their performance.

However, this leadership needs to be coupled with a governance structure that facilitates bottom-up approaches to sustainability because people at the top do not necessarily have (or have the detailed levels of knowledge to be able to easily identify) the best or the optimal sustainability solutions to each detailed operational challenge. Input is therefore needed from below when deciding the most effective ways in which the organization as a whole can move towards becoming a more sustainable (or less unsustainable) organization. So commitment from the top is vital, but this needs to be coupled with encouragement of bottom-up approaches. The case studies highlight the importance of connecting and cascading responsibilities for the implementation of the strategy from senior management down to the individual job specifications, performance objectives and remuneration of managers and staff.

A number of organizations have tried to foster an environment where employees are supported and encouraged to become involved in sustainability – for example, involvement in the Staff Sustainability Group at West Sussex County Council or the establishment of champions across the organization within Aviva. The benefits from such initiatives may be reduced, however, if there is no specific recognition for taking on such responsibilities. When this is the case, those volunteering are highly likely to be restricted to only those with a strong personal commitment to sustainability, and this does not necessarily help to achieve the changes in behaviour and culture needed across the whole organization. In particular, for those participating as champions on a voluntary basis, unless recognition was formalized as part of their role and reward, 'embedding sustainability' was seen as separate from, rather than part of, the 'day job', which would inevitably be given priority when faced with work pressures.

Articulating the business case

In building sustainability into the business cases underlying decision-making, the business case needs to be clearly articulated in language that can be understood by different stakeholders and in terms that help them to understand the relevance of sustainability. The case studies demonstrate that different business cases need to be made at different levels and for different types of decisions within each organization. These business cases are considered to be vital in convincing people within an organization (who individually might not be personally committed to broader notions and an understanding of social and environmental sustainability) to embed sustainability considerations within their decisions and actions. Therefore, the business case needs to be articulated in such a way that it addresses a stakeholder's personal interests. And if those stakeholders are not people who have a particularly strong personal commitment to issues of social and environmental sustainability, the business case needs to be put in such a way that it shows how and why effective addressing of social and environmental issues is going to help them achieve their targets, budgets or other objectives.

A number of the case study organizations highlighted that this ability to articulate the connection to their value chain was particularly important in engaging suppliers. In the case of the Sainsbury's lamb supply chain, where sheep farmers are focused on short-term economic survival, it was essential to demonstrate that acting sustainably made economic sense.

In many areas of sustainability, it is likely that some aspects of the business case cannot be readily or reliably captured through metrics or quantified in financial terms. In the case of BT's Sourcing with Human Dignity Initiative, for example, despite initial questioning from those who perceived there to be very little risk related to the issues covered by the initiative, buy-in was achieved through clear articulation of the linkage between the social issues around sourcing and the impact on the financial and reputational risk of the company. However, BT also found it necessary to appreciate that individuals need to be given the space and encouragement to develop their understanding of the benefits.

Business case information communicated through internal connected reporting at board level was generally considered to be important in helping boards of directors and senior executives to better appreciate the connection between economic, social and environmental impacts in terms of organizations' broad strategies. It thus facilitated a more effective response at board level to the likely overall economic impact for an organization in the short, medium and longer terms of embedding commitments to a greater or lesser degree of social and environmental sustainability into the organization's overall strategic direction.

Role of accounting processes to support behavioural change

One of the key challenges in embedding sustainability is to change underlying behaviours within an organization. An organizational culture where this is actively encouraged is a prerequisite, but still has its limitations, particularly where individuals do not have any personal interest in sustainability issues. The setting of targets, use of formal reporting systems, etc. were seen as essential to achieving behavioural change; but unless presented with the same regularity, rigour and timeliness as financial information, sustainability-related targets were perceived as less important and stakeholders, including employees, were less likely to respond in line with the organization's stated objectives.

Investing in systems to support the collection, management and analysis of relevant data has been seen by the case study organizations to be an effective means of supporting behavioural change. West Sussex County Council introduced its Sustainable Workplace Tool to improve the overall sustainability of staff behaviour by enabling the collection and analysis of data in specific areas on a routine basis. Like HSBC's online data collection system, the tool also integrates a training function to raise awareness and educate those responsible for implementation.

Integration of sustainability decision-making protocols and considerations as part of standard systems and processes was seen as vital to effective incorporation and implementation. Through this integration, it was important to make it easier to adopt sustainable decisions and to express them in language relevant to the individual. For example, as part of its travel booking system, the Environment Agency has ensured that an employee is guided towards the most sustainable travel option first (including challenging the need to travel) and requires increasingly more effort and justification to take less sustainable options.

Assurance – either via internal compliance or audit procedures, or through independent external providers – was seen as a key factor in reinforcing the importance of non-financial data by a number of organizations. EDF Energy saw this as important from an internal credibility and engagement perspective, as well as for external stakeholders. Perhaps the ultimate example of this is Novo Nordisk's decision to apply the principles of the Sarbanes–Oxley Act to its non-financial reporting – an approach that clearly puts non-financial data on the same level as financial data.

Selecting appropriate key performance indicators

Determining what information should be collected, measured and then reported – both internally and externally – is not always obvious. The selection of appropriate key performance indicators (KPIs) requires careful considera-tion, and organizations need to apply a structured approach to assessing the significance of specific issues to different stakeholder groups, and the implica-tions of this assessment for the company. There are a very large number of possible KPIs that could be looked at in terms of sustainability. This is partly due to the fact that in the case of issues such as sustainability, 'materiality' may be affected as much, if not more, by non-financial or qualitative factors as by financial or quantitative ones. This concept of materiality – taking into account both quantitative and qualitative factors – does not differ significantly from 'accounting' materiality; but organizations may find that there is a broader range of 'material' items due to the wider perceptions and objectives of different stakeholders. In determining and selecting appropriate KPIs, it was seen as essential that they were relevant to individuals within the organization, as well as to external stakeholders and, through this, that there was a connection between the KPIs used to manage the business, set targets and measure perfor-mance internally and those used to report externally.

   BT, for example, has adopted a structured approach to determining what its 'material' issues are, quantifying in financial terms the size and likelihood of individual issues. It validates this view through independent sources such as media coverage of issues, investor questionnaires, employee focus groups, etc. before subjecting it to final review by an internal senior-level committee. In particular, this validation process enabled BT to adjust the assessed level of materiality for impacts considered important but hard to quantify, for example, through indirect impacts such as reputation enhancement or damage. Novo Nordisk takes a similar approach, identifying emerging issues that are poten-tially material and reviewing the implications for its long-term business. Aviva has found that implementing the Connected Reporting Framework (CRF) forced the company to think about what is important to its stakeholders and should therefore be reported. Likewise, EDF Energy found that by encouraging the organization to think about what it wants to achieve, how this can be best communicated and how performance might be measured and reported, the CRF was instrumental in addressing some of the challenges of translating its more strategic ambitions into measurable employee goals that were both relevant to individuals and within their control.

Role of qualitative and quantitative financial and non-financial information

Measurement is a key part of embedding; but it should be recognized that although financial data can be an important element of the business case, in particular at middle manager levels, not everything that is significant in managing operations in a more sustainable manner can necessarily be measured in financial terms.

There was strong recognition in many of the case studies that qualitative assessments of economic, social and environmental sustainability impacts, and reporting in qualitative terms, in conjunction with use of quantitative information, are in many instances the appropriate, and sometimes the most suitable, ways to communicate a connected understanding of sustainability. Qualitative information has a vital role, particularly at the higher levels of an organization, because many strategically and operationally important sustainability impacts are not amenable to quantification. In some cases, as observed in the Sainsbury's case study, senior management needs to have the vision to accept this fact and to be able to make decisions without the 'security' of financial measures.

At the more operational levels, while qualitative information from narrative reporting was also recognized as important, there was generally seen to be a greater role for accurate quantified information in reaching day-to-day decisions. This information was sometimes quantified in financial terms and sometimes it was quantified in non-financial terms using a variety of different metrics. This greater reliance on quantitative data at less strategic levels was consistent with a need to have more routine practical decision protocols. These helped people at operational levels to embed considerations of environmental and social sustainability into their day-to-day decision-making, where standardized, and therefore often quantified, information plays a key role in routine decision protocols. Sainsbury's considered that investing in 'hard facts' and sufficiently detailed data was important to understanding and balancing the risks of decisions faced. In the case of EDF Energy, the company found that accounting controls such as budget-setting seemed to exert a significant influence on performance, particularly at middle management levels. In contrast, the Environment Agency's experience was that non-financial measures could be equally effective – for example, targets to reduce staff mileage, as well as the costs of staff travel. With the complex nature of sustainability and the evolving understanding of the environmental and social consequences of actions taken, it was generally considered important to identify and act on the 'best truth' at that point in time rather than postpone action while striving for the perfect outcome or answer.

The role of information systems

Formal reporting systems are a powerful mechanism for embedding organizational practices and driving behavioural change. The integration of
sustainability-related information within financial data collection processes
results in data that is reliable, verifiable and auditable and helps to give the
credibility needed in order to be taken seriously, both internally and externally.
The Environment Agency identified the importance of gathering data at the
lowest point of entry and as part of financial systems as key to having the information necessary to link financial and sustainability outcomes. Adopting this
bottom-up approach to data and reporting, and matching financial spend data
to environmental data from point of entry up has facilitated the identification
and tracking of significant cost savings from projects to improve environmental
performance. In addition to finding this approach to be at lower cost than
implementing a standalone system, it enabled sustainability performance to be
broken down into relevant functional, service or individual employee levels.

Many of the case study organizations recognized the importance of appropriate data collection systems. Those organizations that had invested in a
computer-based system for the collection of financial and non-financial sustainability-related information found there to be significant advantages from doing
so. These are in addition to those noted above in the section on 'Role of accounting processes to support behavioural change'. Aviva and HSBC have both
invested in web-based systems that facilitate the input of data, reduce the
potential for error, increase consistency, enable the performance of variance
analysis and allow the organization to monitor whether all areas of the business
are adhering to the required standards. Both companies also noted the value of
having information that was readily verifiable by a third-party assurance
provider.

Innovation, competitiveness and experimentation

The role of sustainability in driving innovation and competitive advantage was
underlined through the case studies. In many cases, it was important to start
with small initiatives, to encourage a culture of experimentation and to accept
that some of these initiatives would not succeed. Where successful, these 'small
wins' could be built on and rolled out more widely within the organization. A
culture where broader thinking is encouraged and there is an acceptance that
not all ideas will end up being successful is one where the behavioural change
needed to achieve more sustainable outcomes is more likely to occur.

For example, Aviva has sought to experiment with different customer insurance products that reward more sustainable behaviour. It found that products
worked in some markets, but not in all, learning from and building on this
experimentation in future product development. Similarly, it integrated perfor-

mance sustainability considerations within its shareholder voting strategy for responsible investment funds first, before rolling this policy out to all funds under Aviva's management. HSBC adopted different business case criteria as part of the implementation of its Global Environmental Efficiency Programme, enabling higher risk, more experimental environmental technologies to be developed and employed. It saw this as delivering intangible benefits such as changes in culture and behaviour, in addition to improved environmental outcomes and, in some cases, financial bottom-line outcomes.

Connected reporting

To facilitate the embedding of sustainability into the DNA of organizations, the importance of accounting for sustainability in making clear the connections between economic, environmental and social impacts of organizational decisions and actions is demonstrated by the case studies. Clear portrayal of these connections was found to be important not just in external sustainability reporting, but also in internal reporting practices within organizations. In this latter role, connected reporting was a key factor in making visible, and helping managers and other employees to understand, the economic impacts of managing their operations in a more (or a less) environmentally and/or socially sustainable manner.

Many organizations have found the Connected Reporting Framework, and the principles underlying it, useful in helping them to focus on those issues that are of significance to them and to structure the links between financial and non-financial reporting – whether internal or external – in a clearer and more meaningful way. Connected reporting was also found to be a very useful way of demonstrating the indirect impacts of sustainability, as well as the direct ones. The CRF was also valuable in demonstrating and communicating to people and external organizations at different levels in the value chain (over which the reporting organization has less direct control) the role and positive impact of a connected understanding of sustainability.

Overall, therefore, connected reporting was seen to have an important role to play in helping to communicate and coordinate commitments and solutions to sustainability issues between different levels and divisions within an organization and, as part of this, in articulating effective business cases. In practice, the procedures and practices underlying both internal and external connected reporting helped in the identification and communication of sustainability impacts at all levels within the case study organizations. This provided information linking the financial with the social and environmental aspects and impacts of decisions at the broad strategic level, as well as at many different operational decision-making levels.

To fulfil this role most effectively, it was found that the nature of information captured and communicated by accounting for sustainability processes and practices needs to change and adapt within each organization at any point in time. This will ensure that the connections between economic, social and environmental impacts are communicated in a way that is understandable for each type and level of decision that is being taken. In other words, it is important that connected sustainability information is articulated in a way that will be readily understood by the type and level of manager taking each particular type of decision. In this regard, connected reporting information needs to be of a nature that helps managers at each level to identify, and not just in economic terms, the risks associated with a lack of sustainability. By doing so, accounting for sustainability helps these managers and their organizations to identify and understand the risks and financial costs incurred through failing to operate in a socially and environmentally sustainable manner. The connected reporting information also needs to be of a nature that helps managers at every level to identify, assess and realize the many economic benefits and opportunities presented by adaptation and transition to a less environmentally and socially unsustainable society and economy. There are a significant number of such positive business opportunities within the sustainability agenda that are important to recognize in articulating the overall economic impacts of sustainability through connected reporting – both internally and externally.

Summary

By highlighting the above common themes, in addition to the detailed and diverse insights provided by each of the eight case studies reported in this book, we hope to have provided some crucial signposts to aid a wide range of organizations in developing and implementing their own effective accounting for sustainability processes and practices in order to help embed sustainability in a way that is tailored to their individual organizational needs and circumstances. Through developing such effective accounting for sustainability processes and practices, organizations will be much better equipped to systematically identify and interlink the economic, social and environmental costs and benefits of their strategies and actions through integrating a broad concept of sustainability within their mainstream financial processes. This identification and interlinking will help organizations more effectively to communicate to their stakeholders in a connected manner how they have addressed and discharged their economic, social and environmental responsibilities. It will also help organizations to embed a connected understanding of sustainability into their strategic and operational decision-making, and thus will play an important role in helping and encouraging organizations to adapt if they are to address the significant risks and opportunities posed by the challenges and needs of sustainability.

Glossary

Accountability
The duty of an organization (or individual) to provide an account of its activities to those to whom it has responsibilities, both as an explicit record of the way in which it has discharged its responsibilities and as an acceptance of responsibility for them.

AccountAbility
A global, not-for-profit, self-managed partnership founded in 1999 that works to promote accountability innovations for sustainable development (www.accountability21.net).

AccountAbility 1000 (AA1000) series
A set of principles-based standards for accountability, assurance and stakeholder engagement. AccountAbility's AA1000 AS assurance standard is a process standard for the assurance of sustainability reports. The engagement standard (AA1000 SES) provides guidance and best practice for stakeholder engagement and organizational reporting, including ways in which to assess the completeness, materiality and responsiveness of an organization's systems and processes (www.accountability21.net/aa1000series).

Accounting for sustainability
The provision of information and associated management practices and processes that enable organizations and their stakeholders to identify, understand, incorporate and report on both the implications of environmental, social and economic factors on the organization's performance and success, as well as the organization's contribution (positive and negative) to sustainable development.

Balanced scorecard
An analysis technique, developed by Robert Kaplan and David Norton, designed to translate an organization's mission statement and overall business strategy into specific quantifiable goals and to monitor the organization's performance in terms of achieving these goals.

Behaviour change
In relation to sustainability issues, the change of attitudes and actions of individuals and organizations to support positive sustainability consequences.

Building Research Establishment (BRE) Environmental Assessment Method (BREEAM)
A widely used environmental assessment method for buildings. It sets a standard for good practice in sustainable design and has become a well recognized measure used to describe a building's environmental performance (www.breeam.org).

Business in the Community (BITC)
One of The Prince's charities, a group of not-for-profit organizations of which The Prince of Wales is president. BITC works across four areas of expertise in the workplace, marketplace, environment and community, and its members commit to improving the way in which they manage their resources (www.bitc.org.uk).

Carbon dioxide (CO_2)
A naturally occurring gas and one of the most abundant greenhouse gases in the atmosphere. It is also a by-product of burning fossil fuels, industrial processes and land-use changes, and the resultant increase in concentrations of CO_2 in the atmosphere is accepted as a major cause of global warming. For convenience and more effective communication, other greenhouse gases that contribute to global warming are often expressed in terms of their CO_2 equivalence (see CO_2 equivalent below).

Carbon Disclosure Project
An independent not-for-profit organization that was launched in 2000 to collect and distribute high-quality information that motivates investors, corporations and governments to take action to prevent dangerous climate change. It operates the only global climate change reporting system, under which 2500 organizations in some 60 countries around the world measure and disclose their greenhouse gas emissions and climate change strategies (www.cdproject.net).

Carbon footprint
The total amount of carbon emissions for which a person, product, service, organization or country is responsible, both directly and indirectly. So, for example, in terms of products, it represents the emissions over the whole life of a product or service, from the extraction of raw materials and manufacturing through to its use and final reuse, recycling or disposal.

Carbon neutral
Having a net zero carbon footprint through balancing the total greenhouse gases emitted (by an organization, product or service) against an equivalent amount of carbon offsets or carbon sequestered.

Carbon Reduction Commitment (CRC) Energy Efficiency Scheme
The UK's mandatory carbon trading scheme, which started in April 2010 and covers both private- and public-sector organizations. It aims to reduce the level of carbon emissions currently produced by the larger 'low energy-intensive' organizations by approximately 1.2 million tonnes of CO_2 per year by 2020 (www.carbonreductioncommitment.info).

Chartered Institute of Purchasing and Supply
An international organization, based in the UK, which exists to promote and develop high standards of professional skill, ability and integrity among all those engaged in purchasing and supply-chain management (www.cips.org).

Climate change
The variation in the average global or regional climate in relation to average temperature, rainfall and similar measures over the long term. Commonly, the term climate change is used to discuss the consequences of global warming (see below).

ClimateWise
The collaborative insurance initiative through which members aim to work together to respond to the risks and opportunities of climate change. Members commit to action against the ClimateWise Principles (www.climatewise.org.uk).

CO_2 equivalent (CO_2e)
A universal standard of measurement against which the impacts of releasing (or avoiding the release of) different greenhouse gases (their 'global warming potential') can be evaluated on a comparable basis.

Corporate responsibility (CR); corporate social responsibility (CSR)
An approach by which a company recognizes that its activities have a wider impact on society and the environment and takes responsibility for the management of those impacts by taking account of, and responding to, stakeholder concerns.

Culture change
Refers to the structural and social changes in the basic behaviour, values, norms, beliefs, ethical structure, etc. within an organization. This is often sought in order to improve organizational performance.

Dow Jones Sustainability World and Stoxx Indexes
Launched in 1999, the first global indexes tracking the financial performance of
the leading sustainability-driven companies worldwide (www.sustainability-
index.com).

ESG
A term used to discuss environmental, social and governance (ESG) factors,
particularly in the context of financial markets and investment decision-making.

European Union Emissions Trading Scheme (EU ETS)
One of the policies introduced across the European Union (EU) to help it meet
its greenhouse gas emissions reduction target under the Kyoto Protocol through
the allocation and trading of greenhouse gas emissions allowances throughout
the EU (www.ec.europa.eu/environment/climat/emission/index_en.htm).

Externalities
Consequences of an economic activity that are experienced by unrelated third
parties (or the ecosphere), where the cost is borne by one party and the benefit
enjoyed by the other. An externality can be either positive or negative (although
is most commonly negative).

FTSE4Good Index Series
A series of benchmark and tradable indices facilitating investment in companies
with good records of corporate social responsibility, which assesses businesses
on five areas: working towards environmental sustainability; developing positive
relationships with stakeholders; upholding and supporting universal human
rights; ensuring good supply-chain labour standards; and countering bribery
(www.ftse.com/Indices/FTSE4Good_Index_Series/index.jsp).

Gangmasters (Licensing) Act 2004
An act passed by the UK government to make provision for the licensing of
activities involving the supply or use of workers in connection with agricultural
work, the gathering of wild creatures and wild plants, the harvesting of fish
from fish farms, and certain processing and packaging (www.opsi.gov.uk/acts/
acts2004/ukpga_20040011_en_1).

Genetically modified organism (GMO)
An organism (plant, animal, bacteria or virus) that has had its genetic material
altered, either by the duplication, insertion or deletion of one or more new
genes, or by changing the activities of an existing gene.

Global Reporting Initiative (GRI)
A network-based organization that has pioneered the development of an inter-

national sustainability reporting framework that sets out the principles and indicators that organizations can use to measure and report their economic, environmental and social performance (www.globalreporting.org).

Global warming
The progressive gradual rise of the Earth's surface temperature due to the greenhouse gas effect under which increasing concentrations of 'greenhouse gases' in the Earth's atmosphere trap energy from the sun, reflected back from the Earth's surface, rather than allowing it to escape into space.

Greenhouse gases (GHGs)
Atmospheric gases, including water vapour, carbon dioxide, methane, nitrous oxide, ozone and chlorofluorocarbons (CFCs) (perfluorocarbons, hydro fluorocarbons and sulphur hexafluorides), increasing concentrations of which cause global warming. Carbon dioxide, methane, nitrous oxide and CFCs are subject to international control through the Kyoto Protocol.

Greenwash
When an organization projects an image of acting in an environmentally responsible manner – in particular, through external branding, advertising, reporting and marketing – that is not consistent with internal practices, strategies and behaviour.

Gross domestic product (GDP)
The total market value of all final goods and services produced in a country in a given year.

IGD Food Industry Environmental Sustainability Award
A registered charity dedicated to developing the food and grocery industry. Its Environmental Sustainability Award recognizes positive initiatives developed by food or non-food companies with regard to their impact on environmental sustainability (www.igd.com).

International Finance Corporation (IFC)
A member of the World Bank group that provides investments and advisory services to build the private sector in developing countries. It applies environmental and social standards to all the projects that it finances in order to minimize their impact on the environment and on affected communities. These standards include performance standards that define their clients' roles and responsibilities for managing their projects and the requirements for receiving and retaining IFC support (www.ifc.org/ifcext/sustainability.nsf/Content/EnvSocStandards).

International Labour Organization (ILO) Standards
The tripartite United Nations agency that brings together governments, employers and workers of its member states in common action to promote decent working conditions and practices throughout the world (www.ilo.org/global/lang--en/index.htm).

Key performance indicators (KPIs)
A set of quantifiable measures used to assess an organization's performance in critical areas.

Liquefied petroleum gas (LPG)
A gas mixture used for fuel purposes, containing propane, propene, butane or butene as its main components, which has been liquefied to enable it to be transported and stored under pressure.

Materiality
A matter is material if it will influence the decisions, actions or performance of an individual or an organization. In a financial reporting context, a matter is material if it would be likely to influence investment decisions taken by current or prospective shareholders. In the context of sustainability reporting, the concept is extended to incorporate environmental, social or economic factors relevant and significant to the organization and its stakeholders.

MSCI World Index
A free float-adjusted market capitalization weighted index that is designed to measure the equity market performance of developed markets (www.mscibarra.com/products/indices/).

National Farmers' Union (NFU)
An organization that champions British farming and provides professional representation and services to its farmer and grower members (www.nfuonline.com).

Non-governmental organization (NGO)
A not-for-profit or civil society organization which operates on a local, national or international level.

Polyethylene terephthalate (PET)
Recyclable plastic often used in packaging.

Private Finance Initiative (PFI)
A mechanism that provides a way of funding major capital investments without immediate recourse to the public purse. Private consortia, usually involving large construction firms, are contracted to design, build and, in some cases,

manage new projects (www.dh.gov.uk/en/Procurementandproposals/
Publicprivatepartnership/Privatefinanceinitiative/index.htm).

Sarbanes–Oxley Act (SOX)
US legislation enacted in response to the high-profile Enron and WorldCom
financial scandals to improve corporate governance. Under the act, the chief
executive officer and chief financial officer must certify in writing the effectiveness of the company's internal financial controls.

Social justice
Recognition in policy, regulation and practice that all persons, irrespective of
ethnic origin, gender, possessions, race, religion, etc., are to be treated equally
and without prejudice.

Socially responsible investment (SRI)
An investment strategy that integrates social, environmental and/or ethical
criteria within the processes of financial analysis, investment selection and fund
management.

Stakeholder
A person, group or organization who can affect or be affected by an organization's actions, objectives or policies. Stakeholders in a business organization
may include creditors, customers, directors, employees, government, shareholders, suppliers, unions and the community from which the business draws
its resources.

Stonewall
A professional lobbying group acting to protect and advance recognition of the
human rights of lesbian, gay, bisexual and transgender members of the community (www.stonewall.org.uk).

Supply chain
The system of organizations, people, technology, activities, information and
resources involved in delivering a product or service.

Sustainability
Actions and approaches adopted by organizations compatible with, and
contributing to, sustainable development.

Sustainability report
A report produced by an organization to report the (positive and negative)
impacts of its operations on society and the environment and its performance in
this regard.

Sustainable development
Considering what we do not only in terms of ourselves and today, but also of others and tomorrow. This concept of sustainable development recognizes the need to meet society's needs, particularly in response to poverty, without exceeding the environmental limits of a finite planet. This underlines the interdependence between achieving social, economic and environmental outcomes.

Triple bottom line (TBL)
The measurement of an organization's performance taking into account economic, environmental and social dimensions, often referred to as 'profits, people, planet'.

UK Climate Change Act
A legally binding long-term framework to cut carbon emissions in the UK. This sets a target of an 80 per cent reduction in UK greenhouse gas (GHG) emissions from 1990 levels, by the year 2050, in line with scientific consensus on the required reduction levels for developed economies.

United Nations Global Compact
A strategic policy initiative for businesses that are committed to aligning their operations and strategies with ten universally accepted principles in the areas of human rights, labour, environment and anti-corruption (www.unglobalcompact.org).

United Nations Principles for Responsible Investment (UN PRI)
A set of voluntary principles that provide a framework for incorporating ESG issues within mainstream investment decision-making and ownership practices (www.unpri.org).

Water footprint
The total volume of freshwater used to produce goods and services consumed by an individual, community or nation. Water footprint can apply in a similar way to a particular product or service.

Index